Jan-Olav Henriksen

Representation and Ultimacy

Nordic Studies in Theology
Nordische Studien zur Theologie

edited by / herausgegeben von

Prof. Dr. Kirsten Busch Nielsen
(University of Copenhagen)

Prof. Dr. Dr. Jan-Olav Henriksen
(MF Norwegian School of Theology, Oslo)

Dr. Hans Bringeland
(NLA University College, Bergen)

Volume / Band 5

LIT

Jan-Olav Henriksen

Representation and Ultimacy

Christian Religion as Unfinished Business

LIT

This book is printed on acid-free paper.

Bibliographic information published by the Deutsche Nationalbibliothek
The Deutsche Nationalbibliothek lists this publication in the Deutsche
Nationalbibliografie; detailed bibliographic data are available in the Internet at
http://dnb.dnb.de.

ISBN 978-3-643-91168-1 (pb)
ISBN 978-3-643-96168-6 (PDF)
ISSN 2311-1194

A catalogue record for this book is available from the British Library.

© LIT VERLAG GmbH & Co. KG Wien,
Zweigniederlassung Zürich 2020
Klosbachstr. 107
CH-8032 Zürich
Tel. +41 (0) 44-251 75 05
E-Mail: zuerich@lit-verlag.ch   http://www.lit-verlag.ch
Distribution:
In the UK: Global Book Marketing, e-mail: mo@centralbooks.com
In North America: Independent Publishers Group, e-mail: orders@ipgbook.com
In Germany: LIT Verlag Fresnostr. 2, D-48159 Münster
Tel. +49 (0) 2 51-620 32 22, Fax +49 (0) 2 51-922 60 99, e-mail: vertrieb@lit-verlag.de
e-books are available at www.litwebshop.de

Representation and Ultimacy:
Christian Religion as Unfinished Business

Jan-Olav Henriksen
2019

Contents

Acknowledgments..7

Introduction 9

What is religion?...15
Introduction: Unfinished business 15
Jonathan Z. Smith on religion..16
Kevin Schilbrack on religion 18
Can philosophers help us understand religion? 19
Transcendental and pragmatist reflections on religion 24
Religions as practice-based (Christian Smith and Martin Riesebrodt)....28
Defining religion between functional and substantive definitions (Schilbrack).....35
Religion, the ultimate, and human experiences (Neville)........................41
Can religions be understood in full when they are not practiced? 44
Conclusion..50

God reveals: On experiencing God 53
Representation as revelation...53
Representation: Starting from a layman's reflections.............................55
Further on representation – Hegel again..57
Mediating God's presence: The Christological perspective 61
Symbols as a manifestation of the finite-infinite contrast: Neville........63
Beyond natural theology – from thinking towards the acts of God.........64
Representation and relationality: The subjective experience of God 68
Schleiermacher – dependency, freedom, and agency 69

Ana-Maria Rizzuto: God-representations and their impact on human life 73

Revealed conditions for human agency (C. Schwöbel) 84

Revelation and semiosis 89

God mediated in signs: Semiotics and transcendental reasoning 92

Experience of God – from a semiotic perspective 97

Transcendentalia and belief – an intermediate conclusion 102

Sacramental panentheism and different realms of human experience 104

God's power: Presence and transcendence 107

God as love: a transcendental condition for experience 109

Deep incarnation (Gregersen) 112

Further on panentheism: A Trinitarian vision 116

Supernaturalism revisited 118

The Triune incarnated God 126

God – Conclusion 131

Desire and vulnerability: The human condition 135

Introduction 135

Desire, flourishing, goodness 139

Representation, desire, and the order of the created world 150

Eschatological desire for God 154

Vulnerability 162

Ontological and situational vulnerability 165

Vulnerability and religious representation 169

Vulnerability: Its different dimensions 172

Vulnerability and the responsibility for justice 174

Theological resources for critical approaches to vulnerability 177

Love as the means for coming to terms with desire and vulnerability 183

Love as a process, love as a mode of growth (unfinished business) 189

Emergence as the condition for agency manifesting faith, hope, and love 197

Divine agency as human practice: Relation and participation 201

Preliminary conclusion 205

Practicing the divine image: Forgiveness as transformation 206

Forgiveness: Fundamental considerations for theological discourse 208

Forgiveness, symmetry, and justice 212

A difficult practice 215

Using Sacred Scriptures as a practice of orientation (mainly descriptive) 222

On the practice of using texts (mainly normative): Six theses 230

God as the ultimate in human reality 233

The importance of what we care about: H. Frankfurt as philosophical theology . 234

Conclusion 249

Literature 251

Index 265

Acknowledgments

This book would not have come to a completion unless some important people made it possible: First of all, my good friend for many years, Olav Fykse Tveit, and his wife Anna, who invited me to stay in their house at the campus of Bossey Ecumenical Institute outside Geneva for some intense weeks of work in May 2019. Their hospitality and generosity will be an enduring memory, and the stay provided the best opportunities for finishing the draft of this book.

Furthermore, thanks also to my employer, MF Norwegian School of Theology, Religion and Society, Oslo, which has always been supportive of my research and provided me with time and resources to pursue the interests behind it.

Thanks also to the other editors of *the Nordic Studies in Theology*, to whom I turned this book over in order to take care of the necessary referee business and handling of the manuscript, and to the anonymous reviewer for valuable suggestion for improvement. Thanks to my wife, Hilde Marie, who accepted my absence from home during the writing of the draft, and to Anne Marie Hovland Aschim, who again took care of improving my English. Whatever flaws remains are mine.

Oslo, Fall 2019
Jan-Olav Henriksen

Introduction

Some years ago, I saw an ad in a Princeton cinema, which attributed the following quote to the actor Jennifer Lopez: "Life is about two things: to love and to learn." The point is well taken. Love is crucial to human life and to that from which we understand ourselves, and learning is a basic element in human growth and transformation. This book is about how we can perceive reality in this way, and what kind of role religion and belief in God may play for a life lead by this insight.

The quote also suggests, implicitly, that human flourishing depends on the fact that reality is open-ended, and that we do not depend solely on what has determined us from the past. To live is to be in a state not fixed. It offers us new chances for learning, growth, transformation. Reality faces us constantly with something new, and consequently, it challenges our need for orientation as well. Without these chances for new experiences – a reality open-ended and shaped by creativity, alternatives, and freedom – we would not have a good life. Religion, in a variety of forms, offers us resources for orientation and transformation that keep us on track towards such life – if it succeeds.

This book draws together some main trajectories in my previous research and thinking. One line of reasoning relates to how we can think of God and the human condition. Another is how we are to understand religion, and more specifically, what we call Christianity, as one version of articulating what it means to be human. Hence, the following is in many ways an attempt to continue the enterprise of a philosophical theology that sees religion as founded in practices of orientation, transformation, and reflection. It does so by drawing together three inter-related topics: Religion, God, and Humanity. In terms of these topics, the enterprise I undertake here is not very original – I guess most theologians and philosophers of religion do similar things at a certain stage in their careers. However, what I try to do in the following is to show how we need to consider these three topics together as constituting what in principle is the unfinished business of theology and a dynamic concept of religion that can contribute to theological reflection about it. Underlying this point is the conviction that a theological concept of religion is necessary in order to understand what theology is all about. Such an understanding entails, with necessity, a normative position: it becomes a proposal about how one best should understand religion from a theological point of view, and why one should do so.

The unfinished business of religion, and therefore of theology, shapes the interrelation in this triangle in a way that can only be suggested briefly here:

- God understood as *semper major,* as the transcendental condition for concrete human agency, and the origin of all representations in which God manifests Godself.
- Religion as expressed in practices which serve as representations by which we can relate to the divine, and which we need to appropriate repeatedly exactly as representations in order to avoid idolatry (be it with regard to what we do, the physical entities we use, or sacred scriptures).
- The unfulfilled human desire that roots the quests for meaning, significance, and things that help us see what matters, and help us come to terms with our finitude and vulnerability in our struggle to live and realize our lives as images (representations) of God (*imago Dei*).

God reveals Godself in religions that can shape and motivate human agency and desire – and God is, therefore, also dependent on human thought and action in order to manifest Godself in a recognizable mode in the world. God is not finished revealing Godself – there is always more to experience about God, learn about God, learn from God, and receive from God.

Religion, at its best, can direct humans towards the divine and ultimate. Religions provide practices, symbols, narratives, and ideas that guide humans on what matters most – and thereby makes it possible for us to manifest the divine in the world as images of God (*imago dei*). We can never take religions, as representations of the divine, at face value as containing the full truth. Nevertheless, they provide resources by which humans can accomplish the way of living that follows from the realization of the insight into *Deus semper major* and *imago Dei* indicated above. The employment of these resources requires critical appropriation – and therefore, religion cannot be other than unfinished business, as well.

Humanity can employ religious symbols and ideas to orient and transform themselves and their reality in ways that not only speak about important features in the human condition (love, desire, vulnerability, relationality, dependence, etc.) but also, and thereby, can contribute to how God manifests Godself in the world. This task is never completed.

Consequently, it is important to think of religion as unfinished business and not as something easily pinned down, for several reasons:

a) From a theoretical point, religions represent a reality that implies that there is still more to explore.

b) From a theological point, the notion of *Deus semper major* suggests that God can never be grasped fully but is a reality that goes beyond human conceptualization and understanding, without being incomprehensible, because God manifests Godself in the reality of human experience.

c) From a socio-political point, the unfinished character is important to underscore in the face of, and against, secularism and fundamentalism, and against the desire to cling to ideas about imagined communities and nations in ways that exclude others.

d) From a cultural point of view, religious practices are ongoing processes that shape and develop in the course of human life.

e) From an anthropological point, religions are enriching or impeding human life and flourishing, and neither of these alternatives. Religions are ambiguous in principle.

Some further words are required on how this study relates to my former scholarly contributions. I have previously tried to relate the contents of Christian dogmatics to other fields of scholarship, especially psychology, philosophy, and some evolutionary theory and sociology, This work came to its fruition in a "first trilogy," in which I developed topics on theological anthropology, Christology, and the relation between God and human experience.[1] This work was followed by more intense engagement with the psychology of religion, which resulted in a study published in 2013. Here I read contributions to the psychology of religion with a concern for how these were also relevant for the philosophy of religion.[2] One could see my attempts to adjust or supplement Hegel's understanding in what follows as the result of the latter, as it wants to acknowledge a stronger place for the emotional dimension in relation to religious representations than he did, without leaving behind his valid insights into the role that such representations have as the necessary semiotic mediation of the ultimate reality to which religion as a human phenomenon relates. Moreover, the present study develops further *the* central element for understanding the reality we call God, namely that God is love, and thereby, intrinsically related

---

[1] Jan-Olav Henriksen, *Imago Dei. Den teologiske konstruksjonen av menneskets identitet* (Oslo: Gyldendal akademisk, 2003); *Desire, Gift, and Recognition : Christology and Postmodern Philosophy* (Grand Rapids, Mich.: William B. Eerdmans Pub. Co., 2009); *Life, Love, and Hope : God and Human Experience* (Grand Rapids, Michigan: Eerdmans Publishing Company, 2014).

[2] *Relating God and the Self : Dynamic Interplay* (Burlington: Ashgate, 2013).

to the most important element that creates, sustains, and shapes human life in a positive manner.

Furthermore, the following also builds on work that explores the topic of religion more in detail. This work, which has resulted in a "second trilogy," dealt with the topic of how to understand religions in general, based on a theory of religion as a cluster of practices for orientation and transformation. Some of this work is strongly reflected in what follows, and it was also, after the generic theory was published in 2017, followed by an investigation of Christian practices and a study on what such a theory meant for a Christian understanding of religious pluralism.[3] In these studies, I developed a position increasingly more inspired by pragmatism, and especially the semiotics of C.S. Peirce. In the present volume, these studies are pursued further by employing more explicitly the notion of *ultimacy* (Neville) or the *superempirical* (Schilbrack), both of which I hold important to spell out the specific religious character of the practices of orientation and transformation. The advantage of this theoretical approach is that it allows us to see religions as intrinsically interwoven with human practices and experience, and not as separate from the everyday of believers. As such, this bulk of my work is an adjustment of an understanding of religion that sees it primarily as *belief*.[4]

However, both these bulks of scholarship are also related to a third trajectory of research that I have pursued throughout my career, namely the interest in theological anthropology.[5] The following can therefore also be read as my most recent attempt to spell out what I hold to be the most important features within the framework of theological anthropology, and especially the central

---

[3] This "second trilogy" consists of the following volumes: *Religion as Orientation and Transformation : A Maximalist Theory*, (Tübingen: Mohr Siebeck, 2017); *Christianity as Distinct Practices: A Complicated Relationship* (London: Bloomsbury, 2019); *Religious Plurality and Pragmatist Theology – Openness and Resistance.* (Leiden: Brill, 2019).

[4] Henriksen Jan-Olav, "Everyday Religion as Orientation and Transformation: A Challenge to Theology," *Nordic Journal of Religion and Society*, no. 01 (2016).

[5] This interest has, in addition to what has been mentioned above, resulted in e.g., Jan-Olav Henriksen, "Mennesket Som Natur : En systematisk-teologisk analyse av forholdet mellom antropologi og naturforståelse i Wolfhart Pannenbergs teologi," (Dissertation, Det teologiske Menighetsfakultet, 1989); *Finitude and Theological Anthropology : An Interdisciplinary Exploration into Theological Dimensions of Finitude*, Studies in Philosophical Theology (Leuven ; Walpole, Mass.: Peeters, 2011); "Distinct, Unique, or Separate? : Challenges to Theological Anthropology and Soteriology in Light of Human Evolution," *Studia Theologica* 67, no. 2 (2013); "Love as the Power with Which God Shapes the World: Theological Anthropology and Human Experience," *Louvain studies* 41, no. 3 (2018); Jan-Olav Henriksen and Karl Olav Sandnes, "The Vulnerable Human and the Absent God the Stories About Gethsemane as a Possible Source for Theological Anthropology," *Kerygma und Dogma : Zeitschrift für theologische Forschung und kirchliche Lehre* 64, no. 3 (2018).

notion of *Imago Dei,* which I would argue still has significance, and not so only from a theological point of view, but also because of its cultural impact. My understanding of desire, vulnerability, and in spelling out what matters most to us as humans as something more than knowledge or ethics, is the reason why the last chapters in the present book develop these themes. Moreover, my engagement with Harry Frankfurt's work in the last chapter not only supports this position, but it also confirms my conviction that theological anthropology, as well as religion in general, represent attempts to spell out or articulate a mode of life that builds on, and is conditioned by, interests and phenomena that all humans are interested in, or at least would have good reasons for being concerned with.

It follows from the above that not everything on the following pages was written for this book originally. However, everything has been re-written and altered in the course of developing the overall argument. Furthermore, as the reader will realize, re-reading of Hegel's philosophy of religion is among the things that have contributed to the actual result of what one can find here. Thus, the book is one more contribution to philosophical theology, i.e., to theology that utilizes philosophical insights and tools in order to develop and shape a theological position. Nevertheless, it does not aim to say a final word on these matters – a fact that follows from the book's topic about unfinished business.

What is religion?

Introduction: Unfinished business

Religions matter only if they change peoples' lives, and have consequences for how they live and relate to themselves, to others, and the world. In this sense, religions must be understood from the point of view of their consequences, just as a tree can be judged from its fruits. The present work builds on this pragmatic approach to religion. This approach entails what C.S. Peirce wrote about how the whole meaning of a (clear) conception consists of the entire set of its practical consequences.[6] Thus, we must consider religion with regard to its experiential implications. What we say about it must be possible to relate to some sort of collection of possible empirical elements, although not being reduced simply to empirical observations. Peirce insisted that the entire meaning of a meaningful conception consisted of the totality of such specifications of possible observations. This approach challenges us to specify the consequences that religious symbols, narratives, rituals, and conceptions have for human life. It means that we have to view religious features with regard to their implications for, and their shaping of, human practices.

This approach may be at odds with other positions. In the twentieth century, theological thinking more or less ignored the fact that peoples' religious engagement is determined not so much with ideas and beliefs as with concrete practices. However, religions are not only about what people believe or hold to be true. Religion is about doing good, praying, going to church, the mosque or the temple; it is about singing in choirs, reading the scriptures, etc. In all such practices, beliefs are an element, of course, but belief and its formulations in doctrine are only part of what is involved. More than being about what to believe, or accepting all parts of a pre-established doctrine, religion is about what to do. On the other hand, doctrines and theological reasoning help us to understand, reason about, and provide warrants for practices we have – and sometimes, they even help criticize practices, when they are misleading in terms of how they affect people. An obvious example of the latter is how theological

---

[6] Charles Sanders Peirce, "How to Make Our Ideas Clear," in *Peirce on Signs: Writings on Semiotic by Charles Sanders Peirce* ed. Edited by James Hoopes (Chapel Hill: University of North Carolina Press, 1991), 169.

reasoning about the role of women in the Church has led many churches to reconsider their position on women ministry. This change would nevertheless not have been possible unless there was already some existing practice that made it necessary to rethink and reconsider the effects of keeping women out of ordained positions. Hence, theology is not – from this point of view – an enterprise that is settled or finished once and for all: theology constantly needs to reflect on the actual practices of which religions consist, in order to provide them with the necessary underpinning or address them critically in order to provide opportunities for change.

This book tries to think theologically about religions as clusters of practices. To think theologically is in itself a practice, and often it is a *religious practice*, although it need not be. To reflect theologically is to think according to procedures, patterns, and modes of communication that involves specific resources, a community of peers, and a context of other practices to which this reflective practice is related in some way or another (be it constructively, critical, normatively guiding, or simply descriptive). Theology needs to have a clear idea about what religion is – empirically – in order to address its topics in a way that proves adequate and relevant to peoples' ordinary lives. However, empirically speaking, what religion is cannot be determined without an adequate *concept* of religion. Here, a problem immediately presents itself: what belongs to the concept of religion, and *how* can we conceptualize religion? Only if we can answer these questions can we in turn also determine some of the relevance that an adequate understanding of religion may have in a distinctively *theological context* that is also oriented towards a normative approach to religious beliefs, ideas, and practices. The following sections aim at discussing how we can conceptualize religion.

Jonathan Z. Smith on religion

In a much-quoted paper, religious studies scholar Jonathan Z. Smith argues, among other things, that religion has proved to be a most flexible concept with a wide diversity of connotations. From an anthropological angle, one has used "religion" as a concept to describe those who are "others" – those who live and worship in other contexts and cultural settings than one's own. The more one has learned about other religions, the more one has had a use for the concept. Furthermore, after the Reformation, religion did not so much describe the cultic and ritual dimension in religion, as it aimed at subjective piety and belief. From a more critical angle, e.g., in Hume, one has asked what it is in the human condition(s) that causes humans to have religion. This approach could also lead to a thematization of elements in nature in general that deserve attention because they represent basic conditions for life outside the strictly human realm.[7] A major result of Smith's survey of the use of the terms religion, religions, and religious is that "'Religion' is not a native term; it is a term created by scholars for their intellectual purposes, and therefore, it is theirs to define. It is a second-order generic concept that plays the same role in establishing a disciplinary horizon that a concept such as 'language' plays in linguistics, or 'culture' plays in anthropology."[8] This conclusion leads him to the consequence that it is always up to the scholar to define what religion is, and there is an infinite number of ways to do so. Religion is not impossible to define but needs to be defined in a certain respect, with regard to something specific that one wants to address. Accordingly, religious studies scholars and theologians alike need to be pragmatic in their definition of religion: they cannot define religions' essence but need to refer to pragmatic definitions that suit their specific interests and what they see the need for bringing to the table.[9]

The diverse approaches to what one conceives as religion thus yield different results. A major point resulting from J. Smith's survey is that religion, or religions, are constructs. One cannot understand them apart from the human activity that defines it/them as such. However, this does not mean that religion/s only exist in peoples' minds, just as language or culture do not. We need to acknowledge that the activity that defines religion is rooted in, or is a cognitive response to, the need to orient oneself in the reality in which one finds oneself. Therefore, it is not surprising that religious people also need to define religion, and that this is part of religious and theological activity: Puzzles about what religion is, shape the need for orientation also among religious people who consider it an important element in their lives.

---

[7] Jonathan Z. Smith, "Religion, Religions, Religious," in *Critical Terms for Religious Studies*, ed. Mark Taylor (Chicago: University of Chicago Press, 1998), 277.

[8] Ibid, 281f.

[9] Christian Smith makes this point clearly, when he writes: "In short, the categories religion and something-other-than-religion need not be either/or but may be both/and. Thus, for another example, we can rightly understand Hinduism to be a religion and, in various aspects, a civilization, a worldview, and a philosophical tradition." Christian Smith, *Religion : What It Is, How It Works, and Why It Is Still Important* (Princeton: Princeton University Press, 2017), 50.

Kevin Schilbrack on religion

From a philosophy of religion perspective, Kevin Schilbrack comments on the topic of defining religion by pointing to how "the very existence of religion depends on historically emergent concepts."[10] Therefore, "the reality of religion is itself a social construction, what religion is, depends upon social recognition."[11] The concepts of those who observe religion are entangled with what these observers intend to grasp. Consequently, we need to assess definitions of religion according to how they serve the purposes of those who use them. No definition can be seen as the final: the employment of definitions must be open for adjustment, according to the purposes behind their use. A good definition depends on its practical value.[12]

Hence, if one thinks that religion is simply a vast array of more or less peculiar ideas that people have in their minds and that mainly are concerned with entities or conceptions that are more or less unrelated to this world, this notion needs reconsideration. Although religion is, as suggested, often considered in the West mainly as *belief,* to think only in those terms about it may be misleading. Religions are, or rather, offer, a cluster of practices (including reflective ones) in which people engage, and which shape and form their lives in different ways. Moreover, as I will argue in the following, religions are processes more than fixed systems, practices more than theory, and more about signs and significations than about things or entities in themselves. Altogether, this means that religions provide us with resources for being in, relating to, and engaging with the world in a wide variety of ways. Religions put us on quests for truth and the good life (process). They inform us about what matters and what not; about what must change and how to accomplish change in personal life and in society (in practices of orientation and transformation); and they provide resources for reflection, interpretation, and understanding that allows us to see the world as more than what is in front of us.

This is a dynamic understanding of religious traditions. Therefore, it runs counter to ideas about religions as rigid systems for thinking and disciplining. In the following chapters, I will argue that religion is open and continuous processes (unfinished business), and implies more unfinished work than one gets the impression of when it is presented as a system of thought that can "explain" what we cannot otherwise explain, or as rituals that are unrelated to quotidian

---

[10] Kevin Schilbrack, *Philosophy and the Study of Religions : A Manifesto*, Wiley Blackwell Manifestos (Chichester, West Sussex: Wiley Blackwell, 2014), 115f
[11] Ibid.
[12] Ibid.

life. Not only are there theological conceptions implied in religious practices that still require work and which one has to recognize as in need of further pondering, clarification, and reflection. Religions also point to unfinished business in human life, and to the need to work on oneself and one's life conditions.

However, the unfinished character of religions does not end here. Also on the theoretical level, religions represent unfinished business. To put it simply, if the reality to which religions point and with which it engages is real, it means that the concept of religion, and how we understand it theoretically, are not yet completed. Hence, religions deal with unfinished business in human life, but religions also point to hitherto unfinished scholarly engagement.

What kind of vantage point can enable us to see both theology and religious practices as dealing with unfinished business? I suggest that philosophy can help in this task, and especially the philosophical insights related to *pragmatism*. Why this is so, I will argue in one of the following sections of this chapter. After having presented the philosophical insights that may help us in this regard, I present some recent contributions that are important to be aware of if one is to argue for religion as being about unfinished business, which is then the thesis that the bulk of this chapter aims to advance.

Can philosophers help us understand religion?

What do we look for, or think of, when we search for or speak about religion? As indicated above, the answer to these questions depends on our *concept* of religion, but also our experiential context, as that which has informed our concept. No one has shown this more clearly and in-depth than Hegel.

According to T.A. Lewis, for Hegel, "objects are constituted by the concepts that define or determine them. Without these determinations, these delimitations, they would not be the objects that they are. They would be different objects or – in the complete absence of such determinations – no object at all." The consequence is that not only our concepts rely on and is dependent on the practices of thinking – "all objects of thought are necessarily conditioned by the activity of thought" as well.[13] As long as we realize that "religion" is a concept and not an entity, this is easy to acknowledge.

There is presently a range of views on reason as context-dependent. Since reason and reasoning both determine concepts and is determined by them, we need to observe this fact. If one wants to approach the understanding of religion

---

[13] See Thomas A. Lewis, "Overcoming a Stumbling Block: A Nontraditional Hegel for Religious Studies," *The Journal of Religion* 95, no. 2 (2015): 205.

as related to reason and as evolving based on social and historical processes, reasoning about and conceptualizing religion cannot be done without taking context into consideration. The historicity of reason is also the historicity of the concept of religion, and accordingly, of our understanding of it.

Hegel's insights into the historicity of concepts may benefit considerations about the conditions for the understanding of religion. These insights are related mainly to how he understands the dynamics behind the development of what he calls the concept (*Begriff*): When he historicizes the concept (in our case, the concept of religion), he shows that it is the result of processes in which one cannot remain in the immediacy where we originally find ourselves. Our concepts are always developed in negation to other concepts, and therefore, the context plays a significant role in how their content is shaped. Thus, whatever we try to understand is conditioned by contextual and historical processes. Our understanding builds on, and is rooted in, previous, insufficient forms of thinking that have attempted to come to terms with the object that constitutes its content. Because it is the concept that is the basis for our understanding of a phenomenon, the development of our understanding (of religion) is based on the concept's content, and it is the concept that allows for further understanding.[14] We can understand Hegel's approach here as one that, accordingly, explains the reasons why Max Müller could say about religions that "the one who knows one, knows none."[15]

In both Hegel and his contemporary, Schleiermacher, their "conceptualization of religion depends upon their accounts of human feeling, cognition, and action."[16] Hence, both of them addresses issues that are important in order to concretely understand how religion may point to unfinished business in human life. As they make explicit what remains merely implicit in a great deal of theorizing of religion, they point to features that must be addressed in order to explicate more fully what is at stake in religious belief and practice. "Conceptions of the human subject – of our cognition as well as the relation between our practical and theoretical activity, for instance – are integral to conceptions of religion. In this respect, even theorizing of religion that seeks to abstain from

---

[14] Hegel, *Enzyclopädie* I, 307; *Wissenchaft der Logik* II, 264, in Georg Wilhelm Friedrich Hegel, *Werke in Zwanzig Bänden*, neu ed. Ausg. ed., Theorie – Werkausgabe (Frankfurt am Main: Suhrkamp, 1976).

[15] Friedrich Max Müller, *Einleitung in Die Vergleichende Religionswissenschaft* (Strassburg: Trubner, 1874), 14.This famous quote of Müller's may be understood against the backdrop of his studies in philosophy, in which he was especially influenced by Hegel and Schelling.

[16] Cf. Thomas A. Lewis, *Why Philosophy Matters for the Study of Religion-and Vice Versa* (New York, NY: Oxford University Press, 2015), 76.

these philosophical questions will draw upon particular sets of answers to them, whether conscious of doing so or not. Philosophy is thus unavoidable in the conceptualization of religion."[17]

When making the observation in the quote just given, Thomas Lewis then also argues implicitly for highlighting that religion is about more than it articulates when we understand it simply on its own premises, as is the case in immediate beliefs and practices, and in theologies that take the reality to which these relate for granted. This point is what philosophy and reasoning that addresses pragmatic and transcendental preconditions for human life can bring to the fore. One important consequence of this is that philosophical reflection can explicate that religion is not only about a world beyond, or about belief in supernatural entities. Hegel illustrates this well, in Lewis' opinion:

As much as Hegel's project seeks to validate inherited religious claims, it does so by justifying them as representations. Their genuine significance lies not in their relation to particular historical events or literalistic readings of the representational claims but in their representational expression of the truths treated most adequately in philosophy. In perhaps the most important example, Hegel preserves much traditional language about God, validating and justifying it; yet, over the course of his philosophical system, he argues that this absolute is to be understood in terms of the social practices of the human community rather than the superhuman being frequently presented in religious representations.[18]

To understand religions thus, however, implies that what one identifies as religious features can become articulated in the self-conscious and critical reflection where philosophy offers the chances for identifying something as *representations*. The character of such reflection is tied closely to how Hegel understands the conditions for the concept – in this case, the concept of religion, to which we will return shortly. However, the philosophical insight into religion cannot be the starting point for what we know about religion. Actual, practiced, empirical religion is "a necessary stage in our learning and appropriation of these insights."[19] However, one cannot remain by these immediately present appearances of religion if one is to understand what it is. Religious practices, images, narratives, etc., must be understood as ways to represent a deeper dimension of reality that always brings forth something new. Thus, philosophy as the reflective response to these representations will, by necessity, not be able to round up and bring to closure religions' dealing with the open-ended character

---

[17] Ibid.
[18] Ibid., 77.
[19] Ibid.

of human life. Instead, there are main reasons for thinking that philosophy itself will need to explicate why such closure is not its task to bring about in its dealing with, and reflection on, religion.

Hegel's notion of the concept implies that all understanding of finite phenomena is insufficient. This insufficiency is the main reason why he is critical to a mere empirical approach to religion since it leaves out the chance for seeing the empirical as conditioned by the absolute or the infinite, i.e., God.[20] Although his philosophy is not specifically concerned with empirical realities as such, they serve as immediate instances that one needs to overcome in the development of an understanding that allows for the appearance and the conceptualization of the absolute, or the totality. This appearance and its result are still outstanding, or deferred, though. Nevertheless, some elements in this approach can prove relevant for the understanding of religion:

First, as already indicated, the concept 'religion' is itself an abstraction, based on a limited number of experiences and cases that have contributed to the development of what we hitherto have been able to grasp as 'religion.' This limited access to the full phenomenon has implications for the concept of religion as well. However, instead of abstracting from the historical and empirical in order to develop a concept of religion, we need to consider its concrete historical forms and functions within a given context in order to understand and conceptualize it further.[21] Accordingly, it is impossible to operate with a generic and ahistorical notion of religion.

Furthermore, Hegel's insistence on the overcoming of immediacy means that we cannot remain by the phenomenon as it appears. We need to assume, with him, that we do not know what religion is, only from what we observe in front of us. Not only do we need to know something about its historical development and origin, but we also need to know something about its present contribution to the context and to human life – how it works and thus, what it *represents* in a given context. This latter, pragmatic element is necessary to address in its concreteness, but it is also important to make the generalizations necessary

---

[20] Cf. for more on this point below, 65ff.

[21] These remarks can be substantiated further by the following insights by Thomas A. Lewis: "[H]istorical and social scientific studies of religion necessarily presuppose responses to the kinds of philosophical questions about the nature of reason, belief, and practice that lie at the heart of much work in philosophy of religion. Any attempt to theorize religion depends upon prior commitments – implicit or explicit – about how to construct the object that needs investigation. And these commitments involve non-trivial claims about the nature of reason and its relation to other, related forms of human sensibility. There is nothing wrong with such reliance, but it should be more than implicit." Lewis, *Why Philosophy Matters for the Study of Religion– and Vice Versa*, 81–82.

for shaping an adequate concept of religion. Otherwise, our understanding of religion would not be possible to develop. The concept of religion that informs the interpretation of what is at hand is of vital significance: without it, we would not be able to understand either what religion is or to develop and adjust our understanding of it. Not only is religion itself a contextual and historical phenomenon; so is the preconditions for our understanding of it as well.

Lewis argues that Hegel uses the term 'religion' for elements that refer "to the representations and other practices through which we come to know the absolute."[22] Although Hegel focuses on knowing here, and we need to expand that by saying that religions, furthermore, also is about *engaging* the absolute, this nevertheless points to the important *pedagogical* role of religion in Hegel's thinking. He "develops a vision in which religion plays a central role in shaping our deep intuitions about social and political life,"[23] and this role seems to problematize or contradict contemporary approaches to religion, which argue that it should be separated from the political sphere in principle. It is not possible because of its rootedness in the deep psyche of the human. The value commitments from which we orient ourselves are not something we can bracket or ignore in parts of our lives without severe consequences.[24] On the other hand, Hegel "argues adamantly against conceptions that would offer religious or theological legitimation for particular political claims."[25] "With respect to the conceptualization of religion, a crucial point is that religion will be closely connected to politics. Both social and political institutions, on the one hand, and religion, on the other, manifest our conceptions of the communal social practices that collectively constitute spirit or the absolute."[26] It is hard not to read these insights in Hegel as a comment on those who argue for a normative position that secularization implies that one should keep religions and politics separate – as this cannot be the case, even at the empirical level. Religion influences all areas of human life, since it is in principle about orientation in all of them.

---

[22] Ibid., 77.

[23] Ibid.

[24] Ibid. "Because religion shares philosophy's content but is more closely connected to feeling, religion – particularly a child's early religious formation – frequently powerfully informs the subject's most firmly held commitments about our relations to others – how we depend on them, what we owe them, how we ought to act toward them, and so forth. While these commitments can in principle be revised, they are often deeply habitual and pre-reflective. They constitute what we take for granted (and do not articulate) as much as or more than views we espouse in words."

[25] Ibid., 78.

[26] Ibid.

Of course, the fact that value commitments, including those that inform our political stance, are rooted deeply in our personal feelings, judgments, and psychological dispositions does not mean that they cannot be altered or revised. Philosophical reflection may criticize or offer justification for them, and thereby make them more transparent. However, such later reflective practices can lead to different results. "Depending on circumstances the result may be a reformation of habits or a divided self split between deeply ingrained habits and pre-reflective responses, on the one hand, and explicit, theoretical commitments, on the other," writes Lewis.[27] In both cases, an element of transformation is required, and religious practices of formation and reflection may provide the means for it. Thus, we see again how religion contributes to the manifestation and articulation of unfinished business.

According to Hegel, religion is not directed toward a transcendent, superhuman subject. Religion works to express and shape our self-understanding. Hence, it is a "set of practices through which we reflect upon and express our essence, spirit."[28] Therefore, religion is related to more than the cognitive dimension in human life and practice: religion is "an interrelated set of feelings, representations, rituals, and other social practices that mold and express a consciousness of our own essence."[29] Moreover, when Hegel focuses on religious practices, he does not exclude belief because "religious practices cannot be understood without reference to the content of religious representations – and vice versa. Hegel thus challenges the reduction of religion to either belief or practice."[30] Hence, he opens up to a wider space for considering what religion is all about than what is the case when one focuses on religion as primarily about peoples' beliefs. In this way, he seems to combine a pragmatic and a transcendental approach to religion – since it implies that he then can focus on the effects religious practices has on peoples' lives and self-understanding as the presupposition for their agency.

Transcendental and pragmatist reflections on religion

The complexities and difficulties in defining religion suggest that it is not possible to understand it by means of an easily defined category or a fixed concept.

---

[27] Ibid., 77.
[28] Ibid., 215.
[29] Ibid.
[30] Ibid., 209–10.

The very concept of religion must reflect that we need to see religion as a historical and processual phenomenon, which is implied in or shaped by different experiential contexts. The "implied in or shaped by" here suggests that what religion is about, goes beyond what these contexts contain from a mere empirical point of view. If religion, as I will argue further below, is about human orientation and transformation by means of engaging what Robert Neville calls 'ultimates,'[31] it means that *religions deal with the transcendental conditions for human experience and attempt to formulate and engage those in ways that shape, form, and expand human life, agency, and understanding.* Sometimes, religious practices and reflections may cover up the fact that such transcendental conditions are what religion symbolically articulates and engages. But theological and philosophical reflection need to explicate this fact. It is by doing so we can see that the unfinished business of religion is related to how these transcendentals or ultimates are implied in human life, whereas simultaneously slipping away from consciousness or even being contradicted in the actual and immediate experiences we have of them.

The phenomenon of love, which I hold to be central for a theological notion of religion, is an example of what I am after here. I will return to it as the main topic later. Here, the intention is only to point to how experiences of love, present or absent, shape our mode of being in the world. Love is as an important element from which we orient ourselves – even when it is not there. Love can serve as an ultimate point of orientation, but also as something that contributes to the transformation of human life. Love, or the need for love, may be shaping life even when it is not articulated or recognized. Love is more than present – it shapes life also when it is not. Therefore, it is more than an actual phenomenon, although it is that, as well: it is a transcendental condition for experience, agency, and understanding of self and world.

If we see religions as clusters of practices that provide us with resources for engaging 'ultimates' that contribute to orientation in, and transformation of, the human condition, then more is implied in religions than what appears first hand, or only by focusing on their symbols, rituals, narratives, and practices in their immediate presence. Also, as already suggested, more is implied than what doctrine and moral guidance explicate. This "more," I argue, one needs to explicate along two already suggested different lines of thought: one that concerns the transcendental conditions for flourishing human life and experience, and the

---

[31] See Robert C. Neville, *Ultimate Realities* (Albany: State University of New York Press, 2001).

other the actual pragmatic dimension inherent in religion. These two lines of reasoning support each other and can illuminate each other.

What do I mean by *transcendentals* here? How can we understand religions as providing access to, articulating and mediating transcendental conditions of human life? Transcendental elements condition and shape our actual experience of the world, and our agency, as well as our self-understanding, without themselves being immediately present or accessible, under our control or something that we can generate. Kant spoke about transcendental conditions for reason, morals, and aesthetics, and something similar is meant here, but not as conditions existing in the mind.[32] At this point, it is necessary to recall the difference between transcendence and the transcendental: the transcendent is simply that which is beyond our world, that which is not part of our realms of experience, but which we sometimes can get a glimpse of in our actual experiences. The transcendental is, on the other hand, that which is implied in, and *necessary* for our actual experience, its content and shape. Of course, from a theological point of view, it is difficult to maintain a rigid distinction between the transcendent and transcendentals. E.g., one could say that God as transcendent is also the transcendental condition for human experience. However, such a characterization would make God part of the created order, and it should, therefore, be avoided. The transcendentals I speak of here and in the following are part of the created order, and therefore intimately related to the actual experiences we have of the world.

Pragmatism is not a philosophical system or a specific set of methods or convictions but identifies some main concerns and interests on which most pragmatists seem to agree. "The pragmatist tradition, like any philosophical tradition, is dynamically evolving, living, and changing, not fixed once and for all."[33] It represents an open-ended approach that does not provide final or ultimate answers to anything. Instead, it is concerned with understanding human practices and the specific human mode of being in the world, including how

---

[32] Some may also call this type of reasoning, because it does not see the transcendentals as existing only in the human mind (as did Kant), for retroduction. For a discussion on this type of reasoning, based in critical realism, see Berth Danermark and Mats Ekström, *Explaining Society : Critical Realism in the Social Sciences*, Second edition. ed., Routledge Studies in Critical Realism (Abingdon, Oxon ; New York, NY: Routledge, 2019), 96–98.

[33] The following presentation of pragmatism draws heavily on elements in S. Pihlström, "Introduction" in Sami Pihlström, *The Bloomsbury Companion to Pragmatism*, Bloomsbury Companions (London: Bloomsbury Academic, 2015), 5 et passim. For in-depth studies on different aspects of pragmatist approaches to religion, see Hermann Deuser et al., *The Varieties of Transcendence : Pragmatism and the Theory of Religion* (New York: Fordham University Press, 2016).

this mode comes to expression in ethics and religion. Pragmatists are concerned with human practices and habits.[34] They are interested in philosophical views and concepts as these are examined in practical, experiential terms. They do not recognize a sharp dichotomy between theory and practice, as "even the most theoretical scientific or philosophical matters are examined in the light of their potential connections with practical human action."[35] The emphasis on practice means that pragmatic approaches to being human do not find the transcendental conditions for human understanding of and engagement in reality in fixed structures of the human mind. These conditions are located "in historically changing human practices, which nevertheless have provided us with contexts within which it (only) is possible for us to experience an objectively organized world."[36] Hence, pragmatism opens up to a historicist approach to religious traditions and implies that there is no neutral position from which to evaluate these. In addition, this historicist perspective is the basis for the emphasis on semiotics we find in pragmatism: We are constantly involved in semiotic practices in which we try to make sense of the world – a point we will return to below.

Although pragmatism therefore explicitly denies the possibility for a "God's eye view," it does not exclude normative judgments about what positions and ideas are good or not. However, the focus on the practical implications of ideas provides a basis for this assessment. The advantage of this approach is

---

[34] As for habits, pragmatism understands them as socially produced and mediated. Hence, they are "not simply individualistic responses to the world; they are also socially instituted, reinforced, and transmitted." Moreover, "The unconscious routines of individual agents are acquired through experiences that are not solely individual but are, at least to some extent, social." Accordingly, pragmatism sees "the individual herself, the self as the unit of action and organized experience, [as] socially constituted." See John McGowan, *Democracy's Children : Intellectuals and the Rise of Cultural Politics* (Ithaca, N.Y.: Cornell University Press, 2002), 208. To what extent this dialectic between the individual and the social is recognized is a debated theme, cf. e.g., the discussion about W. James' individual approach as criticized in Charles Taylor, *Varieties of Religion Today: William James Revisited* (Cambridge, Mass. ; London: Harvard University Press, 2002).

[35] Cf. Pihlström, *The Bloomsbury Companion to Pragmatism*, 4. Pihlström points, as do others, to the overlap between the features of pragmatism and the insights articulated in Wittgenstein's philosophy. With regard to religion, "no account can be given of belief which does not take note of the way in which it is interwoven with the surrounding features of human life. It is how a religious belief is acted out in this context which determines what kind of sense, if any, it may have." Furthermore, "What happens to a religion in a form of life cannot be laid down in advance. It is a matter of its fate in a complex network of influences and counter-influences." D. Z. Phillips, *Belief, Change, and Forms of Life* (Atlantic Highlands: Humanities Press International, 1986), 79. A detailed account of Wittgenstein's relation to pragmatism is Sami Pihlström, "A New Look at Wittgenstein and Pragmatism," *European Journal of Pragmatism and American Philosophy* IV, no. 2 (2012).

[36] Pihlström, *The Bloomsbury Companion to Pragmatism*, 10.

that we can avoid questions about the extent to which a religious practice is "true" in any abstract or context-less sense. Instead, one can ask to what extent it is justified under specific conditions, given its practical implications.[37] The main element in normative assessments is the focus on how practices enable and support human flourishing. In the present context, this is of crucial importance, since one main element in how to assess religion is to consider to what extent it contributes to this aim, and since a significant portion of criticism of religion claims that it does not.

Religions as practice-based (Christian Smith and Martin Riesebrodt)

Sociologist Christian Smith contributes further to overcome the theoretical and cognitive-based approach to religion from an empirical angle. He reminds us that religion – and what we think of as such – is not only the result of cognitive processes and concepts that we have developed but also the result of social practices. In his view, religion "is best defined as a complex of culturally prescribed practices that are based on premises about the existence and nature of superhuman powers. These powers may be personal or impersonal, but they are always superhuman in the dual sense that they can do things that humans cannot do and that they do not depend for their existence on human activities."[38]

Although Smith does not self-identify as a pragmatist, there is a lot to say about how his approach coincides with this movement. In *The Varieties of Religious Experience*, William James argues that under every religious creed is a basic experience or sense that something is wrong about us as we naturally stand. The solution to this predicament is that "we are saved from the wrongness by making a proper connection with the higher powers."[39] In this connection, it is the notion of "higher powers" that interests us. James' claim sheds light over the role of religion in several ways. First, religious practices can contribute to identify, articulate, and even enhance the sense that there is something wrong with humans or what they do. Moreover, the possible access to solutions to this predicament: the connection with higher powers necessary for solving it, is

---

[37] The position that religion should be assessed with regard to how it can present justifications for its practices, instead of asking about to what extent it is true, is argued by D.-M. Grube in Dirk-Martin Grube and Walter Van Herck, *Philosophical Perspectives on Religious Diversity Bivalent Truth, Tolerance and Personhood* (London: Routledge, 2018).

[38] Smith, *Religion : What It Is, How It Works, and Why It Is Still Important*, 3.

[39] William James, *The Varieties of Religious Experience : A Study in Human Nature*, Penguin Classics (New York ; London: Penguin Books, 1985), 508.

never established directly but is mediated by practices in which others are involved. Hence, the one who wants to overcome religiously mediated experiences of wrongness needs to relate to practices that facilitate such overcoming. These practices may be of a different kind, depending on how one understands the "wrongness." No matter how this is done, one needs to establish an alliance with superhuman powers that does not depend on humans for their existence.

Religious traditions deal with the human predicament and wrongness in diverse ways. M. Riesebrodt argues that the promise of salvation is among the elements that are constitutive to what we call religion.[40] I concur with this claim, if we, as suggested, extend that description and speak instead of the promise of some deliverance from evil and achievement of some good, given that it implies "a proper orientation of life towards a transcendent reality and the hopes connected with it."[41] Thus, a pragmatic approach identifies different views about salvation as the possible plural modes in which the human condition is mirrored, developed, and transformed by a diversity of practices that aim to mediate it.[42]

This detour via William James and Martin Riesebrodt is not only pointing to how Smith's understanding of religion seems to concur with certain pragmatist themes. It also suggests that they agree in terms of substance. Smith's understanding of religion aims at avoiding some of the problems connected to other definitions of religion. He writes:

Religious people engage in complexes of practices in order to gain access to and communicate or align themselves with these superhuman powers. The hope involved in the cultural prescribing of these practices is to realize human goods and to avoid bads, especially (but not only) to avert misfortunes and receive blessings and deliverance from crises. *Key to this definition is the dual emphasis on prescribed practices and superhuman powers, which distinguish it from other approaches that focus instead on people's beliefs or meanings (rather than practices) and on the supernatural, sacred, transcendent, divine, or ultimate concern (rather than superhuman powers). This emphasis helps to avoid problems that plague other theories of religion.*[43]

---

[40] See Martin Riesebrodt, *The Promise of Salvation : A Theory of Religion* (Chicago: University of Chicago Press, 2010).

[41] Perry Schmidt–Leukel, here quoted from Frederiek Depoortere and Magdalen Lambkin, *The Question of Theological Truth : Philosophical and Interreligious Perspectives*, Currents of Encounter (Amsterdam ; New York: Rodopi, 2012), 279.

[42] Thus, it becomes understandable why a Christian understanding can differ from a Hindu one: salvation restores the basic problem in Christianity that is lack of community with God. In Hinduism, the achievement of *nirvana* is the solution to the problem about how to exit the eternal cycle of reincarnation. These notions are, accordingly, in one sense incompatible, although from a pragmatic point of view they represent different solutions to "wrongness." For the understanding of different 'salvations' from the point of view of a philosophy of religion inspired by pragmatism, see Henriksen, *Openness and Resistance* (forthcoming, 2019).

[43] Smith, *Religion : What It Is, How It Works, and Why It Is Still Important*, 3. My italics.

Several elements are worth noting in this quote: First, a point that we will have to return to in a later chapter, namely that Smith, like others, see religions as attempts to deal with specific challenges that are inherent in the human condition. Religions are, therefore, not possible to understand simply as something that has to do only with a non-existent or imagined reality – a point that I have already suggested above in the identification of religion as dealing with transcendental conditions for human life. Second, and furthermore, Smith approaches religions from the point of view of practices instead of beliefs and uses the notion 'superhuman powers' in order to avoid notions of the divine, supernatural, etc. By prioritizing these elements in his definition of religion, he moves the understanding of religion closer to empirical realities: practices are observable, and humans are not the only source of powers in the world.[44] To define them as "superhuman," though, means that he recognizes that religious people see themselves as interacting with powers that influence them and shapes them, without having their origin only in themselves or in something of which they are in control.[45]

W. James' notion of 'Wrongness' may suggest that there is something inherently destroyed, impeded, or incapacitated in human life that should not have been, and that religious practices provide a solution to or repair for this situation. However, at this point, C. Smith offers another, and I would argue, more open and empirically validated interpretation of what is at stake and why engagement of superhuman powers appear as desirable. That does not presuppose some previous, initial, or original state of being human that is now left behind. Instead, religion originates from "humans' unique possession of a complicated combination of natural capacities and limitations." These capacities "make it possible for humans to conceive of and believe in superhuman powers that are

---

[44] Ibid., 23.

[45] Smith defines these powers further by saying that "'Superhuman' here means that these powers are (believed to be) able to influence or control significant parts of reality that are usually beyond direct human intervention. That is why humans need their help. Normally these superhuman powers are also not directly observable by human senses. Their sphere of influence may concern personal experiences, human social life, the natural environment, and life after death. Superhuman powers can make happen things that human powers cannot, at least in some situations – that is what makes them superhuman." Ibid., 22. Moreover, they are not human creations (ibid., 23). I cannot go further into that topic here, but this point may have some resemblance to what Charles Taylor means when he talks about how a pre-modern mode of being in the world (as religious) meant having a porous self as opposed to a modern, buffered one. See Charles Taylor, *A Secular Age* (Cambridge, Mass. ; London: Belknap Press of Harvard University Press, 2007), 33, and https://tif.ssrc.org/2008/09/02/buffered-and-porous-selves/ .

not immediately present, and to find ways to try to access their help."[46] The recognition of the natural limitations in our mode of being "provide good motivations for seeking such help."[47] Thus, Smith provides an explanation for the evolvement of religion that takes into account how religion represents a response to the human condition and its limitation as this is perceived by human imagination. In this connection, he uses the notion "space" for that mental context in which religion originates: "The uncomfortable existential space created by the collision of amazing human powers and severe human incapacities provides the grounds in which religions germinate, grow, and flourish. Seeking the help of superhuman powers to live in that difficult space – and to realize humanly good and avoid bad things within it – is the central reason why people practice religion."[48]

One advantage of this approach to religion is the aforementioned foundation of it in practices that do not require personal commitments or special beliefs to exist. Practices create the space in which religions take place: By pointing to religions as "culturally prescribed religious practices," Smith thus approaches religion in a way that does not only focus on "people as religious practitioners and what they may or may not believe."[49] A major advantage of this approach is that he can identify religion also where such practices are not dependent on how much "people embrace or dissent from their religious traditions."[50] Hence, it is not their thoughts and feelings about their religions, including their critical, alienated, and dissenting positions, that make religion, but the cultural traditions that mediate the practices in which they partake for different reasons, and with a variety of different beliefs, criticisms, and dissent.[51]

The consequence is that religion appears as porous and without any specific essence, whereas simultaneously possible to detect, identify, and analyze as an empirical phenomenon. From the point of view of an outsider perspective, it is not difficult to argue, as I have done elsewhere, that religions contribute to orientation about fundamental features of human life, and to the understanding of and the tools for necessary transformations at a personal as well as at a social level. When Smith identifies religion as "a complex of culturally prescribed practices, based on premises about the existence and nature of superhuman powers, whether personal or impersonal, which seek to help practitioners gain

---

[46] Smith, *Religion : What It Is, How It Works, and Why It Is Still Important*, 5.
[47] Ibid.
[48] Ibid.
[49] Ibid., 15.
[50] Ibid.
[51] Ibid.

access to and communicate or align themselves with these powers, in hopes of realizing human goods and avoiding things bad"[52], it substantiates this approach and specifies it further. According to him, "to avert misfortunes and receive blessings and deliverance from crises of many kinds," be it in terms of mundane or more "spiritual," other-worldly terms.[53]

A further advantage in Smith's empirically oriented approach is that it allows for recognizing that religions focus on elements that are part of the world as we experience it, and not only focus on the supernatural or transcendent. This allows him to identify elements in religion that can count as "ultimates" even when they are empirically accessible. Examples of such ultimates that are providing conditions for human life can be found in religious traditions that focus on superhuman powers linked to natural phenomena like the spirits of trees and streams – elements that suggest that human life is also dependent on water, plants, and nature.[54]

I have suggested already that we need to see religions as clusters of practices. Smith's view on religion seems to correspond well with this understanding, as he sees religions as consisting in part "of a complex of culturally prescribed practices." According to him, such practices "are culturally meaningful behaviors that are intentionally repeated over time."[55] These elements – meaning, behavior, intentionality, and repetition – are all constitutive for what can count as a genuine practice. Accordingly, he writes:

Religions are formed from networks of practices grouped together into complexes. A single practice does not make a religion. One does not simply burn some incense or read the passage of a text and thereby have a religion. Religions are composed of conglomerations of interrelated practices, sometimes so many that it takes a lifetime to learn to perform them well. Each of the practices has its own meaning, and each usually adds extra meaning to the others in the larger complex of practices to which they belong.[56]

The issue of complexity should not be underestimated here: the combination of individual and self-explanatory practices can allow them to enrich each other's meaning, e.g., in religious worship: "The combined meaning is more than the sum of its parts. Complexes of religious practices, which are part of even the

---

[52] Ibid., 22.
[53] Ibid.
[54] Ibid., 24.
[55] Ibid., 25.
[56] Ibid.

simplest of religions, thus generate synergies and experiences that individual practices alone do not."[57]

Practices cannot exist without, or independent of cultural patterns and traditions that are shared by communities. They "are never random, idiosyncratic, or arbitrary. If they were, then they could not be meaningful."[58] Moreover, they are mostly *social activities,* dependent upon "communities of memory engaged in carrying on particular traditions."[59] Traditions are of significance because they legitimize the practices and provide the point of reference in the past that gives authority to the present.

Practices are dependent on beliefs in order to be culturally meaningful. However, Smith underscores how "meaning is more than beliefs, but it always depends upon some beliefs." Accordingly, "to initiate some religious practice, some people at some time must hold some beliefs."[60] Such beliefs are also related to the purpose of the practices. Here we see, again, how Smith develops his understanding of practices in a way that is similar to the one referred above as William James': "The presupposition of religious practices specifically is some premises about the existence of some superhuman powers that those practices aim to access. Thus, some beliefs are essential to religion's constitution, even if, again, they are not central to its performance and study."[61]

Religious practitioners do not need to "authentically believe in the premises and cultural meanings behind the practices they perform."[62] It is sufficient "that the practice itself is institutionalized in a complex of repeated actions that are culturally meaningful in religious terms, that is, oriented toward gaining access to superhuman powers."[63] Hence, Smith can maintain that for religious practices to be meaningful, it is not required that they are constituted by "cognitive assent of the people engaged in them at any given time but from a variety of

---

[57] Ibid., 26.
[58] Ibid.
[59] Ibid., 26–27.
[60] Ibid., 30.
[61] Ibid., 30–31. He specifies the purpose further, thus: "This purpose should be broadly construed to include steps like making contact with, sustaining a relationship with, attuning oneself to, learning the will of, worshipping, attempting to manipulate, winning the attention of, honoring, pleasing, appeasing, feeding, bargaining with, and more."
[62] Ibid., 32.
[63] Ibid.

institutional sources, including historical traditions, sacred texts, and explanations by religious specialists."[64] Accordingly, such practices cannot be reduced
to the beliefs of the people who enact them."[65] Smith goes on, writing:

Attempting to define religion theoretically by referencing practitioners' subjectivities is a misguided enterprise. By contrast, the intended meanings of religious cultures, traditions, and institutions are more or less objective, public, and focused, and so provide firmer grounds for conceptualizing a definition of religion. Empirically – that is, what we can observe about people's
actual practicing of religions – what religious institutions prescribe and why people practice religions are nearly always coupled, but we often observe only a "loose coupling," not a tight fit.
Our theoretical account of religion needs to account for that loose coupling. Again, an interest in
understanding the subjective motives of religious people is entirely valid and often necessary.
But that shifts our attention away from defining religion analytically – what we are trying to do
in this chapter – and toward studying religiousness empirically, a key distinction […] that we
need to grasp and maintain.[66]

Smith's approach to religion as clusters of practices allows him to avoid the
idea that beliefs come first, and practices follow. Beliefs are not more fundamental than practices.[67] Instead, one has to recognize the mutual influence that
practices and beliefs have on each other. Thus, his is not a mere cognitivist
theory about religion that builds on the premise that religion originates from
beliefs and cognitive assumptions only. In his view, although religion also requires cognitive activity, it is "embodied practices oriented toward superhuman
powers [that] define the core of religion."[68] The dynamic character of religions
is linked to how the practices rooted in traditions and culture interact and are
changing over time and due to context:

Clusters of religious practices are always diverse, converging, and diverging. The boundaries of
religious traditions are porous, the premises and practices themselves often contain glitches and
unanswerable questions, and the human cultures prescribing and persons performing the practices are by nature creative. A realistic concept of religious traditions, therefore, must grasp that
their temporal continuities are relative, so religious cultures and institutions are always located

---

[64] Ibid.
[65] Ibid. Hence, Smith holds that "Religion is not most fundamentally a cognitive or existential
meaning system. Rather, it is essentially a set of practices aimed at accomplishing things that
humans consider to be good and avoiding bads." Ibid., 41.
[66] Ibid., 34–35.
[67] Ibid., 44.
[68] Ibid., 45: "It is not that people first think or comprehend something religious and subsequently
undertake a practice. Rather, the idea of many practices is to work the other way around: People
need to start engaging in the prescribed practices and, it is hoped, as a result they should over
time find themselves transformed in spirit and mind. Practices, in other words, are formative, not
simply expressive."

somewhere in the middle range of a spectrum between the extremes of absolute flux and permanent changelessness.[69]

Smith's analysis of religion thus makes visible its rootedness in practices, tradition, and culture, and not in individual beliefs, although beliefs are not without importance. The dynamic character of religions cannot be underestimated and is related to, I argue, how the practices in question are oriented towards both orientation and transformation with respect to contemporary challenges. Moreover, although not advocating a cognitivist theory of religion, Smith also provides good reasons for seeing religion in a pragmatist frame that makes it necessary to hold together its substantial and functional dimension, as we shall see below that Schilbrack argues. This dynamic character is also a testimony to the unfinished or open character of religious engagement.

Defining religion between functional and substantive definitions (Schilbrack)

It follows from the understanding of religion presented via Hegel above that religion is rooted deeply in different realms of human existence. It has the consequence that even when we interpret religion from a pragmatic point of view, this approach should not be mistaken for a mere functionalist approach to religion. Religious practices and representations are not easily exchanged or substituted with alternatives that provide exactly the same effects. However, when we understand religions from a pragmatic point of view, and primarily as clusters of practices, what consequences does this understanding have? The classical discussion about approaches to religion from a functional versus a substantive perspective is relevant when we try to answer that question. We can get a better grasp of this topic by looking into the recent discussion by Kevin Schilbrack. His treatment recommends itself because it allows us to see some of the nuances and possibilities when we address the practices within a larger context that also includes beliefs.

Schilbrack's definition of religion rests on the combination of a functional and a substantive definition: The functional he calls promissory (cf. Riesebrodt's notion of religion as the promise of salvation as well as James' notion of wrongness as overcome by an alliance with higher powers), whereas the substantive focuses on the empirical. He sees the combination of these two as the most fruitful for the study of religion. The former identifies "certain beliefs, practices, institutions, and communities as religious in terms of what such

---

[69] Ibid., 48.

phenomena do for the participants." The latter "define certain beliefs, practices, institutions, and communities as religious in terms of their focal object."[70]

If one wants to address religion across cultures, the functional approach recommends itself. Functional definitions do not require that cultural phenomena must include a belief in God, and they are dynamic and "permit one to study religions in whatever forms they take from one culture to another, and they permit one to recognize the emergence of new forms of religion."[71] Nevertheless, the challenge related to this approach is that it needs to be developed in order to be able to differentiate religion from other cultural phenomena – a problem that does not present itself in the same way when one operates with substantive definitions.

Does one need to choose one of the approaches? Not necessarily. Schilbrack holds that the choice between functional and substantive definitions overlooks the fact that "many of the beliefs, practices, institutions, and communities that are called religious actually satisfy both kinds of definition."[72] This overlap, as he calls it, in the extension of the two definitions, shapes an "area in which one can find cultural phenomena that are religious according to either strategy."[73] Hence, in this area, we find cultural phenomena that are both functionally and substantively religious. According to Schilbrack, "They have to involve both an ontological and a pragmatic commitment. [...] Together, they articulate what might be called a mixed definition that identifies two features that are necessary for something to be recognized as a religion."[74]

From a critical point of view, the distinction between these two approaches does not contribute to a better understanding of religion(s), but to dissecting religion by focusing only on certain aspects that do not contribute to better understanding. Hence, Schilbrack holds that "the most useful definition of religion for the academic study of religions is the one that identifies these two aspects as both being required."[75] He goes on:

One aspect concerns why a belief is held and a practice done, the functional or pragmatic aspect of religion. The other aspect concerns what the beliefs and practices are about, the substantive or ontological aspect of religion. If one does not insist on a pure functionalist or a pure substantive definition, then one can see that the two can overlap, in the sense that a belief or a practice or an institution can be both functionally religious (providing certain kinds of benefits) and also

---

[70] Schilbrack, *Philosophy and the Study of Religions: A Manifesto*, 116–17.
[71] Ibid., 117.
[72] Ibid.
[73] Ibid., 117–18.
[74] Ibid., 119.
[75] Ibid. 120.

substantively religious (concerning certain kinds of realities). The best definition for the future of philosophy of religion, in my view, is therefore a mixed one.[76]

This approach may be seen as irenic, but it does not imply that Schilbrack sees the approaches or definitions as being on equal terms. We can approach religions from the point of view of people's agency, by asking what they hope to get out of it. Thus, a functional or pragmatic approach sees religions as composed of actions that people do in order to accomplish something. "Religious people believe that religious actions help them."[77] The question is, in what way? With what? At this point, it is possible to link up Schilbrack's pragmatic approach with the one I have suggested, which sees religion as basically about orientation and transformation. Religious practices, therefore, cannot be isolated from the purposes, aims, and agency of those who practice. Problems call for transformations that overcome them. It is against this backdrop that Schilbrack suggests that the pragmatic approach may also be seen as "therapeutic" or "promissory." The notion "therapeutic" captures how religions are "typically composed of embodied social practices that seek to heal one's life as a whole but also to cure and protect the body, the community, and the natural world." Here, religions offer different diagnoses and different solutions. The "promissory" dimension in religion is expressed in how they are "composed of embodied social practices that promise benefits." None of this can be done without seeing religion as normative and prescriptive with regard to practices that "teach people how to act wisely, properly, or best. Religion is therefore here defined not simply as a set of beliefs about religious realities but also as a set of practices that promise right living."[78]

Schilbrack's decision to approach religion from the point of view of practices implies that one can identify moral, cognitive, and aesthetic dimensions in these practices[79] and that a religious practitioner is not only a believer, but engages in a specific mode of life, or of being in the world. Thus, some of the ways he describes religion here come close to the Wittgenstein-inspired approach to religion as formulated by D.Z. Phillips. Phillips argues that "no account can be given of belief which does not take note of the way in which it is interwoven with the surrounding features of human life."[80] Thereby he makes a point that is important to highlight, but he also adds something to Schilbrack's

---

[76] Ibid., 120–21.
[77] Ibid., 121.
[78] Ibid., 122–23.
[79] Cf. Ibid., 124.
[80] Phillips, *Belief, Change, and Forms of Life*, 79.

analysis: Namely, that religious practices only have meaning in relation to other practices, from which they can be differentiated as religious. Thus, for religious practices to be what they are, a certain negation is needed (cf. Hegel, above). Moreover, "It is how a religious belief is acted out in this context which determines what kind of sense, if any, it may have."[81] In other words: Religion is conditioned by a pragmatic context that goes beyond its own boundaries. Phillips points to this fact aptly when he writes that, "It is a misunderstanding to speak of a religion as a form of life. What can be said is that it is impossible to imagine a religion without imagining it *in* a form of life."[82]

For the overall argument of this book, the point Phillips makes here is important because it underscores the openness in religious practices; the unfinished and open-ended character of its meaning within the diversity of contexts where they appear, are practiced, and manifested: "What happens to a religion in a form of life cannot be laid down in advance. It is a matter of its fate in a complex network of influences and counter-influences," he writes.[83] Accordingly, both Schilbrack and Phillips provide a reminder of how religion is dependent upon the cultural context, and cannot be considered as independent or separated from the cultural and societal conditions to which it belongs.

The critical front, against which this approach can be utilized, is, of course, an approach to religion that treats it as mere propositions – an approach that can tempt one to think of religion in terms of what is private and above history. However, a practice-based approach that sees religions' meaning as intertwined with historical, social and cultural conditions that are not religious, but nevertheless contribute to its significance, contradicts this approach and allows for a historicized, dynamic and processual understanding that sees religious practices as "patterns of desires, as emotional and volitional commitments, as investments in styles of living. Religion here involves people who develop projects with others over time, thereby creating individual and group identities."[84]

The open-ended variety of functions we find in religious practices nevertheless have not yet been identified with regard to their specific *religious* character. Schilbrack sees this lack of specification as a good thing because it does not preclude, by definition, what religious communities care about from the outset.[85] Nevertheless, one needs to define something as specific to religion in

---

[81] Ibid.
[82] Ibid.
[83] Ibid.
[84] Schilbrack, *Philosophy and the Study of Religions : A Manifesto*, 124.
[85] Ibid., 125.

order to distinguish it from other cultural (and thereby normative) practices. Hence, the *ontological* questions about what religious communities presuppose as *being the case* in their practices and teachings cannot be bracketed out or ignored.[86] In my words: When religions is understood, analytically, in terms of practices for orientation or transformation, these practices will unavoidably presuppose some ideas about what it is that one needs to orient oneself in relation to, and what the starting point and end point are, for transformative practices. In all of this, values and ontological presuppositions are intertwined. Schilbrack describes this well:

> People have beliefs insofar as they take something as true, and they take something as true as soon as they act in any purposive way. Therefore, even in cases in which a religious community has not developed an explicit ontological account that justifies its practices, identifying practices by their ontology is still appropriate. This is so because agents have a prereflective understanding of the world in which they operate. It is precisely this pre-reflective engagement with the world that one seeks to make reflective when one's practices fail or are challenged… For this reason, we can define religion as normative practices that at least implicitly make ontological claims in terms of which the practical norms are authorized.[87]

Both reflective and prereflective religious practices are therefore operating on conditions in which practical and ontological aspects are interdependent. It is against this backdrop that one must understand discussions about truth in religion. Schilbrack, therefore, claims that "making truth claims is intrinsic to religion and one cannot identify religious practices without them."[88] Nevertheless, the analytic differentiation one has to make from a scholarly point of view with regard to religious practices, and the understanding of the world that gives them sense does not imply that religion, as it is lived, is dichotomous.[89] The question is, then, what are the ontological commitments or assumptions that can be defined as religious? It is at this point that *substantive* definitions of religion are needed.

We need not refer to all the definitions that Schilbrack rejects as being inadequate for a substantive definition. His concern is to establish an inclusive definition that can encompass empirical elements, and which needs not ignore the "worldly" elements that are understood as religiously significant for religious practitioners. Moreover, it should not necessarily have to be based on

---

[86] Ibid., 126–27.
[87] Ibid., 128–29.
[88] Ibid., 129.
[89] Cf. Ibid.

some kind of dualism. Also, it is not sufficient to speak of "nonempirical" elements, as such elements and judgments based on them are also found outside
the context of religious practice.[90] "All forms of culture are evaluative and will
seek to speak through symbols and metaphors to describe invisible orders of
significance and value. Consequently, one cannot say that the difference between what is and is not religion is that religions speak of nonempirical realities."[91] Instead, one must define religion in terms of how the conditions for these
nonempirical realities (such as the norms of goodness, beauty, and justice etc.)
are understood: do they depend on humans and other empirical beings, or do
they exist independent of empirically identifiable conditions? In the latter case,
we have a religious position.[92]

Hence, the substantive content of religious practices is primarily defined
by Schilbrack as *values*. That makes sense in relation to my own suggestion
about clusters of practices for orientation and transformation: Values tell us
what matters and what does not, define importance, goods and bads, why transformation is needed and towards what, etc. What makes these practices *religious* is that they constitute and exist in communities "that adopt values that
they do not believe depend on human or other empirical forms of agency."[93]
Schilbrack calls these aspects of reality whose existence allegedly does not depend on empirical sources for *superempirical*. "Thus religions are composed of
those social practices authorized by reference to a superempirical reality, that
is, a reference to the character of the Gods, the will of the Supreme Being, the
metaphysical nature of things, or the like. In short, I define religion as *forms of
life predicated upon the reality of the superempirical*."[94]

Thus, Schilbrack contributes to understanding religions from a pragmatic
point of view, that allows for an open-ended approach that does not preclude or
limit what kind of reality (ontological) and what practices (functional) religious
commitments manifest themselves in and through. What we need to do in the
following, is to look closer at in what respect the assumptions of these superempirical elements provide the means for orientation and transformation. That
cannot be done without addressing their ultimate character. That is what Robert
C. Neville does in a recent book about the definition of religion.

---

[90] Cf. ibid., 133–34.
[91] Ibid., 134
[92] Cf. ibid.
[93] Ibid., 135.
[94] Ibid., My italics.

Religion, the ultimate, and human experiences (Neville)

Robert C. Neville defines religion as "the human engagement of ultimacy." According to him, such engagement "requires harmonizing semiotic cultural systems, aesthetic achievements, social institutions with their own dynamics, and psychological structures, along with intentional relations with what is ultimate. All these things can be present, but not harmonized so that something ultimate is engaged."[95] Two main elements in this definition are worth a comment. Firstly, when Neville speaks of religion as engagement with *ultimacy*, he qualifies further the role that the superempirical realities that Schilbrack identifies as the constituting elements for religion. Their realities do not only exist independently of humans and their agency, but they also provide humans with a relationship to ultimate significance and meaning, in a way that suggests that there is no going beyond these ultimate factors (which is why they are ultimate). What is ultimate is the elements that provide human life and human practices with a meaning that goes beyond the individual life and its contingencies. It seems reasonable to see these ultimates as something that is not easily exchangeable for an individual – if they were, they would not be considered worth engaging as ultimates. Secondly, agency is involved in such engagement, and this engagement with ultimates relates to pre-existing elements in the life-world of the religiously practicing person. Hence, religious engagement of the ultimate includes a relation to elements present in the everyday. As a consequence, religion cannot be seen as separated from ordinary life or existing in a sphere of its own – religious engagement is rather to be understood as a sacralization of everyday features. Accordingly, Neville can speak about how the human engagement of ultimacy is "expressed in cognitive articulations, existential responses to ultimacy that give ultimate definition to the individual, and patterns of life and ritual in the face of ultimacy."[96]

Since humans live under different conditions and with different cultural patterns and social institutions, the ways in which engagement of ultimacy happens will vary as well. Accordingly, what religion is cannot be defined once and for all, because religion will appear differently, not only from an empirical

---

[95] Robert C. Neville, *Defining Religion: Essays in Philosophy of Religion* (Albany, NY: State University of New York, 2018), 1. As for the psychological dimension that he mentions here, I do not develop it in the following. However, it should be noted that he explicitly relates to the different psychological dimensions of religion in the following manner: They have to do "with existential choice, spiritual quests, unifying bliss, and the dark night of the soul" (Ibid., 31).
[96] Ibid., 19.

point of view but also from the point of view of its more philosophical definitions. Neville consequently suggests that "religion is best defined heuristi-
cally."[97] When religion is defined thus, it can guide inquiry and help identify
what counts and not in it, without precluding investigations that focus on other
elements. Hence, religion itself is an open-ended concept that cannot be final-
ized conclusively in one definition. Neville expresses this point well when he
writes about how inquiries into religion should focus on "the connections
among the components of religion, and the components of components, and
how they harmonize in cases of engagement of ultimacy."[98]

Neville underscores that the "heuristic" approach he suggests does not imply a denial of realism in inquiry – a point that is important with reference to
positions that see religion merely as a construct of the West and often labeled
as 'postmodern.' He differentiates a postmodern from a pragmatic position, and
argues that "Inquiry in pragmatism is interaction, transaction, or engagement
… with things as guided by interpretations that employ signs,"[99] and these signs
can be corrected as their objects give feedback – a point that also Hegel seems
to realize in his understanding of how a concept is constituted.

Furthermore, Neville points to how "there is no obvious phenomenological
description of religion that is not itself a function of heuristic commitments."[100]
However, in order to develop a good heuristic definition of religion, he finds it
necessary to look at how religion relates to human experience. Thus, one can
find an answer to the question about how "any of the dimensions of human
experience are involved as components in ultimate engagements." The advantage of this approach is that one then can address the components in ultimate
engagements as an inquiry into religion insofar as such experiences are involved. [101]

There are two important obstacles to the study of religion from the point of
view of a heuristic definition like the one Neville suggests, and he addresses
both. The first is that "most of the disciplines that claim to be studying religion
do not acknowledge or have any internal way of dealing with ultimacy."[102] Although metaphysical forms of philosophy and religious philosophies and theologies may provide an exception to this lack of internal perspectives, it is not
given that one can comprehend the impact of religious engagement simply by

---

[97] Ibid.
[98] Ibid.
[99] Ibid., 20.
[100] Ibid., 21.
[101] Ibid., 23.
[102] Ibid.

studying it from an external perspective. This topic will occupy us further in the next section. The latter challenge is that "just about any dimension of experience, including politics, tradition, and the flow of consciousness, might or might not involve engaging ultimacy."[103] In other words: Elements of the everyday may, or may not, be considered to be of religious importance and be engaged accordingly.[104]

What is it then, if anything, that allows for something to be considered as religious or as having religious significance? Against the backdrop of what he calls semiotic cultures, Neville holds that various semiotic components "are religious insofar as they help articulate how the world achieves an actual identity that has the value of actualizing the possibilities it does."[105] Thus, it becomes possible to appreciate what good the world holds, and the origin of this goodness for which experiences of the world offer the possibility. This origin or source of goodness is worshipped in religious practices.[106]

Neville suggests that there are five ultimate realities: "an ontological creative act that creates everything that is determinate and four transcendental traits of anything whatsoever that is determinate: namely, form, components integrated in the form, existential location relative to other determinate things, and achieved value-identity."[107] A religion that has achieved a certain level of depth and reflective subtlety must cope with each of the ultimate realities.[108] It can be argued that the following chapters' analyses of love can serve as a way to interpret and explore the experiential as well as the transcendental dimension on the "ontological creative act."

Against the backdrop of this description, that Neville unfolds in far more detail than presented here, we can assess the quality in religious engagement with reality on the basis of what it helps us achieve. The quality is dependent on "how well it orients all the important domains of life with regard to the ways its sacred canopy facilitates engagement with ultimate realities."[109]

When Neville develops the understanding of how experiential engagement is to be understood, he not only points to how the different elements are interpreted in a wide diversity of ways, and thereby express different religious traditions as semiotic cultures. It furthermore implies that any interpretive act is

---

[103] Ibid.
[104] Cf. Ibid.
[105] Ibid., 33.
[106] Cf. Ibid.
[107] Ibid., 37.
[108] Ibid., 40.
[109] Ibid., 49–50.

shaped by the signs it employs. "Engagement takes the object engaged to be as the sign says in the respect in which the sign refers to the object. This means, among other things, that the experiencer always brings to engagement a semiotic set of signs that mediates the relation between the experiencer and the object."[110] A pragmatist position implies that diverse experience must be understood against this backdrop, as the interaction of human beings with their environment.

Furthermore, these features are also pointing towards the character of religion as open-ended and religious practices as unfinished business. Neville writes:

> Because engagement is dynamic, a kind of transaction, signs sometimes are modified in the engagement, old signs found wanting, new signs invented by analogy or wit. But there is no unmediated experience. Signs are always involved because we only engage the world in certain respects, relative to our contexts and purposes, and as enabled by the signs we have at our disposal.[111]

Because the elements that mediate religion are found in the world in which we exist, their ability to mediate the ultimate realities described above is always under revision, critique, or reconsideration. It is the very composite relationship between these ultimate realities and the present, experienced world that makes religion an unfinished business. Hence, it is not without reason that medieval theologians spoke about *Deus semper major.* This is why the character of all religion or religious practice as *representation* cannot be emphasized enough. If this is forgotten, religion becomes idolatry.

Can religions be understood in full when they are not practiced?

Although it is possible to assess religions from an external position according to their functions, This fact does not mean that it is possible to get full access to the experiences of how one relates to, or base oneself on, something of ultimacy in religion. Thus, a pragmatic perspective on religion that seeks to address more than its functional dimension needs to take into account that the reality of religion is dependent on a first-person perspective that involves the person in ways not accessible by mere observation. Accordingly, to approach it from the point of view of a third-person perspective seems insufficient. In one way, this point

---

[110] Neville, *Defining Religion : Essays in Philosophy of Religion,* 97.
[111] Ibid.

was articulated as early as Plato, when he stated that one could not know any-thing about the good in a qualified sense unless one participates in it. Corre-spondingly, one cannot fully know what religion is about without engaging in its practices of orientation, transformation, and reflection. If this point holds, engagement with ultimacy means that we need to consider more in detail the different ways to understand it. Some of this task may be completed by employ-ing further the resources developed earlier in this chapter, whereas there may also be other means that can help us with this task.

When Hegel points to how any understanding of religion relies on our con-cepts as contextually conditioned, he implicates that to understand religious en-gagement is dependent on already existing contents in our understanding. Reli-gion is a concept, based on, and a result of attempts to grasp some elements – or clusters of elements – in our reality. The concept is, however, not only a result of these attempts but also what shapes it beforehand. Thus, the anticipa-tory character of concepts, based on what experience and engagement one has already had, or not, determines one's understanding of religion. Heidegger has contributed further to elaborate on this point.

Although Heidegger's preference for immediacy may seem to set him apart from both Hegel and the pragmatists, some of the elements in his analysis of the human constitution (*Dasein*) merit attention in our context. He sees under-standing (*Verstehen*) as a fundamental *Existential*, expressed in the immediate relationship with the world as given in the life-world of employment of tools in practices. Against this backdrop, the objectifying, distanced mode in our rela-tionship with the world is derivative or secondary and based on the bracketing of our immediate, practice-based understanding.

Heidegger's understanding of engagement in and understanding the world is based on his identification of the intentional and anticipatory mode of being. We always understand something as "something in-order-to." Hence, we al-ways participate already in the world as something definite, as it exists for our (preliminary) understanding. "In the 'in-order-to' as a structure, there lies an assignment or reference of something to something."[112] Accordingly, agency based on participating in religious practices cannot be understood apart from this assignment and its intentional content. Substantial content is always pre-supposed by the agent. However, for Heidegger, this reference is not the only

---

[112] Martin Heidegger, *Sein Und Zeit* (Tübingen: M. Niemeyer, 1967), 68. Although references are to the German edition, some quotes are based on the English edition, which contains the original paging as well. See Martin Heidegger, John Macquarrie, and Edward Robinson, *Being and Time* (Malden: Blackwell, 2013).

point in question. He makes a distinction between the phenomena with which we engage as "ready to hand" and those that are "present at hand." Against the backdrop of this distinction, he argues that a mere "objective" approach will not do. If we try to understand something apart from its use and the way it presents itself in the intentional and practice-based structure of the agent, we miss the role it plays there. Although he makes this point with reference to the use of tools, we can employ a similar analysis to engagement in religious practices, although they may not only consist of things (but will have to be about things, as well).[113] He writes:

> No matter how sharply we just look at the 'outward appearance' of things in whatever form this takes, we cannot discover anything ready-to-hand. If we look at things just 'theoretically,' we can get along without understanding readiness-to-hand. But when we deal with them by using them and manipulating them, this activity is not a blind one; it has its own kind of sight, by which our manipulation is guided and from which it acquires its specific thingly character. Dealings with equipment subordinate themselves to the manifold assignments of the 'in-order-to.' And the sight with which they thus accommodate themselves is circumspection.[114]

If we consider the implications of this analysis with regard to religion, the following gives itself: Religious practices exist in a wider network of references that contributes to their distinct character, shape, and meaning. They are actualized and appear as meaningful only within this wider network of signification and engagement, including the effects they have on human life orientation. Consequently, religious agency presupposes other types of agency that cannot be understood apart from the intentionality that conditions the practice. Moreover, this means that religious practices "must employ theoretical cognition if it is not to remain blind"; because the mode in which the world appears as ready-to-hand is primordial. On the other hand, an exclusively theoretical approach to what appears to others as religious will not appear as religious at all, because the ready to hand-character is not present but has to be assumed as present in others. Heidegger writes: "The ready-to-hand is not grasped theoretically at all, nor is it itself the sort of thing that circumspection takes proximally as a circumspective theme. The peculiarity of what is proximally ready-to-hand is that, in its readiness-to-hand, it must, as it were, withdraw in order to be ready-to-hand quite authentically."[115] In other words: the context of intentionality that

---

[113] For the role of *things* in religious practices, see Henriksen, *Christianity as Distinct Practices: A Complicated Relationship,* passim.
[114] Heidegger, *Sein Und Zeit,* 69.
[115] Ibid., 69–70.

shapes agency is something from which one must detach oneself if one is to approach something from a merely theoretical point of view. In his words, Heidegger writes, "To lay bare what is just present-at-hand and no more, cognition must first penetrate beyond what is ready-to-hand in our concern."[116] Hence, theoretical and practical concerns depend on different intentions, both of which shapes the actual character of what is in focus. Moreover, the ready-to-hand character of something is by implication also always a sign that allows for what is ready-to-hand to appear in or point to its context of significance/use. Hence, there is a fundamental pragmatic and semiotic element in the way Heidegger conceives the human condition. The context of use constitutes the primary context of significance and meaning, on which theoretical approaches have to relate in order to get off the ground.

Furthermore, in his development of the *existential* of Understanding (*Verstehen*) as a fundamental mode of being in the world, Heidegger analyzes how one's engagement with the world is not only fundamentally shaped by the intentional character in understanding itself, but these intentions also shape the mode in which beings are encountered *as the world* as well. The pre-theoretical and primordial relationship with the world that constitutes the world as such for the human being, which Heidegger calls *Dasein*:

...the structure of that to which [woraufhin] Dasein assigns itself is what makes up the worldhood of the world. That wherein Dasein already understands itself in this way is always something with which it is primordially familiar. This familiarity with the world does not necessarily require that the relations which are constitutive for the world as world should be theoretically transparent. However, the possibility of giving these relations an explicit ontologico-existential Interpretation is grounded in this familiarity with the world; and this familiarity, in turn, is constitutive for Dasein, and goes to make up Dasein's understanding of Being.[117]

Accordingly, to relate to the world implies that one already understands something as something or understands that one does not understand something. Given this familiarity with the world, which is co-given with human existence, the world and what is in it already appears as something specific. That which exists in the world is primordially understood in terms of involvement and agency. This is of crucial importance for the possibility of understanding concrete religious practices, as these presuppose a primordial involvement that gets lost when one steps back from this stance. "These relationships are bound up

---

[116] Ibid., 71.
[117] Ibid., 86.

with one another as a primordial totality; they are what they are as this signifying [Be-deuten] in which Dasein gives itself beforehand its Being-in-the-world
as something to be understood. The relational totality of this signifying we call
'significance.'"[118]

The most important implication of this analysis of Heidegger's is that we
cannot bracket out the one who understands from the content of understanding.
In other words: to relate to religion as an observer or as participant means, basically, that one relates to contexts of signification that are constituted with different content and against the backdrop of different possibilities of being in the
world.[119] "When something within-the-world is encountered as such, the thing
in question already has an involvement which is disclosed in our understanding
of the world, and this involvement is one which gets laid out by the interpretation,"[120] he writes. Hence, he suggests that there will always be a plurality of
possible interpretations, depending on what angle and which context of use one
addresses and understands oneself in relation to when interpreting. Accordingly, there is no one interpretation of religious practices, but how these are
understood may depend on which intentions we have and how we understand
ourselves in relation to that which requires interpretation: "In every understanding of the world, existence is understood with it, and vice versa. All interpretation, moreover, operates in the fore-structure, which we have already characterized. Any interpretation which is to contribute understanding, must already
have understood what is to be interpreted."[121]

It may be a leap, but if we consider the topic of religion and relate what
Heidegger points to here to the above-mentioned insights in Plato and Hegel,
respectively, consider the following: What is understood as religion depends on
the already pre-given concept of religion with which one is familiar. This concept may be adjusted, but it is the given starting-point for any involvement with
religion. Furthermore, such a concept presupposes that there are, in principle,
several different interpretations of religion, depending on how the interpreter
understands religions' relation to his or her own possibilities for being. A theoretical, detached approach to religion will imply that one takes a step back
from the type of involvement one already has and brackets one's own relationship with what one addresses as religion. Such bracketing also implies that both
engagement with religious practices, and the concomitant agency based on the

---

[118] Ibid., 87.
[119] Ibid., 87, cf. 144.
[120] Ibid., 150.
[121] Ibid., 152.

pre-understanding of the world that religious signs and narratives promote, are left out of sight as an option for the observer. Hence, the very point of religion, i.e., to provide resources for orientation, transformation, and reflection for concrete persons, is not fully grasped.

Hence, Plato's claim that we do not know the good unless we have participated in it may make sense with regard to religion as well. However, to repeat, this is not to say that everyone will have to experience religious practices as good. Some may have experienced them as destructive and negative.[122] This may have caused them to view their engagement with religion as something profoundly negative. However, also this familiarity with religion will be a mode of interpreting it from a certain point of view in which one's own intentions and being are involved – and therefore, not provide a basis for an objective approach to religion.

In sum: What Heidegger helps us see with regard to religion is that, from a phenomenological point of view, the idea that one can approach religion from an objective or theoretical point of view is not only a derivative mode of approaching it. It is also an approach to religion that seems to a) ignore the multitude of individual interpretations that it opens up to and possibly also requires, and b) that the so-called objective approach to religion, which brackets engagement and intentions of employing it, in fact undermines the pragmatic dimension that makes religious practices meaningful. This does not, however, preclude that one can relate to and investigate how people experience religion from a first-person perspective. A theoretical approach to religion is both possible and necessary. However, reports about such experience is not a substitute for experiencing religion oneself. But no matter how and to what extent religious practices are engaged, they will never be without contextual and individual traits. Religions offer resources for individual engagement, appropriation, and articulation, and this dimension both challenges the normative standards it conveys and allows for its dynamic adaptation in individual and collective contexts.[123]

Moreover, this also implies that it is impossible to develop an adequate understanding of religion detached from any first-person perspective. Such a perspective is, furthermore, indispensable not only when we try to understand religion, but for our general perception of the world. That we always experience

---

[122] Cf. Henriksen, *Relating God and the Self : Dynamic Interplay,* passim.

[123] This is the reason why I have pointed to the similarity between religious traditions and music scores and scripts for plays, as well as role-play among children. Some parameters are fixed, but what they contribute to and enable, may differ considerably. Cf. ibid., last chapter.

the world as mediated, and therefore from a first-person perspective that has a capacity to interpret the world on the basis of its semiotic character, in which significance cannot be isolated from the meaning of the one who relates to it, just as Heidegger also argues. In another context, D.B. Hart therefore argues:

The first-person perspective is not dissoluble into a third-person narrative of reality; consciousness cannot be satisfactorily reduced to physics without subtracting something. The redness of the red, red rose in my garden, as I consciously experience it while gazing at the rose in a poetic reverie, has objective existence not in the molecules or biochemical events that compose those petals, that stem, or those thorns, or that compose my synapses, my sensory apparatus, or the electrochemical reactions going on in my brain. The phenomenal experience is in my mind but has no physical presence in my brain or in the world around me [...] [I]t is probably logically impossible to address this issue meaningfully in purely quantitative and physicalist terms. This is because the essential mystery here is not that the encounter between a particular physical object and a particular kind of sensory apparatus should generate data of a very particular kind [...]. But the real mystery lies on the other side of that process, entirely in the subjectivity that is the site of those impressions, and hence in their irreducibly subjective character.[124]

Semiotics, which I will develop further in the next chapter, suggests a solution to this mystery: The world is a sign only because the sign means something for someone.[125] This someone is bound to experience herself as an "I" because the symbol "I" is pointing to the experiencing instance that is other to any other experiencing instance. The first-person perspective is not independent of other perspectives on the world and is not only relating to the "inner world" of the self but to the specter of experiences in the social/cultural and the physical world. Furthermore, it is dependent on our ability to relate to and interpret the world as signs.

Conclusion

As long as humans are in need of orientation and of founding their commitments and engagements in values and considerations that can shape coherence and continuity and enhance their sense of value and significance, they will need to relate to ultimates that inform and shape those commitments. Thus, they will

---

[124] David Bentley Hart, *The Experience of God : Being, Consciousness, Bliss* (New Haven ; London: Yale University Press, 2013), 175.

[125] Hence, the first-person perspective cannot be eliminated from science or philosophy. This is well argued also by Lynne Rudder Baker, whose basic argument is that as long as one does not recognize first-person properties and include them in an ontological account of reality, science cannot provide a complete inventory of reality. This point, she holds, makes ontological naturalism false. See Lynne Rudder Baker, *Naturalism and the First-Person Perspective* (Oxford ; New York: Oxford University Press, 2013).

need religions, as the space where practices of orientation and transformation are present and provided. Religious symbols, no matter how they are articulated, offer the chance to go beyond the immediate, to continue quests for meaning and value. Ergo: religions disclose themselves and human life as unfinished business. They tell us that we cannot remain by the immediate present and that the absolute is still beyond our present state. As processes and continuous engagement with symbols that provide the means for orientation, religions remain as unfinished business. Orientation is about more than registering what is the case. It has to do with what we do and how we relate to that which is, and what use we make of what we know, or think we know, about the world. This approach allows us to see religions primarily as specific types of human practices that orient us in ways that are mediated through different types of *signs:* storytelling, symbols, rituals, reflection, and communicative co-operation. Religions thereby contribute significance that transcends the immediately given of the everyday, but without leaving the everyday behind. To become religious is to learn how to process and act on the signs that open up the world to more than what is immediately at hand, as, e.g., in a promise. It is to relate to and to interpret the present in light of that which transcends the immediate.[126]

According to John Dewey, Hegel took a "generally pragmatic approach to religion" and was "ultimately concerned with individuality and the social conditions requisite for the growth of individuality." This is an important observation, as it implies that religion, in Dewey's view, is related to human growth and development.[127] Because religion – at its best, at least – provides chances for such growth and development (transformation), it also builds on the premise that humanity's unfinished business with religion has a correlate in humanity's unfinished business with itself. The following chapters will try to develop an understanding of how this is the case; first by looking into what the symbol 'God' entails for human life, and then into what main elements in human life appear as important to thematize by means of religious symbols.

---

[126] The approach to religion suggested here is developed more extensively in my *Religion as Orientation and Transformation: A Maximalist theory.* It builds on the work of C.S. Peirce, and more specially, on the reception of Peirce's work in recent contributions by Andrew Robinson. See especially Andrew Robinson, *God and the World of Signs : Trinity, Evolution, and the Metaphysical Semiotics of C.S. Peirce* (Leiden ; Boston: Brill, 2010).

[127] See John Kaag and Kipton E. Jensen, "The American Reception of Hegel (1830–1930)," in *The Oxford Handbook of Hegel,* ed. Dean Moyar (Oxford: Oxford University Press, 2017).

God reveals: On experiencing God

> *Hegel insisted that the proper topic of philosophy of religion is precisely the nature and reality of God. Philosophy of religion cannot properly limit its concern to the phenomenon of religion; rather it must recognize that religion itself encompasses the relationship of human beings to God. Religion intends an actuality that lies beyond it.*[128]

Representation as revelation

Whoever speaks about God, speaks about herself as well – about her points of orientation, her commitments, her view of what matters and not, her relationships with the elements that are contained in the *concept* God. We cannot speak about God without having – at least – a preliminary concept of God. This concept is necessarily a composite one: God is the source of life, love, goodness – and God is all these things, as well. The different elements that compose this concept are also those that matter in human life – and this is why we cannot speak about God without also saying something about how we understand the conditions for human life. Hence, when human beings, in their religious practice, relate to God as the ultimate, it is because this has an impact on the way they understand their own lives and relate to those features that make their world. This is the reason why religions must be understood not only as about God or the ultimate but also as practices that aim at shaping the human condition – a topic I will deal with extensively in the next chapter.

There may be religious practices that can do without a concept of God, but religions cannot do without some idea about *the ultimate* – what matters most,

---

[128] Peter Crafts Hodgson, *Hegel and Christian Theology : A Reading of the Lectures on the Philosophy of Religion* (Oxford ; New York: Oxford University Press, 2005), 12. Cf. Hegel, *Vorlesungen über die Philosophie der Religion* (G. Lasson), Vol 1, 7.

what are the unconditioned condition for all that is. Accordingly, we can elaborate on the concept of God at the heart of the Christian religion adequately from a philosophical point of view based on the understanding of religion that Robert Neville argues in favor of.[129] He defines religion as "human engagement of ultimacy expressed in cognitive articulations, existential responses to ultimacy that give ultimate definition to the individual, and patterns of life and ritual in the face of ultimacy."[130] It is how we conceive of ultimacy as it is reflected in our conceptions of God that determines what we perceive as relevant and central to human life. The understanding of God as the ultimate is then the main instance that we employ when we want to orient ourselves about what should matter. However, unlike Feuerbach, who understood God and religion to be about nothing else than humanity,[131] a relational approach to reality, which rejects understanding anything as existing in and for itself, has to take another route: to see humanity, and its religious practices as instances that point beyond themselves towards the ultimate reality that Christians call God. This is why it is difficult to think about religion without making God a theme. This point notwithstanding, how to understand God still needs to be determined.

The present chapter, which admittedly is a rather large one, will develop some basic features in the idea about God, thereby pointing to the relevance of these features for orientation in human life. When God reveals, God does not only reveal Godself, but also some of the basic conditions for our experience of reality, and thereby, a deeper dimension in reality itself. The approach here chosen will then also provide a bridge to the content of the next chapter, on religion and the human condition. This is so because how we understand the features of ultimacy has profound consequences for how human beings lead their lives. Perhaps this is most obvious in the case of thinking of God as love, but it also has consequences for how we understand the representations of God in light of conceptions of ultimacy and infinity, and for understanding our own agency in terms of God's creativity and human dependence.

---

[129] Neville is not the first one to think along these lines, though. Already in Hegel, the common object shared by religion and philosophy is God. "For Hegel, it must be said that the content of philosophy, its need and interest, is wholly in common with that of religion. The object of religion, like that of philosophy, is the eternal truth, God and nothing but God and the explication of God. Philosophy is only explicating itself when it explicates religion, and when it explicates itself it is explicating religion.... Thus religion and philosophy coincide in one. In fact philosophy is itself the service of God, as is religion. Religion and philosophy are both efforts to grasp 'the absolute,' which religion has tended to express with the language of God." Lewis, *Why Philosophy Matters for the Study of Religion–and Vice Versa*, 74-75.

[130] Neville, *Defining Religion : Essays in Philosophy of Religion*, 9.

[131] See Ludwig Feuerbach, *The Essence of Christianity* (New York: Continuum, 1990).

A tacit implication of the above way of reasoning is the following: whether God exists or not, does not matter for what religious *conceptions* of God can do to shape and form human life. Among the points that follow from understanding God as ultimate (or as Firstness, in Peirce's terms) is that God is only accessible by representations that are not themselves God. It is the impact of these representations on human life and mind that causes religion and faith to work and have consequences. The reality of God may thus mirror the consciousness for which God appears, but consciousness may also mirror the reality of God with which it is engaged.[132] Accordingly, the understanding of who God is cannot be isolated from the ways in which we know and relate to reality. God is present as represented in the sphere that is our experienced reality. However, God is, in a certain respect, not a part of reality but the condition for it. Thus, God is also the condition for the modes of human relationality that express themselves in intuition, knowing, desire, and feeling in general, and more specifically for the experienced relationship with God via these modes. Therefore, we need to reflect on what it is that makes not only thinking about God but also all types of relating to God preliminary and mediated by transient representations. It is against this backdrop that we can get a better understanding of what it means that God *reveals*.

Representation: Starting from a layman's reflections

Instead of starting from a conception of God that Richard Dawkins has become infamous for promoting his lack of belief in (and it is not difficult to completely support him in distancing oneself from the notion of God that he rejects), we can start this section by listening to a voice slightly more sympathetic to religious imagery about God. In an interview with Steve Hogarth, the singer in the UK rock band *Marillion*, he speaks about his relationship with religion. He reflects on images of God. Although he does not think of himself as a religious person "in the traditional sense," he makes a remark similar to the one many others have done, about God as "the man with a beard in the sky." He argues, not surprisingly, that it is an image one has to leave behind. Hogarth could have remained at that, but he reflects further, and says, with reference to ex-Beatle George Harrison's words, "God is everything. God is everything that has life or spirit, so if for you God is a man in the sky with a beard that's absolutely fine."

---

[132] Cf. Hodgson, *Hegel and Christian Theology : A Reading of the Lectures on the Philosophy of Religion*, 7.

Without accepting that image as an adequate description of God, Hogarth reflects further on how God's presence manifests itself in a flower or a grizzly bear or forest in a mountain valley. He sees God as a "life force thing. God is what binds us all together. It's the energy that makes us believe in the impossible." He goes on to say that God "has a lot to do with the kind of indescribable energy that's contained in beauty and nature, and also in empathy and mutual understanding."[133] Thus, Hogarth provides a layman's reflections in a way that opens up to profound reflections about God as beyond all, but still related to all that exists.

Moreover, Hogarth's reflections illustrate Paul Ricœur's famous dictum, "The symbol gives rise to thought, and thought returns to the symbol."[134] Instead of remaining by the reified symbol as an adequate conception of God, he uses the conception or symbol to start reflecting and develops an almost transcendental reflection, which identifies God as a composite ultimate, expressing Godself in beauty, goodness, empathy, and the energy that allows everything to be. Hence, Hogarth not only uses the symbol as a cause for thought and reflection, but this reflection also allows him to view the experiences of God as mediated by means of what is present in the world. Thus, instances of goodness, beauty, etc., become signs that point beyond themselves towards their own transcendental condition. In other words, the symbol that he starts out with allows him to engage in a reflective and semiotic process in which the symbol from which he takes his point of departure is not reified, but allows for a dynamic process that opens up to experiencing the world in another way than what would have been the case if not. Hence, the symbol itself (e.g., the man with a beard) becomes destabilized and rejected as a reified or iconic sign, whereas on the other hand, the experienced world is introduced into a semiotic process in which its significance consists of more than what is present, without its mere presence being without significance (index-sign). The inference from and consequence of this line of reasoning is that we have to acknowledge that if there is any experience of God at all, it has to be mediated by means of relating to the world in ways that thematize its transcendental conditions as ultimates.

Accordingly, if 'God' is related to the transcendental conditions of the world, there are two important things to note. Firstly, that God's transcendental character cannot mean that God is part of the created world. This, however, does not mean that God is separate from this world, or that we can think about

---

[133] See http://www.dirtyimpound.com/2012/10/omg-interview-marillions-steve-hogarth/. Accessed Feb. 20, 2019.
[134] Paul Ricœur, *The Symbolism of Evil* (New York,: Harper & Row, 1967), 247f.

the world as independent of God. We will return to this topic later when we discuss the notion of a panentheist God. Secondly, if God is related to the transcendental conditions as mentioned by Hogarth above, it means that to develop an understanding of God as a symbol requires developing a symbol that is composite in the way already suggested: Such a concept has to include love, energy, power, creativity, goodness, beauty, etc. These different attributes may all suggest something about what we speak when we speak of God, but in a way that goes beyond the empirical reality in which we experience phenomena that we use such words to describe. When connected to the conception of God, these features point to or suggest an ultimate reality that we cannot grasp in a conclusive manner by the words and conceptions employed.[135] Thus, from the outset, we can see how thinking about God requires a process that has no clear end, and where one is constantly called to reflect upon what it means to experience the world in light of the conception of God, and experience God in light of how the world presents itself to us. God is part of the unfinished processes that practices of religious reflection have to take up and deal with, infinitely.

Further on representation – Hegel again

Hogarth's pondering above can serve as an entry point into more profound reflections of related issues, presented by Hegel. In his *Lectures on Philosophy of Religion*, Hegel sees *representation* as the form of cognition most closely connected to religion. What are representations? They are images, stories, symbols, rituals, etc. Such elements play a crucial role in religion. In Hegel, however, the type of cognition they provide the basis for is of interest, and not the actual or immediate presence of these elements. Thus, he provides a form of demythologizing of religious representations, including doctrine. This move makes it possible for him to account for the transformation of representations into thought, which for him is the highest way of relating to the ultimate. However, despite his own preference for thought, Hegel holds, probably very realistically, that most of humanity cognizes the content of religion through representations.[136]

In Hegel, the subjective aspect concerning the certainty of God is established in *feeling*, whereas the objective dimension is established by means of *representation*. As he says, "For human beings, God *is* primarily in the form of

---

[135] For more on this, see Robert C. Neville, *The Truth of Broken Symbols* (Albany: State University of New York Press, 1996), which I will return to more extensively below.
[136] Cf. Thomas A. Lewis, *Religion, Modernity, and Politics in Hegel* (Oxford ; New York: Oxford University Press, 2011), 151.

representation."[137] Several things are worth commenting against this backdrop:
Firstly, that there is a relationship between subjective experience in feeling and
the objective representation. Secondly, the "objective" representation is exactly
that, namely of a God who is not possible to experience directly but only by
means of representation. This means, thirdly, that the fact that God is represented in a way that also stirs the experience of God in feeling by means of
objective representation is due to God being the (transcendental) condition for
experience, and not immediately present in experience. God always exists as
mediated, although Hegel will also say that the content of the experience is
God.[138]

The valid point Hegel makes here is that God is never immediately present.
Even in so-called mystical experiences, which may have an immediate character, God is only present by the way God is mediated in the experience. The
inference we can make from this fact is that the semiotic element that characterizes every experience of God representations (because experience is always
an experience of something for someone) suggests that one has to move beyond
the immediate and sensual or intuitive experience of something towards an interpretation that could be otherwise. There is no way to secure the experience
as a secure experience of God – it will always depend on the capacity for interpretation in the subject who relates to the one she *thinks* is God.

Against Hegel, we have to say that the "outward" representation is not only
a transitory phase or element in the way humans develop their understanding of
God (and themselves). The main element in religion is not the concept, but the
actual experience of God and the world as this is illuminated or made possible
to experience more in depth by means of the concept. Hence, neither the reification of the symbol / representation, or the literal reading of the Scriptures as
such is adequate, but neither is mere philosophical speculation that only uses
the representation or the scriptures as a stepping-stone towards a certain type of
philosophy.[139] The challenge is, therefore, to maintain that representations are
not merely indices of something else – they are also expanding our experience
of the present reality without leaving it behind. To say, as does Hegel, that "they
are only metaphors"[140] is thus misleading, insofar as it only makes the world a

---

[137] Georg Wilhelm Friedrich Hegel and Peter Crafts Hodgson, *Lectures on the Philosophy of Religion : The Lectures of 1827*, One-volume ed. (Berkeley: University of California Press, 1988), 291f.
[138] Cf. ibid.
[139] Hegel is likely to be read thus, cf. his comments on the historical, ibid., 293f.
[140] Ibid., 293.

mere appearance, *Schein*. Important, however, is the insistence that all intuitions we may have about God and which can be formulated in language, is actually not taken in a literal sense in the same way as is the case with objects. God is not wrathful like humans, and even God's love is not like that of humans. But there are some analogies, which are important to maintain.

In his analysis of Hegel's philosophy of religion, T.A. Lewis points to representation as what stretches between intuition and thought: "It begins with the sensible content that characterizes intuition and moves from finding itself determined in this manner toward the free self-determination of the most developed forms of thought."[141] Thus, representations imply the "combination of heteronymous givenness and self-determination," which entails a continuous transformation toward greater determination by the subject, without these connections being determined fully by the subject.[142] Representations are simply what initiates religious reflection – as the Ricœur quote mentioned above suggests.

A representation as a placeholder for the ultimate thus have a threefold function in religion. It contributes to the initiation of religious reflection, it provides some of the content and the boundaries for what is possible in the actual development of such reflection, and it delivers chances for the type of transcendental reflection that goes beyond the immediate present in the representation itself. Thus, one can say that God, who is dependent on representations in order to come to (the believer's) mind, is potentially present in representations – but only if one recognizes the transcendental element in them. The opposite would be to misunderstand their function as representations: "Representation misleads if it is taken literally. Taking them literally both leads us to think that religious doctrines are making (indefensible) claims that they are not and, no less importantly, causes us to overlook their genuine meanings."[143] This is the reason why one cannot remain by what is possible to observe from a mere empirical point of view if one is to understand anything about religion at all. Or, to put it otherwise: A theoretical approach to religion that leaves out God as the possible origin and object of representations is not able to grasp how religion, by means of these representations, provide chances for orienting oneself on the basis of ultimates that are conceived as transcendental and/or transcendent. By inference, this means that the notion of God is – if understood thus – in itself a

---

[141] Lewis, *Religion, Modernity, and Politics in Hegel*, 151.
[142] Ibid.
[143] Ibid., 152.

challenge to any approach to the world that wants to remain exclusively by the empirical.

The fact that God is represented in the world, and that religious faith identifies God in the signs observable or possible to experience in this world, means that the semiotic processes that cause thinking to occur and define the world as related to God, do not themselves produce God, but must be seen as produced by the divine reality. Thinking is grounded in God. What we know about God is based on how God has revealed Godself in the world – and such revelation cannot occur without the semiotic processes that thinking manifests.[144]

What I have above called Hegel's realistic approach to representations implies that the religious consciousness that develops notions of God based on the experience of the world, must build on the natural intentionality of immediate, sensible consciousness. Nevertheless, "the constitution of religious consciousness occurs through a movement of thought out of the confines of immediate consciousness's natural field of awareness."[145] Therefore, this consciousness is not directed towards something in the world as such, but towards the unity of object and thinking. Hegel shows that religion is dependent upon thinking and is aiming at the unity of the thinking subject with God. Or, in other words: a consciousness that thinks on the basis of religious symbols, but does so in a way that excludes God or the ultimate, cannot contribute to the unity he describes and is therefore not religious consciousness in any qualified sense.

At this point, however, a problem presents itself. Although thinking is necessary to perform or carry out the semiotic processes that result in the experience of something like somebody's experience of God, this cannot possibly mean that Godself is dependent on thinking. That would imply that God exists only because there is someone thinking. In order to avoid this problem, it is necessary to see thinking as a response to how the world presents itself to the subject who does the thinking. We should understand thinking against the backdrop of Hegel's emphasis on the intermediary role of representation. The reason is simple: If God is dependent on thinking, the thinking subject is God because it is this subject who is the all-determining reality. This is probably the reason

---

[144] Cf. Philip M. Merklinger, *Philosophy, Theology, and Hegel's Berlin Philosophy of Religion, 1821-1827* (Albany: State University of New York Press, 1993), 4: "Hegel noted that all thinking, including both the Classical philosophy of religion and Enlightenment theology, is grounded in a common object, God. All that proceeds from thought – all the distinctions of the arts and sciences and of the eternal interweavings of human relationships, habits and customs, activities, skills, and enjoyments – find their ultimate centre in the one thought of God. God is the beginning of all things and the end of all things; [everything] starts from God and returns to God."
[145] Ibid., 25.

why Hegel says that God thinks Godself through human consciousness.[146] But if thinking is based on, and a response to, representation, it means that thinking contributes to revealing God in what God is not.

The role of representation, in its generic character, is then to lead to explicit knowledge of God because it is a manifestation of the interstice realm between the 'thinking subject' and 'the immediate subject.' Representation brings these two sides in the subject together.[147] Thus, "religious representations" provide the means for another mode of being in the world, because they manifest another way of experiencing the world, which goes beyond the immediate. It also shapes the cognition of the difference between the finite character of the immediate empirical world and the infinite character of the universal context that consciousness becomes aware of by engaging representations as exactly that – as gestures towards the infinite horizon that encompasses the finite representations.

My point with these reflections, inspired by elements in Hegel's thinking, is not to develop a fully Hegelian concept of God, but simply to point to how much of modern criticism of religion misses the mark when they attack reified representations as if they were themselves the reference of religious belief and that which motivates religious practices. Furthermore, Hegel makes us aware of the role of cognition in the constitution of religion, although his preference for thinking as the main access route to a religious mode of being in the world may cause us to overlook other elements that are important in the carrying out of a religious mode of life. These are the ones to which I will turn in the next section. There are reasons for not seeing thinking as the only mode in which experiences of God are accessible.

Mediating God's presence: The Christological perspective

Since representation is one of the main ways that God mediates Godself, this point sheds important light over the constitutive element in Christian theology, namely that God's representative, the incarnated Son, Jesus Christ, is the one who reveals God in the world. Not only is this person Gods representative, and the true image of God (cf. Col. 1,15), but also a human being. Hence, God's

---

[146] The Hegelian reasoning here has several concerns, among them also the intention of avoiding what Hegel sees as mere subjectivism. See, e.g., Paolo Diego Bubbio, "Hegel, the Trinity, and the 'I'," *International Journal for Philosophy of Religion* 76, no. 2 (2014).

[147] Merklinger, *Philosophy, Theology, and Hegel's Berlin Philosophy of Religion, 1821–1827*, 33.

revelation of Godself for humans and as a human merges representation, humanity, and God into a unity. It allows for all involved to be apparent in another way than they would have been without this unification – as well as for the concomitant reconciliation of God and humanity. Ingolf Dalferth therefore, accordingly, underscores that from the point of view of Christian theology, the fundamental insight that there is no unmediated access to or awareness of God must be seen in relation to Christology. God's presence is hidden for both epistemological and soteriological reasons, he writes. "We can discern neither God's presence nor its true character without mediation."[148] Hence, we are dependent on God mediating Godself to us. The representation of God in Jesus Christ does, therefore, provide the most ultimate means for access to insights into the identity of God.

Dalferth's detailed analysis of the different aspects of God mediating God's presence will not occupy us here. However, he points to one crucial element for the understanding of how representations work that mediate Gods presence to humanity: *Mediation safeguards human freedom of assent.* "God presents himself in ways that allow us freely to respond to him, even though whatever we do or don't do will be a response to his presence."[149] To this insight, which expresses that God must be understood as present in our present no matter what, and without compromising human freedom, he adds another important point: the otherness of God's acts "are so singularly unique that they are in principle beyond our powers of discernment."[150] However, this means that mediation is necessary and that God manifests Godself when we discern how God's presence effects and affect us. Hence, we can interpret God's manifestations in the world in those features, events, and experiences as a result of God's presence, which makes it possible for us to experience God. "God mediates his presence to our particular situations, i.e. relates to our present in his creative, perfecting and salvific activity in ways appropriate to our particular circumstances; and we become aware of God by apprehending how we depend and feed on the possibilities and chances played into our way by God, i.e., by consciously apprehending both our prior apprehensions of God's present with our present and God's present to our present in apprehending it," Dalferth writes.[151] In other words, the experience of God is attuned to our contextual circumstances. God's

---

[148] Ingolf U. Dalferth, *Becoming Present : An Inquiry into the Christian Sense of the Presence of God* (Leuven: Peeters, 2006), 214.
[149] Ibid., 215.
[150] Ibid.
[151] Ibid..

presence in human life is mediated via experiential features that are themselves present and determining for it. He adds one point to this that identifies how it is possible to speak about the *truth* conveyed in such representations. For the Christian message to be recognized as true, "God's self-presentation in the workings of divine love and our apprehension of it on our 1st person perspective must be co-present components of one and the same occurrence or situation."[152] Hence, the main component in the composite notion of God, namely love, is what makes it possible to have a contextually mediated experience of God as represented in the present.

Symbols as a manifestation of the finite-infinite contrast: Neville

Robert Neville's work on symbols can provide us with further insights into what representations do, and into their specific religious character, than what we have been able to do so far via Hegel. For Neville, religious symbols express them-selves in the finite/infinite contrast. Hence, by interpreting them, humans are aware not only of the finite character of their own reality but also how this reality is encompassed by the infinite. Religious representations, or symbols, as Neville calls them, mediate the experience of this contrast. Thereby, not only is the divine reality to which one relates experienced, but so is oneself in one's relation to this reality.[153]

It is the interpretation of representations that can disclose that they, as finite objects, have "some world-constructing importance, either in the cosmological sense or a sense having to do with the ground, meaning, and goal of human life."[154] I take this to be Neville's way of expressing how these symbols or rep-resentations provide means for orientation. However, religious representations and symbols do not only orient us concerning the concrete situation in which we find ourselves. Especially complex religious representations "partially dis-locate us" from the perspectives present in our own culture. A good example is the Eucharist, which "is decentering, dislocating; it pushes participants to the limits of their centered world, and over."[155] Thereby, this and similar practices

---

[152] Ibid., 217.

[153] A religious representation or symbol which is employed in a devotional practice therefore expresses these two aspects at once. Hence, the reference it has is doubled. "The symbol is used in a devotional act to refer on the one hand primarily and directly to the finite/infinite contrast, as an intentional referent and on the other hand secondarily and indirectly to the devotee as en-gaged by the divine so symbolized." Neville, *The Truth of Broken Symbols*, 171.

[154] Ibid., 70.

[155] Ibid., 99.

of orientation relate persons to the infinite as well as the finite.[156] Hence, they do, in a specific way, direct us beyond the present that Dalferth pointed to in the previous section, as well.

Moreover, Neville underscores how important it is to not see the interpretation of a symbol or a representation as a mere repetition of it. The interpretative activity makes the representation's referent effective in the experience of the interpreter. Neville thereby underscores the pragmatic impact of a symbol or a representation – and thus, shows that symbols have experiential content to the extent that they appear as effective. He writes:

> An interpretation consists in the impact of the symbol's referent, usually some one or several finite/infinite contrasts, on the experience of the interpreter or interpreting community, as mediated by the symbol; this impact is the symbol's content meaning integrated into practice. The interpretation is not the repetition of the symbol. Nor is it the naked presence of the divine, as if that were possible in finite experience. Rather, the interpretation is the difference made in experience by the referent, God or related divine matters, as the symbol makes the referent effective.[157]

The crucial importance of representations (Neville: symbols) is underscored not only by how they open up to and orient humans in their experience. "Religious experience is not possible at all without engaging symbols," he writes. Similar to Dalferth, Neville understands representations as necessary for mediating religious content, including the reality of God: "No aspect of divine matters can be experienced for which we lack symbols with which to engage it."[158] Again, we see how representation is necessary for engaging the infinite.

Beyond natural theology – from thinking towards the acts of God

Consider Hogarth's reflections, as referred above in the introduction to this chapter: They are based on how he (and probably many with him) experiences the world, and it gives him food for thought and for transcendental reflection. His version of *natural* theology is not based in specific historical occurrences or events, but on features that, at least in principle, can be experienced by all, everywhere. However, in a Christian context, not only energy and power, goodness, and beauty tell us something about God. Christian theology claims that God is revealed in the story about Jesus Christ; a man whose story is also about

---

[156] Cf. Ibid., 99.
[157] Ibid., 119.
[158] Ibid., 133.

vulnerability, suffering, death, and injustice – and where it is not the glory, power, and energy that is depicted, but defeat and failure. In what ways can we see these features as relevant representations that determine how to understand God? In these negative elements, the *theologia crucis*, is something revealed about God that is important for the human condition and for how humans experience the world?

We cannot engage these questions adequately without bearing in mind the point Hegel reminds us of, namely that representation is the mode in which one is united with the divine – if one acknowledges that representation is exactly that: representation. When the cross represents God – it represents God as God appears under the conditions of this world: as someone who loves, but who also, when met with hate and anger, is failing in the attempts to engender love. Hence, God is vulnerable and not invincible or lacking in susceptibility but exposed to suffering, rejection, and injustice. Accordingly, the *theologia gloriae* of Hogarth must be accompanied and supplied by a *theologia crucis* that reveals God as not remote or distanced from the negativities and vulnerable features of the human condition. As represented by Christ at the cross, God is revealed in a way that goes beyond natural theology's capacities: God is revealed in an "act of revelation that at the same time discloses the human condition and God's hidden identification with it."[159]

My initial point in addressing this point is that when God is revealed in this way, God's revelation of Godself allows for a richer language about the full human condition. When God is represented in a human, under the conditions of injustice, suffering, and death, it provides another context of discovery for who God is than is the case when one only looks at the positive elements depicted in a *theologia gloriae*. Thus, the unity of God and humans are not only constituted in the thinking mind that unites the immediate and the universal (Hegel) but in the way that God, as represented in Christ, reveals Godself as sharing in the full human condition. Hence, the unity, of which Hegel speaks in a somewhat abstract manner, becomes concretized in a way that goes beyond what thinking itself can accomplish. It is revealed by the acts of God in Christ.

Against this backdrop, it also becomes meaningful to speak of the believer's mode of being in the world as one that takes part in God's agency in

---

[159] Cf. Vitor Westhelle, "Luther's Theologia Crucis," in *The Oxford Handbook of Martin Luther's Theology*, ed. Robert Kolb; Irene Dingel; Lubomir Batka (Oxford: Oxford University Press, 2014), 162. Cf. also Jan-Olav Henriksen, "The Crucifixion as Realisation of Identity: The Gift of Recognition and Representation," *Modern Theology* 22, no. 2 (2006).

the world. This is not limited to Christ's agency on behalf of God. We can develop a take on divine agency by means of humans if we look at the famous statement ascribed to St. Theresa Avila: "Christ has no body now but yours. No hands, no feet on earth but yours. Yours are the eyes through which he looks compassion on this world. Yours are the feet with which he walks to do good. Yours are the hands through which he blesses all the world. Yours are the hands, yours are the feet, yours are the eyes, you are his body. Christ has no body now on earth but yours."

Divine revelation is an instance of what God *does*: God reveals Godself in representations. Regardless of how one otherwise understands the idea of God's self-revelation, it seems to require some notion of agency. Even if we admit that God always reveals Godself *indirectly, mediated* through that which is other, created, the fact that God can never be experienced directly and immediately as God means that one must assume that this revelation, as an act, message, event, etc., is in some way or another linked to divine agency. On the other hand, even God's acts need to be recognized and interpreted within a specific context and against specific background assumptions or beliefs in order to appear as the outcome of such agency. So, even when we speak of God's agency ontologically, human involvement is implied epistemologically. However, I suggest that something *ontological* is involved on the side of humans when we speak about God's agency as well.

Before I proceed with developing these points further, a crucial theological notion that is of interest here must be identified: The fact that humans are *created in the image of God*. The basic meaning of this notion is that humans are created in order to *represent* God. Hence, the very being that is able to identify in representation that which is the unity of the immediately given and the universal condition for all that is, is itself representation. And it is a representative of God also in this respect: as identifying itself as the being who is called to be a representative of God.

The fact that God always reveals Godself through the means of God's own creation implies that God as creator relies upon, and is even dependent on, creation to reveal Godself. God reveals Godself through the creation and specific creational modes of being. This indirect mode of revelation might then have implications for how we think about divine agency. It may also help to overcome interventionist conceptions of the relation between God and the world, or the idea that God is only present at specific instances or in specific acts. Hence, by starting out with an analysis of how God reveals Godself through the means of God's own creation, we may achieve a better grasp of how we can think about divine agency.

Though God's revelation may be seen as something that is manifested and mediated in specific events, as well as through inspiration, dreams, etc., all such elements require a wider context in which they can appear and be interpreted as such – as parts of the larger framework constituted by God's actions. Although such elements may reveal God in a specific way, they are always linked to, build on, and confirm or expand, our preconceptions about God and about reality as a whole. The relationship to this totality that goes beyond what is at hand makes these elements eventually appear as instances that reveal a God who has a specific identity.[160]

An understanding of revelation as constituted by the relationship between parts and the whole is crucial to the present argument, as it would be absurd to claim that a single instance or event would be able to reveal the whole,[161] or that one representation would mediate all we need to know about God. On the other hand, it seems more adequate to say that some event may be part of what reveals God as God, without having to entail that the actual event is the final, ultimate, or total revelation of God's identity. Therefore, when humans experience instances that realize specific values or qualities that they identify with God's reality or attribute specific events to the motivation or to the specific purposes of God, these attributions will only make sense against a wider and already established conception of God. This conception may derive from specific learning practices in which the interpreter has already been engaged. These practices, on their part, may have their origin in other events or instances in which people have believed that God did reveal Godself. Therefore, despite its mediated character, one can always think of revelation as having its origin in God, even though it can only be conceived of *as* revelation because of interpretative efforts and practices, as suggested the reading of elements in Hegel in the previous section.

The mediating features in all revelation suggest that God is revealed through specific human *practices*. This does not mean that human agency alone

---

[160] This is one of the lasting results of Wolfhart Pannenberg's conception of revelation; cf. Wolfhart Pannenberg, *Systematische Theologie* (Göttingen: Vandenhoeck & Ruprecht, 1988), Vol. 1, 208–09. See also ibid., 249. Therefore, Pannenberg also underscores how God's revelation in history is realized only at the end of history, despite the fact that it is anticipated in the eschatological event of Jesus. For the latter, see ibid., 251, and especially 270–271.

[161] I take this point to be the basic idea about *finitum non capax infiniti*. However, this should not be understood as if God cannot be present in, with, and under the reality God has created – but he cannot be fully expressed in singular instances of the finite.

reveals God, but rather that humans when they *participate in specific practices,* participate in, or engage, some elements in the reality where God is revealing something about Godself. These practices display more than assumed intentions or values that determine the presupposed divine agency. They manifest *realities*, as humans who are determined by a larger reality carry them out. Thus, this way of looking at revelation may also help overcome a mere abstract or mere cognitive way of conceiving God's revelation, thus allowing revelation to be seen as more than a testimonial.[162]

Representation and relationality: The subjective experience of God

Representations are what they are because they point to something beyond themselves, to something given. Before they can be seen as representations, they are present to perception and in feeling. Feeling may be the subjective aspect of religion, as both Schleiermacher and Hegel are aware. This subjective dimension is of utmost importance to the formation of experiences of God. In the following, I will develop an understanding of how we can see the experience of representations of God as conditioned by subjective factors that, in turn, is important in order to understand the transcendental dimension in experiences about God.

God can only be understood as relational, and as the one who connects and combines reality into a unity. Relationality has – for humans – its most immediate presence in feeling. From a distinct theological point of view, however, it means that Hegel's concept of God sees God as taking part in the development of the self, simply because the development of individual selves is one of the ways in which God expresses Godself as creator. It is only by creating something as set apart from Godself that God can establish God's identity. God's identity is dependent upon God's relation to another. On the human side, this means that the development of the self is part of a process through which God also expresses Godself as the creator. This development cannot be seen as separate from God, or as something in which God is not involved. On the contrary, the development of the self, to put it in Hegelian terms, takes place *in* God. Therefore, the finite and the infinite become integrated when an individual human understands and experiences himself or herself from the point of view of God as the infinite other of this very self – as the result of something given, prior to him or her. Hence, Hegel provides an understanding of the self that

---

[162] Cf. for the latter position, Mats Wahlberg, *Revelation as Testimony : A Philosophical–Theological Study* (Grand Rapids, Michigan: William B. Eerdmans Publishing Company, 2014).

allows us to think of God as part of the constitution of the historical process of becoming a human self. This makes it important to consider more in detail the subjective dimension in feeling and its implications for the experience of God.

Schleiermacher – dependency, freedom, and agency

Schleiermacher developed his position on religious subjectivity as *the self-relation determined by God* in the second edition of the *Christian Faith (Der Christliche Glaube)*. Here, his understanding of the religious subject is developed in two different directions: in § 3, he develops an understanding of the pious subject that makes piety based neither on knowledge nor on action. It is, as he says, "a distinct formation of feeling, or of immediate self-consciousness."[163] Schleiermacher is careful in his exposition of what he means when he combines self-consciousness with feeling. He emphasizes the immediacy of this self-consciousness, as he wants to identify a trait in human subjectivity that is a supposition for, and hence prior to, any kind of consciousness that has an object (including the self as an object for this consciousness). However, "for every instance of self-consciousness, something other than one's 'I' is presupposed, something whence its determinate nature exists and without which a given self-consciousness would not be precisely what it is."[164] In other words: from the outset, the self's experience of dependence is a testimony to the relational character of its existence. This is why we always find ourselves referred to something else in our attempts to trace the origins of our actual existence. Accordingly, self-consciousness consists of two features: "the one feature expresses the being of a subject of itself, and the other feature expresses the co-existence of a subject with an other."[165]

What is common in all those determinations of self-consciousness that predominantly give evidence of a having-been-encountered-from-somewhere that belongs to receptivity is that in them we feel ourselves to be dependent. On the other hand, what is common in all those determinations of self-consciousness that predominantly give evidence of a self-initiated activity on the move is

---

[163] Friedrich Schleiermacher, *Christian Faith: A New Translation and Critical Edition* (Louisville, Kentucky: Westminster John Knox Press, 2016, Kindle Locations 801–802). German ed: Friedrich Schleiermacher: *Der Christliche Glaube*, 2. Aufl., (Berlin: de Gruyter 1960), 14.

[164] Schleiermacher. *Christian Faith* (Kindle Locations 1090–1092). German ed: Friedrich Schleiermacher: *Der Christliche Glaube*, 24.

[165] Schleiermacher. *Christian Faith* (Kindle Locations 1093–1098). German ed: Friedrich Schleiermacher: *Der Christliche Glaube*, ibid.

that we have a feeling of freedom. We feel dependent not only because we have come to be from elsewhere but chiefly because we could not come to be in this way except by some other.[166]

There is reason to emphasize here that Schleiermacher writes about the feeling of *dependence*. To feel dependent is something else than to know that one is dependent, and one probably cannot feel total dependence unless one is also able to think it. Hence, the relational character he analyzes must be mediated by thinking in order for it to become fully acknowledged as religiously relevant, and as an experience of the dependence of God. Against this backdrop, he can claim that "feeling oneself to be absolutely dependent and being conscious of oneself as in relation with God are one and the same thing. This is so because absolute dependence is the fundamental relation that all other relations must include within themselves."[167] God-consciousness and self-consciousness cannot be separated from each other.

One more element in Schleiermacher's analysis is especially relevant to our employment of psychology below: the fact that experiences of being dependent on others are not similar to the feeling of absolute dependence that is mediated in the experience of God in self-consciousness. Whereas others on which we may feel dependent are given in our concrete experiences, for him, "any sort of givenness of God's being remains completely excluded." Therefore, the "rendering of that notion to any sort of sense-perceptible object is always a corruption, unless one is and remains conscious of that notion as a purely incidental symbolization."[168]

Several elements are worth considering here: Schleiermacher underscores the need to not identify any representations or objects with God. This is a warning against idolatry, but it also points to how the experience of God relies on a transcendental experience of absolute dependence, and not on empirical experiences of dependence, be it on parents, material or natural conditions, or similar. Hence, he is not after the psychological dimension in the experience that articulates itself in our relations and dependencies on others. If anyone tries to make themselves the sole instances for determining others, they are in fact, trying to take the place of God.

---

[166] Schleiermacher. *Christian Faith* (Kindle Locations 1110–1114). German ed: Friedrich Schleiermacher: *Der Christliche Glaube,* 25.

[167] Schleiermacher. *Christian Faith* (Kindle Locations 1201–1206). German ed: Friedrich Schleiermacher: *Der Christliche Glaube,* 30.

[168] Schleiermacher. *Christian Faith* (Kindle Locations 1211–1215). German ed: Friedrich Schleiermacher: *Der Christliche Glaube,* ibid.

Moreover, the insistence on the givenness of God in feeling prior to any representation is important for the understanding of how God reveals Godself. Representations of God are possible to experience as such because they can be related to the experience of the absolute dependence that is present in feeling. Thinking can explicate this connection. Hence, even a person who only feels dependence experiences God, but she cannot know that she is experiencing God before she makes the inference in thinking that is mediated by symbols or other types of representation that engage semiotic practices.

Schleiermacher's elaborations on the experience of God makes it possible for him to state that the fundamental element in the structure of subjectivity is not created or constituted by the subject itself. This element has a great amount of impact on the actual fulfillment of the individual's life and is something from which the subject cannot withdraw herself, but which, nevertheless, points to how the subject is related to something that influences it. Theologically speaking, it makes it possible for Schleiermacher to locate the basis of piety (i.e., God) in the very element in subjectivity that is not reducible to the subject's own capacities or activities. Although he is careful to spell out that there is a close connection between feeling, knowledge, and action, he is nevertheless also insistent that feeling not only is prior to the other elements but is the element that makes out the origins of piety (Frömmigkeit) – which none of the other elements do.

Hence, not only in thinking (as in Hegel) but in feeling, the subject becomes aware of the experience of something other than and prior to what is the content of its own activities and its acquisition of knowledge. There are three implications from the fact that feeling contained in the immediate self-consciousness is *a given* that can be summarized quickly:

- There is an element in the subject that is not the result of the subject's control or activity
- Through this immediate feeling, the subject can become aware of a dimension in life that precedes or transcends the one made out by its own activity
- Hence, the subject, as it can experience itself in the feeling of immediate self-consciousness, is not solely a self-constituted entity.

The achievement of the analysis so far makes clear that God reveals Godself in a way that is deeply connected to the human experience of dependency, freedom, and agency. It is, namely, only on the basis of absolute dependence that a person can experience herself as free, i.e., as being herself the origin of things that happen or change in the world.

In § 4,1 in *Christian Faith,* Schleiermacher points out that self-consciousness by implication consists of two elements. On the one hand, we understand ourselves as this or that (as objects). On the other hand, self-consciousness is, as we have seen, related to the presence of some *Other*. It is by ways of this presence that the self becomes aware of itself as an independent entity and receives its determinate character. Without any awareness of otherness, we do not have any access to ourselves as subjects. All action and all awareness of ourselves, thus presuppose a more original receptivity (Empfänglichkeit), and this is the presupposition for the subject as an active entity.

Schleiermacher, therefore, distinguishes between two different experiences in the subject: on the one hand, the feeling of dependence, on the other hand, the feeling of freedom. An interesting point here is that he indicates that the feeling (or experience) of freedom is related to the prior experience or feeling of dependence so that freedom is something that a subject only can unfold and express on the basis of being determined by something else first. In other words; in order to be able to determine something else by our actions, we first have to know and experience ourselves as determined – we have to experience ourselves as what we are due to something other than ourselves:

What is common in all those determinations of self-consciousness that predominantly give evidence of a self-initiated activity on the move is that we have a feeling of freedom. We feel dependent not only because we have come to be from elsewhere but chiefly because we could not come to be in this way except by some other. We do feel free, because something else is determined by us and could not be determined in this way without our own self-initiated activity.[169]

The experience of freedom is therefore only possible on the condition of a more fundamental experience of absolute dependence. From a theological point of view, this is an important point, because it indicates that God's agency is prior to human activity that leads to the emergence of self-consciousness. Christian theology emphasizes that it is God, and not human action that constitutes the world and is the primary instance of experience. To establish an understanding of the world and of everything given on the basis of human agency is therefore misleading. This is not a mere doctrinal statement of Christian faith, but the result of a phenomenological analysis of the conditions for human existence and human freedom.

---

[169] Schleiermacher. *Christian Faith* (Kindle Locations 1112–1115). German ed: Friedrich Schleiermacher: *Der Christliche Glaube,* 25.

In our experience of the "things" in the world, there is no sense of neither absolute dependence nor absolute freedom. The conclusion to his analysis of the relationship between dependence and freedom is the following: An absolute experience of freedom is not possible. The reason is simple: In order to experience oneself as free, one has to be active in relation to an object that is already given. This object, however, is never given without us first being influenced by something else, on which we are then dependent, and from which we receive the influence that presents the object in our consciousness. Hence, to be free is at the same time to be dependent upon given conditions. This is why we can talk of an absolute feeling of dependence, but never an absolute feeling of freedom.[170]

Schleiermacher's identification of the feeling of absolute dependence and Hegel's analysis of how our experiences always point towards the infinite are both important elements in understanding the transcendental conditions for experiencing God in feeling and thinking. What remains underdeveloped in Schleiermacher is the relationship between feeling and representations. Somehow, this mirrors a parallel shortcoming in Hegel, who in my view does not sufficiently develop the relationship between thinking and representation. In order to correct these shortcomings, I suggest that we add another, more psychological perspective, presented by a psychologist who is profoundly interested in the relational character of human beings and has developed a thorough analysis of how representations of God develop in the psyche, with implications for both feeling and thinking.

Ana-Maria Rizzuto: God-representations and their impact on human life

In *The Birth of the Living God*,[171] Ana-Maria Rizzuto calls attention to psychological factors that contribute (or fail to contribute) to the development of an *experience of God*. She sees the development of the conditions for what type of

---

[170] "Accordingly, there can be no such thing as a feeling of absolute freedom for us. Rather, anyone who claims to have that feeling either deludes oneself or separates factors that belong together. This is so, for if the feeling of freedom gives evidence of a self-initiated activity that issues from ourselves, then this activity must have an object that has somehow been given to us, but this process could not have happened without having an effect on our receptivity; hence, in every such case a feeling of dependence that belongs to the feeling of freedom is coposited, and thus the feeling of freedom is limited by the feeling of dependence. The opposite case could arise only if the given object were in every respect to come into being only by our activity; but this is always only relatively, and never absolutely, the case." Schleiermacher. *Christian Faith* (Kindle Locations 1155–1161). German ed: Friedrich Schleiermacher: *Der Christliche Glaube,* 27f.
[171] Ana-Maria Rizzuto, *The Birth of the Living God : A Psychoanalytic Study* (Chicago: University of Chicago Press, 1979).

self one becomes as related to and organized by how representations of God (which she calls the symbol "God," with inverted commas) function within the self. This development is a result of the interaction between different and closely connected strata: The first is what Rizzuto calls "images of God" that are based in the initial stages in the development of the self. She elaborates, but from a more constitutive relational perspective, on Freud's statement that children create images in their efforts to master the initial challenges in their development, and in order to resolve the emotional tensions and challenges with which they are faced. Such images are not formed by the child in isolation, but also by interaction with her immediate environment (family). 'God' enters into the world of the child because God is represented in the social world – God is found in "everyday conversation, art, architecture, and social events."[172] However, Rizzuto adds another element, which may be of major importance for a nuanced view of the complex dynamics with regard to representations of God to which the self experiences herself in relation. The psychologically effective representations that shape the actual experience of God are not only the result of imaginations and psychological conditions or interactions with others, but of religious elements and practices. Practiced religion provides the space where a clearer *use* of representations of "God" is perceived by the child as related to ritual, stories, and other prearranged events.

Hence, according to Rizzuto, the "home-made" God, (who may be similar to the "white-beard God" to whom Hogarth refers), is confronted with another God, the God of religion: The God of religion and the God created by the child's imagination become related in interplay, and this interaction contributes to the diverse ways in which the child has to reshape and rethink God. This process also has an effect on his or her emotional experience of God.[173] It allows God to be re-birthed in both reflection and feeling. "This second birth of God may decide the conscious religious future of the child. No child arrives at the 'house of God' without his pet God under his arm."[174]

Two elements in Rizzuto's approach call for comment. The initial and immature image of "God" to whom the child relates is more an experience than a clear object. This is parallel to Schleiermacher's understanding of the immediacy in the feeling in which one relates to God. It appears only as an unspecified experience. Later, with the introduction of the social and cultural world, the child can also experience God as an "object," and thereby becomes increasingly

---

[172] Cf. Ibid., 7–8.
[173] Ibid., 8.
[174] Ibid.

conscious of the potential and the scope of such a symbol. It is in the interaction between these two elements that we may see a development from the initial and pre-conscious stages of the "God" in the self, toward an increasingly conscious notion of God in the self. Thus, the self may become increasingly more aware of its own content and the implications that such a notion of God entails for her self-experience when she engages with others and reflects on the impact of the symbol by means of what she gains access to in interaction with others, e.g., through religious practices.

Rizzuto indirectly testifies to how one cannot understand the importance of representations of God simply by focusing on God as an object. Thus, she does, as do Hegel and Schleiermacher as well, point to the constitutive relational dimension in God-representations, but she also points to the importance of Heidegger's distinction between present-at-hand and ready-at-hand that I presented at the end of the previous chapter. Focus on isolated representations that do not take the personal conditions and the individual's previous life-experiences into consideration neglects the very potential that the God symbol may have for the self and the appropriation of its significance. Moreover, an exclusively cognitive approach to the symbol God is insufficient for determining the impact of "God" on the formation of the self. Alternatively, as Rizzuto says explicitly, if one wants to understand the progress of an individual child with regard to his or her relation to "God," one needs to have some knowledge of the "private God" which accompanies the child.[175]

Against this backdrop, the challenges facing the God-self dynamic throughout life appear to be a continuous task, or as we have said, unfinished business to be resolved in constant interplay with different factors. These cannot be clearly determined as identical for each human, but nevertheless, they have some common traits. Rizzuto writes:

The natural history of God does not end there. Unless completely repressed and isolated defensively from its complex roots, the representation of God, like any other, is reshaped, refined, and retouched throughout life. With aging, the question of the existence of God becomes a personal matter to be faced or avoided. For most people, the occasion for deciding on the final representation of their God comes in contemplating their own impending death.[176]

Accordingly, the relation between the self and God is not only a question of one's beliefs but also of how one comes to terms with the basic conditions of the self as they are shaped by the confrontation with the representations that

---

[175] Ibid.
[176] Ibid.

causes both emotions and thoughts to develop in certain ways. Representations of God have a crucial role in this regard. This role is overlooked if one, for instance, sees religion merely as some kind of motivating force for what people do, or see it as a specific way of understanding the world. Religious representations, and representations of God, in particular, *shape a specific way of being in the world as a self.* It is therefore never merely a question about what God reveals God as by mediating Godself through different representations. Such revelation cannot be isolated from the conditions of the one to whom God reveals Godself, and the situation and the context in which this revelation takes place. The importance of religious representations lies in how one's beliefs are conditioned by them in ways that create opportunities with regard to being in the world. The significance is not in the object of one's beliefs as such. It is against this backdrop that one can also understand what Rizzuto writes, aptly: "Only detailed study of each individual can reveal the reason for that person's belief in his God."[177]

Furthermore, Rizzuto contributes to the understanding of why people simply do not engage with the God symbol anymore, why they do not perceive a need for it or why initial images of God from childhood are not developed further throughout life but left behind. Thereby, she contributes to a far more nuanced understanding of the God-image than the one provided by Freud. The difference between Rizzuto and Freud lies in the fact that his attempts to explain the formation of the God representation as a way of solving the oedipal conflict with the father reduce God to "a representational fossil, freezing it at one exclusive level of development."[178] Against this simplistic and one-dimensional approach, Rizzuto argues for the "many complex sexual and nonsexual, as well as representational, ideational components present in the child, which contribute to the genuine creation of an imaginary being." Consequently, the dynamics of the creation of the God-image within the self are opened up in ways other than those assumed by Freud. This fact may help us to appreciate different ways of seeing the God symbol. "The sexual and the nonsexual attachment to that representation depend upon the entire series of factors contributing to the symbolic creation of it."[179]

Rizzuto thus presents an alternative to Freud's understanding, the consequence of which is that all believers "must be still longing for the father as he

---

[177] Ibid., 47.
[178] Ibid., 46.
[179] Ibid.

was in reality, whenever they resort to God." Instead, she sees the representation of God as a new and original "representation which, because it is new, may
have the varied components that serve to soothe and comfort, provide inspiration and courage – or terror and dread – far beyond that inspired by the actual
parents."[180] One obvious benefit of this approach is that it provides an explanation for belief in God where people are neither as infantile nor as regressed as
they appear in Freud, and therefore do not "make us suspect that they constantly
reactivate their childhood drama or cling to a parental divinity."[181]

Because it is possible to have different – and mature – relationships with
one's parents, one should also be open to the possibility of a mature relationship
with the God representation. Such an understanding of God representations,
however, suggests that the symbol 'God' may have a wider range of functions
in relation to the self than those acknowledged by Freud. The psychic transformation and use of the God representation will, according to Rizzuto, be closely
related to – and thereby contribute to – the individual's total psychic transformation and reworking in each stage of the life cycle. This point is vital from the
point of view of the philosophy of religion, as it suggests that reified and static
understandings of religion and its representations may not help us to see the
deep roots and basic functions of religion in the creation of the conditions of
human experience. As Rizzuto says, "Those who are capable of mature religious belief renew their God representation to make it compatible with their
emotional, conscious, and unconscious situation, as well as with their cognitive
and object-related development."[182] Hence, the intrapsychic representation of
God also appears as engendered by an unfinished and endless process.

Whereas Hegel points to how representations cause the subject to think,
and Schleiermacher points to how they are manifestations of what is immediately present in feeling, Rizzuto has a different take on these representations as
they are present in the psyche. Given that we allow for the multitude of personal
processes that contribute to the development of religious representations, she
holds that "human life is impoverished when these immaterial characters made
out of innumerable experiences vanish under the repression of a psychic realism
that does violence to the ceaseless creativity of the human mind."[183] Because
representations of God are not merely observed or fixed but have an impact on
the human psyche, they are both the result of and engender creativity. They

---

[180] Ibid.
[181] Ibid.
[182] Ibid.
[183] Ibid., 47

contribute actively to the shaping of the mental space and the conditions of creative human agency. Therefore, it is also misleading to call religion "illusion": instead, "it is an integral part of being human, truly human in our capacity to create invisible but meaningful realities capable of containing our potential for imaginative expansion beyond the boundaries of our senses."[184] This potential is not only inherent in the contents of religion, but in many other symbols used in society. Without them, "the entire domain of culture becomes a flat, irrelevant world of sensory appearance."[185]

It is not only important to see the products of the self as described by Rizzuto as products of the creativity engendered by the representations in which the reality beyond the senses is manifest (theologically: in which God reveals Godself). They also contribute to creativity by engaging the self in the world, and by making possible new ways of relating to the environment. An attempt to censor some of these creations because they are not part of the object world would rely on a constricted approach to both religion and the human world. However, this fact does not give free rein to any notion of God or the symbolic religious order; instead, it is a call for close scrutiny of the functions of this symbol/order, to be able to pass a more solid judgment on what contributes human flourishing or not. The role of religious symbols may still be subjected to a reality check that considers such concerns – based on normative assessments based on flourishing, love, and community.

Rizzuto's approach to the emotional and psychical dimensions of God representations allows her to put forward the strong claim that no person can exist without a God representation in our culture.[186] Thus, the God representation is part of every human's self, regardless of whether or not she or he is a believer. Accordingly, a nonbeliever is a person who has decided, consciously or unconsciously, not to believe in the God representation that she holds.

Whether the representation lends itself to conscious belief or not depends upon a process of psychic balancing in which other sources may provide what the God representation provides for other people. This is not a matter of maturity. Some people cannot believe because they are terrified of their God. Some do not dare to believe because they are afraid of their own regressive wishes. Others do not need to believe because they have created other types of gods that sustain them equally well. Maturity and belief are not related issues.[187]

---

[184] Ibid.
[185] Ibid.
[186] Rizzuto, *The Birth of the Living God*, 47.
[187] Ibid.

Accordingly, to believe in God or not is not merely a question of the cognitive acceptance of a specific objectively presented notion or representation of God. Of course, this does not imply that such representations hold no value – on the contrary, the value that representations, teachings, and other mediations hold for one's image of God may contribute substantially to one's ability to develop a nuanced and liberating faith in God that promotes human flourishing. Theology or religion that underscore the acceptance of orthodox, cognitively accessible and preached doctrine *as the only condition for developing a true faith* may not accept this fact. However, this understanding of religious faith is insufficient both from philosophical and psychological perspectives. In order to grasp the nature of religion, one cannot focus solely on the *result* of the formation of faith, and not on the conditions for this formation within the self, as these in a profound sense is shaped by God as the origin of the representations that engenders the dynamics that make religion unfinished business. We need to understand the creation of the believing self and the believing self's engagement of the God-representation from a much wider perspective than doctrine-shaped approaches to religion provide.

We need to distinguish between a conceptual and emotional layer in the experience of God. This distinction is mirrored in the distinction between the *concept* of God and the *images* of God, which makes it possible to see multiple combinations of concept and image, which "produce the prevailing God representation in a given individual at a given time." Whereas the concept of God is mostly a result of secondary-process thinking, and might even be the result of rigorous thinking, a person who believes intellectually in such a God may nevertheless "feel no inclination to accept him [sic!] unless images of previous interpersonal experience have fleshed out the concept with multiple images that can now coalesce in a representation that he can accept emotionally." Only when this happens can this God relate to the "feelings, images, and memories connected with the earlier childhood elaboration of the representation of God and to that representation's later elaborations."[188] Thus, without the experiential dimension, neither representations nor concepts of God have any function in relation to the self. A merely cognitive, intellectual, or metaphysical approach to God can never, on its own, mediate belief in someone who may be the true God of the individual. This points back to our discussion of what Heidegger

---

[188] Ibid., 47–48. Cf. the extensive elaboration of these distinctions in Leif Gunnar Engedal, "Ecce Homo: En studie av psykovitenskapelige identitetsteorier med særlig henblikk på identitetserfaringens konstituerende elementer og de metateoretiske forutsetningenes funksjon i teoriutformingen" (Faculty of Arts, University of Oslo, 1999), 21.

stages as a conflict between two ways of relating to the world (*Vorhanden* and *Zuhanden*), which imply a tension between more conceptual types of God and the more experientially enmeshed God representations. However, in Rizzuto's case, the psychological significance of the contrast is that the primordial, experiential way of relating to God and the more conceptual one may collide and create conflict. This conflict may nevertheless, according to her perspective, become fruitful and psychologically mature in a way that Heidegger's way of describing the two opposite approaches does not allow for. The reason is that Heidegger focuses on our experience of and approach to the world, while Rizzuto – due to her psychological approach – focuses on the importance of development, integration, and maturation of the self. She writes:

> Integration of the conceptual component of the God representation and some of the images that contributed to it requires a persistent psychic work of soul searching, self-scrutiny, and internal re-elaboration of the representation. This is analogous to what happens in the analytic process, where many of the sources that have provided elements for the formation of a particular representation or experience are reconsidered and divested of some of their real and imaginary danger or appeal.[189]

Rizzuto stresses that her approach does not entail that the phenomenon of actual belief in God as real, existing, alive, and interacting with the believer is called into question in any way by understanding how the God symbol is related to the self psychologically. Moreover, she recognizes that God as a symbol makes God a special type of object, which she describes in the following way:

> This belief makes God a truly amazing object. He [sic] is the only relevant object who has not undergone and cannot undergo reality testing. Belief is usually ego-syntonic, however, although God is not cognized through the senses and cannot be called to a forum to explain himself. The religious person, nonetheless, feels the relation to be real and intense. He does not experience God as a symbol or a sign but as a living being, whose communications the believer interprets. The believer, in spite of the uncommon nature of the relation, is not psychotic, or even necessarily neurotic. He or she may be an emotionally mature person.[190]

It is important to emphasize that the reason why God as an object may function positively is that intra-psychic representations of God are not only a result of psychic tensions and conflicts. Nevertheless, they may also be regulated and reality-checked or tested in relation to practices and experiences in the believer's wider social and cultural world. Unless this check is performed, God

---

[189] Rizzuto, *The Birth of the Living God,* 48–49.
[190] Ibid., 49.

may become a symbolic teddy bear or a mere container for wishful thinking, serving the need for affirmation of his or her immature grandiosity. At this stage, Rizzuto's emphasis on the impact of the social and cultural spheres on the formation and maturation of the child's symbolic order becomes especially relevant. She can identify a psychological foundation for understanding the remarkable phenomenon of actual belief in God, even though God's existence cannot be verified, as is the case with all other symbolic objects of human life. She finds this is how the child's God is realized or mediated by means of his or her parents. In other words, it is by being confronted with her parents' recognition of God that the child is given the opportunity to affirm her own conception of God and develop it further by observing how this conception plays a role in the concrete life of the parents. Thereby, the child can also become aware of a wider repertoire for developing his or her own conception of God and transcend that which may already be accessible in the projections and images that exist in his/her immediate experience of the God image. This process may reinforce and strengthen the conception of God as something more than a mere representative of her parents or a mirror of their demands.

The sense of reality attributed to God may depend upon the dialectical relation of the God representation with the parental representation and with the sense of self. In those cases in which the individual cannot conceive of the universe or himself without God, it seems correct to postulate that the sense of self is in fact in dialectical interaction with a God representation that has become essential to the maintenance of the sense of being oneself.[191]

This analysis entails that the sense of self and its reality is directly and vitally connected to the God representation that is experienced as an existing reality. The challenge this presents to the child when he or she is growing up is related to a process of differentiation, which is tied to the endless process of separation-individuation from the parents. Thus, "the elaboration and reworking (or lack of reworking) of the parental images into a God representation, further elaborated through fantasy and secondary process, is so deeply related [...] that to stop believing in God is to cease to be oneself."[192]

Rizzuto, therefore, provides a reason for warning against speaking of religion in generic terms. We cannot talk about God generically when dealing with

---

[191] Ibid., 50–51.
[192] Ibid., 51. She goes on to say that "This way of understanding religious belief in God illuminates the well-known developmental fact that each new phase in the identity cycle brings with it its specific religious crisis, from the early crisis of doubt in adolescence to the last-minute questions of the dying person." Ibid.

the concept of God in psychoanalytic terms. It is necessary "to specify whose God we are talking about, at what particular moment in that person's life, in what constellation of objects, and in what experience of self as context."[193] Her analysis of the work of religious representations suggests a far richer and more nuanced understanding of the reality of God than we can develop by means of conceptual tools, or access when engaging with the products of the processes of doctrinal formation. It suggests that God's identity in the eyes of an individual may change significantly throughout his or her life, due to elements and circumstances other than those of changing doctrinal resources or worshipping practices: "The God representation changes along with us and our primary objects in the lifelong metamorphosis of becoming ourselves in a context of other relevant beings. Our description of a God representation entitles us to say only that this is the way God is seen at this particular moment of a person's psychic equilibrium."[194]

Rizzuto, therefore, offers a strong and in-depth explanation of why some representations have such a strong emotional impact and are able to shape both individual and collective identities throughout peoples' lives. The self, its God, and its world emerge out of an emotional history that would not exist without the presence of others. While this presence is part of what humans need in order to develop, it is not only a product of their own capacities: others contribute in ways that underscore how the dialectic of recognition we find in Hegel is given a deeper and more empirically elaborate shape through the insights of contemporary psychology:

The representational, experiential, and fantasized history of each individual's God representation lends it its psychological power. God becomes a multifaceted object with some dominant traits. The psychological limitations, and the power of God derive from these characteristics in the original objects as well as from the believer's creative power of fantasy. Wishes, defenses, and fears all shape the clay of the God representation.[195]

Rizzuto's approach to the self provides support for insights in philosophy of religion: given that religion is providing humans with modes of being in the world, her theory shows that "the entire representational process is at the service of making us psychologically viable people in the real world."[196] However, this

---

[193] Ibid., 52.
[194] Ibid.
[195] Ibid.
[196] Ibid., 55.

presents some understandings of religion, and specific religious practices, with some challenges of their own:

First, it suggests that an understanding of religion that sees it as giving rise to emotion only as a by-product of cognitive and cultural processes based on thinking and reflection is deeply misleading. Religion is through and through a system of emotion and emotional investment because it has its origin in the primary (emotional) way in which the self and world are related (as Schleiermacher also suggests, in his way). Understandings of religion that focus merely on doctrine, concrete practices, or ritual, are accordingly in need of correction or supplement from this point of view: not because they are necessarily wrong, but because they do not acknowledge the psychological significance for self-other relationships inherent in the constitutive relationship with the world. Thus, religion is not one of many ways of seeing the world but constitutes a specific world and a specific way of being within it that also has strong emotional components.

Second, and furthermore, the above implies that ways of practicing a religion which do not pay sufficient attention to how both the self and religious representations emerge out of emotional relations to other(s) run the risk of losing access to its potential self-shaping significance. When people today ask: "What is the purpose of religion?", "Why be religious?" or (even more crudely) "What's in it (religion) for me?", an answer that ignores religion's potential for shaping self and world either represents a fairly restricted or constricted version of religious symbols and their significance, or may lead to emotional regimes[197] that favor only specific emotional components, with the consequence that such an answer may contribute to unbalanced self-development.

Religious representations therefore always guide the self towards its origins (as Schleiermacher also points to) and – when functioning properly – open up a future that may be perceived as transcending the self's concrete past. The strength and contribution of a specific religious symbol lie in this double capacity. From a philosophical point of view, this can be articulated in the following claim: "God is the presence of the open future." This depiction of God suggests that a person who has such a God constantly is referred to more than the contents of his or her actual past, and that the God symbol opens his or her perception towards something other and more. This is therefore what creates and sustains this person's need or desire to continue to believe in such a God,

---

[197] For the impact of such regimes on the self, see Ole Riis and Linda Woodhead, *A Sociology of Religious Emotion* (Oxford ; New York: Oxford University Press, 2010).

because this God may inspire the individual to further development and the perception of new possibilities in life – a point we shall develop further when we discuss desire in the next chapter.

I have used so much space on Rizzuto because faith in God is a personal attitude that includes the psychology of trust, anticipation, imagination, and reflection. It is against such a backdrop that we can see the impact of religious representations on persons as being experienced as revelations of God. Whereas Schleiermacher underscores the immediate feeling of absolute dependence as important for religious faith, and Hegel the representations that can be sublated into thinking, Rizzuto takes seriously that actual representations have an emotional impact due to their links to previous experience and their ability to provide resources for creativity, thriving, and growth. Hence, she moves beyond mere feeling and mere thought and shows that it is how the representations exist in the psyche as emotional self-symbols that makes representations important for not only experiencing the self but also for experiencing God as revealing Godself. Moreover, similar to both Hegel and Schleiermacher, she underscores that human beings do not constitute the conditions for their own agency. It is therefore important to move from these contributions towards a more comprehensive understanding of the interrelation between human and divine agency.

Revealed conditions for human agency (C. Schwöbel)

In the previous sections, stories, narratives, symbols, ritual, and other practices have been referred to as instances where diverse representations of God are at work. However, in Christianity, one representation is identified as more central than any of these. It is how the human being, by being created in the image of God, is designated to be a representative of God. This profound designation is crucial for understanding that God reveals Godself in the world. It is also enhanced by the fact that in Christianity, Jesus Christ is seen as God's ultimate revelation of God's being as love.

Moreover, I have suggested that representations are more than symbols that lead to thought. Hence, the immediate feeling that Schleiermacher points to is also a representation. From a semiotic point of view, its significance lies in being an indication of the human dependency on the divine reality. However, we need to underscore an element that both Schleiermacher and Hegel seem to overlook, namely the psychological effect or impact of symbols and signs on human agency. The fact that encounters with other humans have a strong impact on how we understand ourselves and relate to the world is also of relevance when we think of belief in Jesus Christ as that which constitutes the center of Christian faith in God. Against this backdrop, we can now address the relationship between the human being's agency and God's agency.

When God reveals Godself, human beings are the primary mediators of this revelation in more than one respect. They are so by being witnesses to revelation, by bearing testimony to it, by explicating it in practices of orientation, transformation, and reflection, and by being those whom God calls, in all dimensions of their lives, to reflect on who God is. The connection between human agency and God's agency is therefore not an external and arbitrary one but is internal and impossible to dissolve.

Christoph Schwöbel underscores that human agency cannot constitute itself. Moreover, it cannot be explained as the result of other finite agencies either. Therefore, Schwöbel claims, we may see God's creative agency as the presupposition for human agency, since "God invests human beings with the ability to act as free agents."[198] Schwöbel considers the theological notion *imago Dei* to be an expression of this fact and sees this idea as pointing to the similarity and the difference between human and divine agency.[199] Thereby, he points to the main symbol for representing God as constitutive for human agency – a point we will bring to fruition in the next chapter.

The understanding of *imago Dei* as representation we find already on the first page of the Old Testament, in the first designation given to the human being. The idea of the human being as *imago Dei* is to be understood as the idea of humans representing God's reign over the world. The commandment to become many and fill the Earth (Gen 1,28) is not a demand for over-population, but for making manifest a multi-present witness to God as the Creator of all that is.[200] By fulfilling the task of living as the image of God, humans are supposed to make manifest both that they – in faith – recognize God as God, and that they recognize God's recognition of themselves as those making him manifest in the

---

[198] Christoph Schwöbel, "Divine Agency and Providence," *Modern Theology* 3, no. 3 (1987), 232.

[199] "Human agency is similar to divine agency, insofar as it is understood as the ability for free intentional action. The difference between human and divine agency is that, whereas the limitations of divine agency are freely chosen, human agency is limited in its freedom of choice." Ibid, 232.

[200] The understanding of this in the Old Testament draws on the cultural understanding of how different images were erected to make manifest who was the ruling king in the area. Hence, humans live in order to make evident who is the ruler of the world. Further on the OT background here, cf. G.A. Jónsson: *The Image of God. Genesis 1, 26–28 in a century of Old Testament Research* (Stockholm: Almquist & Wiksell, 1988).

world as love, mercy, and care for all that is.[201] The life as *imago Dei* is consequently a life in freedom, in faith, hope and love,[202] based upon both the recognition of God's recognition and upon God's determination of humans as God's
representatives. However, it also presupposes that humans realize that they are
not God themselves (i.e., recognition of difference serves as a basis of identity)
and that they actually destroy the purpose of human life if they live as if they
themselves were God and the ultimate source and end of all things. God is not
human – and the human is not God: This positive-negative-relationship and
recognition is the precondition for both the fullness of human life (as a life representing God) and, moreover, for the fulfillment of the purpose and will of
God.

Two points should be noted in relation to this basic determination of human
life: First, to understand oneself as *imago Dei* means, as indicated, that I am not
God, and God is not me. My identity is in what I am in relationship to another
– and in what I am not. It is an element of both affirmation and negation in this
basic self-understanding. Second, it means that God is both present and absent
at the same time: the very existence of someone as *imago Dei* presupposes that
God makes God's presence manifest in spite of his actual absence.

How can we understand this absence? I suggest it is to be understood as an
absence that makes it possible for humans to partake in the positive functions
of God since God thereby allows humans to fulfill and realize the positive potential of human existence by enabling humans to represent God. Hence, God's
absence is paradoxically also a means of making present the possibilities of
fulfilling God's purposes for freedom in human life, by being dependent on
God, as we saw that Schleiermacher argues. God's positive will for human freedom, love, and faith are given a manifest expression through God's absence or
non-objectified mode of being, which is at the same time functionally present
in the human as the *imago Dei*. Representation consequently involves both absence and presence: the one represented is absent, but as absent, he can still be
present by and through the representative, who has her identity determined precisely by means of the absence of the one she is representing.[203]

---

[201] This is more extensively elaborated in my *Imago Dei: Den teologiske konstruksjonen av
menneskets identitet* (*Imago Dei: The theological construction of human identity*) (Oslo: Gyldendal Academic Press, 2003).

[202] Note that the notion of freedom here is a substantial one as suggested above: freedom is related
to the fulfilment of the substantial relationship with God – not a kind of neutral detachment from
relationship and commitments.

[203] I will return to the topic of absence and presence when I discuss the role of desire in human
life in the next chapter.

When discussing divine agency in relation to the story of Jesus Christ, Schwöbel[204] points to the *prima facie* incompatible character of God's universal agency as creator and what God does through the particular life of Christ. However, Schwöbel holds that there are good reasons for rejecting the claim about incompatibility: Trinitarian thinking maintains a difference between Father and Son, which implies that the Son is not God *tout simple*. Their work is never identical. Therefore, Schwöbel holds that "in Jesus Christ God reveals his faithfulness in sustaining the created universe in spite of the human contradiction against the order that God had created. If this is true, God's creative agency and his redemptive agency cannot be incompatible. Rather, they must be seen as complementary."[205] In the following, I am aiming at not only to show the Christological implications that Schwöbel makes from this position but also point to how this might have implications for thinking about how human agency in general might reveal God.

Schwöbel proposes interpreting God's agency in Christ in terms of revelation. Christ reveals God insofar as his actions disclose that God remains faithful to God's creation "by remaining the ultimate agent who invests finite agencies with the ability to act."[206] This is a crucial point in relation to what I will develop below concerning practices of faith, hope, and love conducted by humans in general. However, as Schwöbel states, the presupposition for such agency is God's relation to humans, as Creator or through the works of Christ. The character of Christ as true God and true human is part of this presupposition: "Insofar as Jesus Christ reveals the relation of God to finite beings which [are] constituted and maintained through his creative agency, Jesus Christ is the revelation of God. Insofar as he discloses in his actions the adequate relation of human beings as creatures to their creator, he is the revelation of what it means to be truly human."[207] As a consequence of this revelation, Christ is able to *restore* the relationship between God and humans that has been disrupted by human sin, i.e., the consequence of *not* recognizing oneself as the image of God.[208]

Hence, revelation is not only closely related to the manifestation of who God is but also shows what it means to be human. When Christ reveals God, he

---

[204] My presentation of Schwöbel here is a reworked version of a section from Jan-Olav Henriksen, "God Revealed through Human Agency – Divine Agency and Embodied Practices of Faith, Hope, and Love," *Neue Zeitschrift für systematische Theologie und Religionsphilosophie* 58, no. 4 (2016).

[205] Schwöbel, "Divine Agency and Providence," 234.

[206] Ibid.

[207] Ibid.

[208] Ibid. .

is the true image of God in a way that reveals the new possibilities for faith, hope, and love that emerge out of the manifestations of God in his own life. God's action in and through Christ shows God as the ultimate agent in the particular actions of this particular human being. Nevertheless, believers may consider the significance of these actions as universal. It is the universal dimension in this particular event that qualifies the appearance of Christ as the revelation of God.[209] Representation and revelation thus become one.

We can identify this universal significance of the particular manifestation of God's agency in Christ as a condition for human agency in general. Whereas the fact that humans are sinners often causes them to misjudge God's intentions for the world, the revelation in Christ provides humans with clearer and less ambiguous conditions for agency, which are all related to faith, hope, and love. "Through the particular action of God in Jesus Christ as God's revelation of God's relation to humankind, human beings can now interpret the world in light of the belief that the motif of God's action is love and that the purpose which determines the patterns of its actions is the Kingdom of God. In this sense, Jesus Christ can be said to be the Word of God or the exemplary Act of God."[210]

An important consequence of Schwöbel's line of reasoning is that it allows us to see God's agency and human agency as closely connected. Christ is not only the revelation of God but is also, as a human, an "*exemplar* for the kind of human action that is made possible by acknowledging the divine constitution of human agency."[211] Schwöbel continues with reflections that are of particular interest in interpreting the conditions for "religious" practices:

Whereas the creative agency of God determines the *scope* of human agency, the revelation of God's motive and purpose determines the *character* of human agency. If we see the purpose of God's agency in Christ as the establishment of an agapeistic community with human beings, Jesus' actions as the *exemplar* of the adequate human relation to God manifest the kind of actions adequate to this purpose. Since the relation of human beings [to] God is constitutive for the relation of a human person to himself, to others and to the world, this revelation does not only concern God and the soul, but the whole set of relationships that make up human life.[212]

Accordingly, the presupposition for understanding human agency as manifesting God's agency is that humans can adopt God's intentions and concerns as their own. That can only happen when one believes in these intentions and trusts

---

[209] Cf. Ibid., 235–36.
[210] Ibid., 236.
[211] Ibid.
[212] Ibid., 237.

that they are the best way of performing agency. Unless faith enables this appropriation of God's will to take place, God's works through humans in the world will not manifest human freedom, and it would be problematic to talk about human agency at all, since there would be no human agent who performed an action on the basis of his or her own intentions, values, concerns, or aims. Such identification is made easier by the fact that the Gospels portray Jesus as one who *embodies* God's relations to the world, whereas Jesus as a bodily agent exemplifies the relation of humanity to God.[213] Revelation is thus also an exemplification of the conditions to fulfill the calling to become a full image of God – revelation enables representation.

Thus, faith is a distinct condition for the type of agency that can reveal God through human agency: not only because it is faith that recognizes God as the agent in the works of Christ, but also because it is faith that discloses and authenticates in the experience of the believer what happens as the works of God. The experiential and authenticating dimension related to God's agency, including God's revelation in concrete human action, is conditioned by, but also conditions faith.[214]

Revelation and semiosis

What does it mean to experience something that can reasonably be interpreted as an experience of God as revealing Godself? This section will present elements in semiotics that may help us further when we deal with questions about how representations may be considered as occasions for experiencing God by experiencing something as God's representation. It is necessary to underscore first what has already been argued above, namely that to experience something as God is not similar to experiencing any other part of reality. Because God is not "part" of reality, we still have to maintain that God is prior to, or encompasses, reality as we know it. Against this backdrop, we can understand the fact that there is no immediate access to God. When Christians say that they have experienced God, they are bound to refer to something that has *mediated* that experience for them – they must point to something in their experience that opens up to an experience that is deeper than what is immediately offered in an experience of the ordinary. This is the reason why we need to consider representations as dependent on semiotic instances that interpret them by means of abduction.

---

[213] Ibid., 237.
[214] Cf. ibid., 237, and also 239.

When I say to my friend, "that concert was a wonderful experience," she can understand that I refer to both an instance in our common world, as well as to my own emotional and musical experience of that instance. I refer to the concert as having meaning and significance in different realms of reality, although these are not accessible to both of us in a similar manner. A concert is an event in our *common* world, and as such, we have presumably at least potentially similar ways of being able to perceive it. However, my own report of its significance for my inner (subjective or personal) world is something she has not access to in a manner similar to what I have (and vice versa, of course, for my access to her experience of it). The latter dimension I cannot convey to her in other ways than by telling her about me. She can nevertheless relate to it and say "I am happy that you had such a good time" – without even starting to question if I had attended the concert in the first place – because she shared that common dimension of the experience with me. We both recognize that we do not refer to the experience of the concert as a mere physical phenomenon – despite the fact that we would have no experience of the music if the physical dimension of reality was not in place. The social/cultural, the inner, and the physical dimensions of experience are important to realize as different but related, and where we put the emphasis is not given. Reality takes on different shapes, depending on what dimensions of it we decide to make thematic.[215]

Experiences of God are not similar to the experience of a concert. God is not an event, although some may say that they believe that an event has its origin in God. When we speak of God, the basis for interpreting something as a manifestation of God is always potentially up for discussion. It could be otherwise. Accordingly, interpretations of something as manifestations or revelations of God are not dependent on inductive or deductive procedures of reasoning, but on abductions. Moreover, as such, they are up for discussion only in terms of the personal, first-hand, or "inner" dimension – which is hard to contest. What is up for discussion is the very experience on which the interpretation rests – the "concert-part." Are wine and bread only wine and bread, or a manifestation of the presence of Jesus Christ? How we interpret and experience practices as the Eucharist depend on what we decide to be the relevant languages of interpretation. Is healing after the laying on of hands a manifestation of God's healing power, or another instance of the placebo effect? Such diverse approaches to reality not only are part of the reason why the existence of God is

---

[215] I have elaborated on the theological relevance of these dimensions more in detail in Jan-Olav Henriksen, "Åpenbaring, Erfaring Og Teologi," *Teologisk Tidsskrift* 2, no. 04 (2013).

up for discussion, but they also testify to the open semiotic character of reality itself. Accordingly, to understand something as God, "God" has to be accessible to us via a sign that we can use, as the representation for the conditions of our experienced reality, and as that which makes something mean something for us. In this sense, belief in God and experiences of God are dependent upon our articulations (similar to ethics, perhaps, as good and bad, right and wrong, and similar concepts are all in need of articulation in order to relate morally to the world).

So-called *religious* experiences are those in which people relate to their world as it presents itself to them as signs of and expressions of that which transcends what is immediately given as accessible to everyone, and which they would not have experienced without employing a specific capacity for *interpretation* of the world. This interpretation, in turn, means that the world is (implicitly or explicitly) understood as *signs; signs* that open up to specific ways of experiencing the reality that can be shared with others who engage in the same type of interpretation. What makes such interpretations religious is not easy to determine. However, as indicated in the previous chapter, religion has to do with the signs that a) offer chances for orientation and transformation mediated by signs that, when engaged within a specific context of significance point towards instances of ultimacy that are grounded beyond the empirical present.[216] In other words, *if we are to talk about experiences of God, they must be regarded as opening up to transcendental features of reality. I.e., they are experiences of that which we can assume to be the conditions for concrete experiences of specific events and entities of this world* (and thus not experiences of the transcendent, which would, somehow then, be a contradiction in terms). When one relates to the world as a sign (and we cannot avoid relating to the world in that way, as we shall see below), it means that a source of meaning and significance prior to my concrete experiences is the condition for my sign-use and interpretations. Furthermore, it means that the world always points beyond what is immediately present in our experience. This semiotic character of the world may help us see more concretely how God is always someone *mediated* by the way we experience specific events and entities in this world.[217] The

---

[216] For further discussion of different ways to approach this topic cf. Wayne Proudfoot, *Religious Experience* (Berkeley: University of California Press, 1985), and Ann Taves, *Religious Experience Reconsidered : A Building Block Approach to the Study of Religion and Other Special Things* (Princeton, N.J.: Princeton University Press, 2009).

[217] For more on transcendental reasoning, its character, and what it can accomplish, see Charles Taylor, "The Validity of Transcendental Arguments," in *Philosophical Arguments* (Cambridge, MA: Harvard University Press, 1995). Taylor concludes his discussion of these arguments thus:

ability to relate to the world as a world of signs is what makes human life distinctive from other modes of being in the world. This is no option among others. Accordingly, human life has an in-built feature that makes religion possible, as this ability to relate to the world as signs, not only works at the biological level (like with animals). It is based in communication and reasoning, that can be developed into thinking and writing[218] – elements that are crucial for reasoning about the transcendental conditions for experience, and therefore, to think of and experience God as something other than a thing or object among other things and objects. The world thus has a transcendental horizon – it is never given only positively, but is also revealing its transcendental conditions – be they recognized or not. Hence, the transcendental character of experiences claimed to be related to God is tied to the immediate claim that God is manifested in experience (albeit then as mediated).

God mediated in signs: Semiotics and transcendental reasoning

It is probable that no one has developed the semiotic dimension in representation and mediation that I have alluded to in the previous sections more elaborately than American philosopher C.S. Peirce. Andrew Robinson has developed the implications of Peirce's theory in order to explicate the theological relevance it entails.[219] A major advantage in his contribution is that Robinson relates God, experience, and signs in a way that does not set the religious experience apart from the everyday experience of the world. Instead, as he writes, "by foregrounding the nature of signs, we encounter the most fundamental aspects of being and thereby meet with the reality and closeness of God."[220] In other

---

"Transcendental arguments thus turn out to be quite paradoxical things. I have been asking here what arguments of this kind prove, and how they prove it. They appear to be rather strange in both dimensions. They prove something quite strong about the subject of experience and the subject's place in the world; and yet since they are grounded in the nature of experience, there remains an ultimate, ontological question they can't foreclose – for Kant, that of the things in themselves; for the thesis of embodied agency, the basic explanatory language of human behavior. When we ask how they prove what they prove, we see another paradoxical mixture. They articulate a grasp of the point of our activity which we cannot but have, and their formulations aspire to self-evidence; and yet they must articulate what is most difficult for us to articulate, and so are open to endless debate. A valid transcendental argument is indubitable; yet it is hard to know when you have one, at least one with an interesting conclusion. But then that seems true of most arguments in philosophy." Ibid., 33.

[218] This point is the reason why we need to consider the challenges that religious texts present to religious practice. See below 224ff.

[219] See Andrew Robinson, *Traces of the Trinity. Signs, Sacraments and Sharing God's Life* (Cambridge: James Clarke & Co, 2014).

[220] *Traces of the Trinity : Signs, Sacraments and Sharing God's Life*, 4.

words, it is by realizing that the world as we live in it is a world of signs that we realize how it is deeply interconnected with the reality of God.

Robinson employs Peirce's way of making a difference between different types of signs. There are three kinds of way in which a sign can stand for an object, i.e., how a "sign-object relation" manifests itself. Signs can be used as indexes, icons, and symbols. In other words, a sign is not "just" a sign, but needs to be specified further with regard to its character and use.

An *index sign* is related to its object by some direct connection, as when some clouds are interpreted as a sign of rain. Here rain is the object, and the cloud is the sign. The direct, causal link between implies that the presence of the sign can indicate the object even when it is not directly observable (yet).[221] When a sign is used as a *symbol*, it lacks a direct connection, be it causal or otherwise. The relation between the sign and its object is established by convention. The contingent character of symbols understood thus means that *anything* can be a symbolic sign.[222] The final way to use signs, as *icons*, points to resemblance or image. "An iconic sign is a sign that represents its object by resembling it in some way." An important function of icons is that they can bring some specific aspect of the object in question to the forefront of attention. When Jesus is understood as the icon of God the Father, it means that Jesus resembles the Father in some way, just as the world's beauty can be an icon of the reality of God.[223]

Both icons and symbols are representations that can open up our experience to something beyond the experiential present. "An icon, then, has the capacity to bring to our attention certain features of the thing represented, often by excluding aspects of the object that are less relevant for the particular purpose in question. More generally, I think we could say that icons make things, or aspects of things, 'present' to us."[224]

To represent things with signs that have no direct relationship to their objects is important because it makes it easier to manipulate them; "that is, they can be presented, moved around, and arranged in different combinations in a way that the objects themselves cannot."[225] Robinson refers to Terrence Deacon, who argues that the capacity to use symbols makes humans unique. "The human mind has a very specific capacity for dissociating signs from the world

---

[221] Ibid., 7.
[222] Ibid., 9.
[223] Cf. Ibid., 14.
[224] Ibid., 15.
[225] Ibid., 10.

and manipulating them independently of the things they represent."[226] A symbol defined in the way Peirce does, as a sign whose relation to its object is given by a rule or convention, allows us to avoid seeing it as something mystical, vague, magical, or lacking transparency. Hence, a clear account of 'symbol' means that "we can say a lot more about religious sign-use than simply that it is 'symbolic.'"[227] The semiotic perspective allows for focusing attention "on some quite concrete and ordinary aspects of religious practices and beliefs."[228] Accordingly, this approach allows for approaching the mystery of the world not "via the arcane and the esoteric. The true mystery would be if the basis of God's self-communication and self-revelation turned out to be [...] the ordinary structure of everyday signs."[229]

Consequently, the semiotic dimensions of everyday experience open up to an approach to the experience of God that "locates" the possibility for this experience in what makes humans distinctive from other species. The capacity to relate to the world as symbols allows us to have different perspectives on what it is, and in that respect, our interpretations overcome the very restricted and finite approach to the world which we would have if we related to the world only by means of indexical signs. Although the finite character of human understanding and interpretation is not overcome, it is nevertheless radically expanded by our capacity for symbolic thought and for relating to the world by symbolic means.

We can now turn to how the semiotic approach to reality also says something distinct about the basic features that so far have been called transcendental, i.e., they are conditions for, whereas simultaneously not in themselves the full content of, our concrete experiences of the world. We see this point illustrated by the very fact that we use signs for a specific purpose: Given that a sign is something that stands for something else, Robinson says, the "'something else-ness' of the sign compared to the object requires as a minimum condition for the occurrence of signs that the world is able to accommodate things that are 'other' than other things. 'Otherness' is, therefore, one of the elemental grounds of signification. The sign is other than the object. Without Otherness, there could be no representation, no signification because nothing could ever stand for something else."[230] In other words, "Without Otherness, the world

---

[226] Ibid.
[227] Ibid., 12.
[228] Ibid.
[229] Ibid.
[230] Ibid., 17.

would be a more comfortable place, but it would also be a place without the possibility of direction or change, and without the possibility of one thing standing for another."[231] This point underscores how the religious practices of orientation, transformation, and reflection are all depending on representations that manifest Otherness as a fundamental transcendental category. Against this backdrop, we are able to consider diverse options and reflect on conditions for change, re-evaluation, guidance, and the possible direction of life-projects. Another consequence of this acknowledgment of otherness is that it constitutes a condition for considering thinking about God and religious practices, including theological reflections, as open-ended enterprises – as unfinished business. Moreover, it is a transcendental feature in the constitution of representation. If human beings or anything else represents God, it is, by implication, an acknowledgment of human beings as being *other* than God – or *vice versa.*

Thus, Otherness is distinctive to all human experience of something as specified or thematic. It is thus fundamental for what makes things matter to us. The function of the sign with regard to this Otherness can be elaborated further:

The sign works by coming between the object and the interpreter. Therefore, the interpreter does not encounter the object directly but encounters a sign. "We may therefore say that the sign mediates between the object and the interpreter. In that sense, signification depends on the elemental ground of 'Mediation.'"[232] Accordingly, *mediation* is the second basic (transcendental) feature of our experience of our reality as a sign-reality. Signs are signs due to their capacity to mediate. "A sign can't mediate between the object and the interpreter without the underlying element of Mediation – the possibility of something joining two 'others' together into a new kind of whole."[233]

As with Otherness, Mediation can be found in the world apart from its specific role in the structure of signs. This is important to point out, as our experience of instances in the world as mediated therefore is suggesting connectivity between the different elements in the world apart from the specific sign-character they might have. "[T]here can be nothing genuinely connected about the world without the operation of Mediation." Mediation is, of course, also implied in the way we think, and in how we make a like between two thoughts.[234] But

---

[231] Ibid., 18. I have developed the theme of otherness with more explicit reference to theological themes than I do here in Jan-Olav Henriksen, "Thematizing Otherness," *Studia Theologica – Nordic Journal of Theology* 64, no. 2 (2010).

[232] Robinson, *Traces of the Trinity : Signs, Sacraments and Sharing God's Life*, 19.

[233] Ibid.

[234] Ibid.

as with the other transcendentals, it is primarily in the world, and not in the mind, that it can be identified.

Taken together, Otherness and Mediation explicate features in the fundamental relationality that is inherent in all being. Since all is not the same, and all that is is connected to something else, we need both categories in order to orient ourselves. When we employ superempirical concepts for doing so, these cannot be utilized unless we also – implicitly or explicitly – employ them as something that mediates and is other. Thus, as transcendental categories, they serve to explicate further the fundamental relationship that, e.g., Hegel identifies between human beings and God. God is Other – but God is also one with whom one is connected because one cannot think of God unless one also thinks of one's origin in God and one's dependence on God (Schleiermacher). The very concept of God makes it impossible to think otherwise.[235]

To experience something as something implies experiencing it as a concrete "what-ness" – a *Quality*. Quality is not simply an assessment of something's value, but a way of identifying its specificity; of saying what it is in itself. Thus, Quality is another transcendental aspect of experience, as we, e.g., then not only experience something as different from other things contained in or conveyed by our experience, but as something with its own distinct character.[236] As such it cannot be reduced to something else: "What we experience when we experience a feeling or an emotion can, if we want to help others know what we are talking about, be given a label. But ultimately the feeling or emotion, as experienced, cannot adequately be translated into anything else. It simply is what it is: and, as such, it is a manifestation of Quality."[237]

Robinson's reconstruction of Peirce's semiotics allows for an explication of the experienced reality, in which the three basic features of Otherness, Mediation, and Quality become the result of a transcendental deduction. These *transcendentalia* are related to our actual experience of the world that signs make possible. If we were not in a position to experience the quality of something as distinct from another something's quality (the capacity for detecting otherness and mediating between different experiences), we would not have the

---

[235] Ibid., 20. Robinson suggests that the theological implication of Mediation with reference to pneumatology would be the following: "The theological correlate of Mediation, I suggest, is the role of the Spirit within the eternal Trinity. The Spirit mediates between the Father and the Son, and this action is mirrored in the way that Mediation operates in the world. More precisely, when a sign mediates between the object and the interpreter, the elemental ground of Mediation is in operation; just as when the Word represents the Father to us, he does so through the work of the Spirit as the ground of mediation." Ibid.
[236] Ibid.
[237] Ibid., 21.

world as we now have it or experience God as we do now. A basic feature in human experience is thus the experience of the world as signs – as representations – and this feature is then also fundamental to the world we share with others. Moreover, the quality of every experience is prior to how it is represented by a sign. The sign thus manifests the Quality as well as the Otherness of the sign from the Quality. "The sign-object relation is grounded in the elemental ground of Otherness. Quality and Otherness are both necessary for something to be represented by something else. A word is an utterance of the heart, and however closely and fully it expresses what is in the heart it is still something that stands, in its Otherness, as separate from the 'heart.'"[238]

This analysis of semiotic elements thus allows for a transcendental deduction that leads to the conclusion that *there are transcendental features involved in all human experience that cannot simply be taken as "facts" along with other "facts of the world."* A main conclusion to the reflections so far is *that if we ignore the transcendental dimension implied in the human use of signs, we are downplaying the human. In turn, we also lose sight of the sources of religion, and the reasons why humans find it necessary to talk about God in their relation to the world.*

Experience of God – from a semiotic perspective

In *The Experience of God*, David Bentley Hart approaches the topic from the point of view of theistic philosophy.[239] His approach opens up to see this experience as manifest in different religious traditions, and not only within the context of Christianity. Hart directs his book explicitly against some of the so-called new atheists. In the following, a selection of his points is interpreted and elaborated in the light of the semiotic approach presented in the previous section.[240]

Hart develops a metaphysical notion of God, according to which God is the "one infinite source of all that is: eternal, omniscient, omnipotent, omnipresent,

---

[238] Ibid., 26.

[239] Hart explicitly distinguishes between metaphysical or philosophical descriptions of God, and dogmatic or confessional descriptions. His book adopts the first approach. Cf. David Bentley Hart, *The Experience of God : Being, Consciousness, Bliss*, 4.

[240] The following analysis of Hart is a reworking of main elements in Jan-Olav Henriksen, "God, Semiosis and Experience," in *Talking Seriously About God : Philosophy of Religion in the Dispute between Theism and Atheism*, ed. Asle Eikrem Atle Søvik, Nordische Studien Zur Theologie (Münster; Zürich: LIT Verlag, 2016).

uncreated, uncaused, perfectly transcendent of all things and for that very reason absolutely immanent to all things."[241] The main point in this definition is to
make clear that God thus understood cannot be seen as a being among other
beings. Therefore, God is not possible to experience in a way similar to what
we do when the conditions Quality, Mediation, and Otherness enable us to relate to an ordered world. Nevertheless, these transcendental features are in some
way also implied in the instances of experience or the representations that we
interpret as manifestations or revelations of God. However,

> God so understood is not something posed over against the universe, in addition to it, nor is he
> the universe itself. He is not a "being," at least not in the way that a tree, a shoemaker, or a god
> is a being; he is not one more object in the inventory of things that are, or any sort of discrete
> object at all. Rather, all things that exist receive their being continuously from him, who is the
> infinite wellspring of all that is, in whom (to use the language of the Christian scriptures) all
> things live and move and have their being. In one sense he is "beyond being," if by "being" one
> means the totality of discrete, finite things. In another sense he is "being itself," in that he is the
> inexhaustible source of all reality, the absolute upon which the contingent is always utterly de-
> pendent, the unity and simplicity that underlies and sustains the diversity of finite and composite
> things.[242]

Against the backdrop of the features in semiotics outlined above, there are several things to comment about this understanding of God: First of all, it makes it
possible to affirm God's Otherness. Secondly, this understanding also makes it
necessary to describe the Quality of God in a specific manner, as beyond the
experiences we have and as not possible to grasp fully with reference to features
of this world. Accordingly, if God is to be grasped (no matter how fragmentarily
and preliminary), God must mediate Godself in a way that makes some of the
beings that we experience in the world signs for God. The point is then, in what
way, what type of signs?

    The answer to this question from the point of view of Christian theology,
is closely related to the historical existence of Jesus Christ. Among its main
claims are that Jesus is not only an *indexical* sign of who God is (i.e., there is a
necessary relation between our understanding of God and our interpretation of
Jesus as a sign of God). Jesus is also a true *icon* of God, someone who is so
similar to God that he manifests the presence of God for those who meet him.
Furthermore, experiences of God as one who is infinitely more than we can
grasp can be mediated by different types of symbols; all of which are flexible,

---

[241] Hart, *The Experience of God : Being, Consciousness, Bliss*, 30.
[242] Ibid.

contingent, and always inadequately able to express who God is in God's full-ness.

Hart points to *infinity* as an important element when it comes to determin-ing God. God is beyond finite comprehension, and therefore, experiences of God, even more than experiences of the world, are not exhaustive, but in need of a supplement that can provide different perspectives. Hence, "much of the language used about him is negative in form and has been reached only by a logical process of abstraction from those qualities of finite reality that make it insufficient to account for its own existence."[243] Furthermore, "God is not merely one, in the way that a finite object might be merely singular or unique, but is oneness as such, the one act of being and unity by which any finite thing exists and by which all things exist together. He is one in the sense that being itself is one, the infinite is one, the source of everything is one." This approach makes it possible to say that from a semiotic perspective, God is the source of quality, otherness, and mediation.[244] But God cannot, like some contemporary atheists seem to think, in any way be likened with anything in this world, or of things that we can imagine in our fantasies as part of this world, like fairies and gods. Writes Hart:

> Beliefs regarding God concern the source and ground and end of all reality, the unity and exist-ence of every particular thing and of the totality of all things, the ground of the possibility of anything at all. Fairies and gods, if they exist, occupy something of the same conceptual space as organic cells, photons, and the force of gravity, and so the sciences might perhaps have some-thing to say about them, if a proper medium for investigating them could be found.[245]

If we take this seriously, it presents Christian theology with a challenge, given what was said above about Jesus. His historical existence does take up some of the same conceptual space as organic cells, photons, etc. But he does this as a human being that Christians insist is also God. If this is to make sense, it is as a human that Jesus takes up such space, and it is as a human that Jesus represents God, i.e., makes God manifest in the world as a reality intrinsically connected with it. Thus, the very concept of representation makes it possible to think of God as present in the world and taking up space there, without having to give up that God is also more, and beyond, what is experientially present in Christ.

However, according to this way of thinking about God's presence in and relationship with the world, it is not possible to suggest that belief in God is

---

[243] Ibid.
[244] Cf. Ibid., 31.
[245] Ibid., 33.

unscientific, or beyond what can count as rational. Exactly the fact that God, as related to the world, is its transcendental condition and the source and origin of our capacities to grasp it in its multitude of different manifestations suggests that science cannot explain God. This notion of God may also help us to understand why there is something like science: Because the world has its origin in a source that is not mere matter, but also ratio, reason, a drive towards order and beauty. God is thus to be identified as the condition for the possibility of the world, and accordingly, *God's function as a transcendental condition is also different from the other transcendental conditions, as neither the world nor our experience of it is necessary.* Whereas the existence of fairies, etc. is a matter of empirical existence, of finite beings, the existence of God is not an empirical question. Empirical science deals with the finite (including the finite world in its totality) whereas philosophy and theology that discuss the question of God, deal with the infinite in a qualitative way.

Consequently, the otherness and the quality of God are different from how these transcendental features appear in our experience of the world. When we determine something as an experience of God, it is not as if we see this something *as* a direct instance of God, but we always see the experience as a sign of God. An experience of God requires for it to be an experience that is mediated (by a sign, symbol, or icon), and the concrete or actual experiential content is never the main content of an experience of God. The most important reference in the representation of God is thus not to some kind of finite quality that expresses itself in a way that makes it accessible to us. The most important reference in an experience of God is that this experience in its finitude is able to manifest itself as being *not* the main content of the experience itself. In this sense, *the reference to God is symbolic because it is not necessary.* However, when it is realized as symbolic, it is also possible to recognize both indexical and iconic elements. The Eucharist is a good example: as symbols, bread and wine manifest community with and the belonging to the crucified and risen Christ. The symbolic character is arbitrary or contingent. Once it has been established, we can also see how the indexical character of the meal displays itself and can be interpreted as a manifestation of a God whose essence is to live in community and to seek communion with God's creatures. Moreover, as an icon, it also resembles the original last supper.

Hart also develops another point, namely the impossibility to interpret the world as we know it simply from an exclusively materialistic or naturalistic point of view.[246] That there can be a natural explanation of existence as such is for him a logical impossibility: "The most a materialist account of existence can do is pretend that there is no real problem to be solved (though only a tragically inert mind could really dismiss the question of existence as uninteresting, un-answerable, or unintelligible)."[247] The reason for this position is simply that he sees the existence of what we call "consciousness" as being "an aspect of reality that constantly eludes the narrative or explanatory powers of materialist thought." And against the backdrop of our previous discussion of the semiotic character of reality, this suggests that "the idea of 'pure' or 'self-sufficient' physical nature is an illusion."[248] *Consciousness* is among the prior conditions that must be in place before anything called nature can be experienced at all. It precedes and exceeds the mechanisms we can experience as natural causality. In that sense, consciousness is also a transcendental condition for experience,[249] but in a sense distinctly different from those identified so far: *Consciousness is both an empirical fact, and a condition for our experience of empirical facts.* Consciousness is also the precondition for articulating or establishing the rela-tionship between the representation and what is represented – and thus, for faith and religious belief.

The fact that we have no direct access to nature as such means that we are bound to reflect on our experiences' transcendental conditions. Metaphysical reflection points to finite things as "being sustained in existence by conditions that they cannot have supplied for themselves, and that together compose a uni-verse that, as a physical reality, lacks the obviously supernatural power neces-sary to exist on its own. Nowhere in any of that is a source of existence as such."[250] However, such metaphysical considerations are also possible to rec-ognize as relevant from a phenomenological point of view because this is ex-actly how the world shows itself to us in its finite character, a point that will be developed further below in relation to Løgstrup.[251] This character of the world in turn opens up to human experience as the place where we can meet the "un-conditioned and eternally sustaining source of being that classical metaphysics, East and West, identifies as God."[252] Thus, the finite points towards the infinite.

---

[246] For a non-believing position, this position has recently been argued also by Thomas Nagel, *Mind and Cosmos: Why the Materialist Neo-Darwinian Conception of Nature Is Almost Certainly False* (New York: Oxford University Press, 2012).
[247] Hart, *The Experience of God : Being, Consciousness, Bliss*, 44.
[248] Ibid., 45.
[249] Cf. Ibid.
[250] Ibid., 104.
[251] See the section below on God's power and transcendence (on Løgstrup).
[252] Hart, *The Experience of God : Being, Consciousness, Bliss*, 106.

To put it even stronger, it makes sense also from a semiotic perspective to state that *finitum capax infinitum* – because the world as signs or representations points beyond itself.

Transcendentalia and belief – an intermediate conclusion

The previous analyses have developed arguments for the position that transcendental reflection is necessary if we are to understand how we understand the world. Moreover, I have suggested that God and religion are instances that both are linked to this type of reflection about conditions for experience. An outcome of the above is that mere positivistic or naturalistic/materialistic accounts of reality end up in inconsistencies. There are two problems at the basis of this predicament: First, its inability to explain *itself* and the basic *transcendental conditions* for its own activity. Second, as pointed out by many, the often-occurring temptation to interpret statements about God and reality as empirical statements seems closely related to this lack of engaging in transcendental reasoning.

The above analysis has developed three different ways in which we may see the human experience of God as having to do with (or is related to) the experience of the world, but without in any way pretending that such experience is an experience of empirical elements as such. It has identified three modes of *transcendentalia* as they appear to the eye of a philosophical theologian:

• The semiotic transcendental conditions, which are displaying themselves through the interrelation between the world (of quality, otherness, and mediation) and the signs (as index, symbol, and icon).

• The empirical fact of consciousness, which is, paradoxically also the condition for experiencing the empirical fact of consciousness, and so in a manner that cannot be done unless this consciousness employs the capacity for signs as spelled out above.

• God, interpreted as the transcendental ground of both being and consciousness, and the one who manifests Godself in all things and thereby makes it possible to interpret some events or instances in the world as representations of God. Accordingly, as we experience the world as significant (in a wide sense of the word), we may also say that we are experiencing God. How God, as such a transcendental ground of being is further understood, may differ in different religious traditions.

We do not necessarily need to assume the existence of God. However, our experience of reality is something which necessarily must imply more than the assumption of mere matter as its ground, and therefore also as the ground of our experience of it. As Hart writes,

Physical reality cannot account for its own existence for the simple reason that nature – the physical – is that which by definition already exists; existence, even taken as a simple brute fact to which no metaphysical theory is attached, lies logically beyond the system of causes that nature comprises; it is, quite literally, "hyperphysical," or, shifting into Latin, *super naturam.* This means not only that at some point nature requires or admits of a supernatural explanation (which it does), but also that at no point is anything purely, self-sufficiently natural in the first place. This is a logical and ontological claim, but a phenomenological, epistemological, and experiential one as well.[253]

Although it can be discussed to what extent language that employs the notion *supernatural* is helpful anymore, the fact that Hart here points to something that is superempirical is in accordance with the analysis we made about the conditions for religion in the previous chapter of this book. Moreover, semiotics could be an addition to the list he makes about how the claim about lack of self-sufficiency can be made explicit in different theoretical realms. There are reasons to think that the lack of ability to account for experience in general, and experiences of God more specifically, on the grounds of how the world appears to us, is in consonance with the incompleteness of understanding and the contingency of what we believe – another point that again reinforces reflections about God and religion as unfinished business.[254] But the fact that there is a world and that it is there prior to our interpretation does not make the world only our interpretation. Hart interprets this point theologically thus:

Even when one suffers some immense "shift of paradigm" in one's understanding of reality, and comes to believe that one must radically alter one's beliefs about things, one continues to act toward the world out of a deeper and unalterable confidence in the (so to speak) nuptial unity of mind and world, and out of an ineradicable joy in the experience of that unity. The indissoluble bond between the intellect and objective reality is forged by this faith that is also a kind of love – a kind of adherence of the will and mind to something inexhaustibly desirable. Seen from the perspective of a variety of theistic traditions, this is nothing less than the reflection of absolute reality within the realm of the contingent. It is bliss that draws us toward and joins us to the being of all things because that bliss is already one with being and consciousness, in the infinite simplicity of God.[255]

---

[253] Ibid., 96.
[254] Cf. Ibid., 247.
[255] Ibid., 247–48.

The knowing and interpreting mind, embedded in an unavoidable process of interpretation, trial and error, failure, and advancement, can be grasped only when we see that the world and our relation to it are deeply intertwined. The world as we know it is a world of signs calling for interpretation in an unending quest for more understanding, and concomitantly, for growth in personal insight. The world as a sign, however, cannot be that unless there is a knowing, interpreting mind. This mind cannot reflect on its own and the world's existence for long before it has to realize that there are transcendental conditions to both the mind and the world. It is in this reflection that God again appears as a theme and as more than a transcendental condition. "God is present in everything because everything abides in God, and that God is known in all experience because it is the knowledge of God that makes all other experience possible."[256] However, from the point of view of Christian theology, this is not enough said. It is because we can experience this world as one in which *love* matters more than anything that we can claim that the God who is love is the God who makes the most sense when it comes to how we want to experience the world. This experience is possible to explicate in the iconic representation of God in Jesus Christ – a theme still in need of development in the following.

Sacramental panentheism and different realms of human experience

Against theological positions that separate God and the world, and emphasizes God's transcendence, it follows from Schleiermacher, Hegel, and Hart that God is intrinsically and internally linked to the world. Hence, we need to consider what God's presence in the world means against the backdrop of its fundamentally relational character. Accordingly, we need to consider what a panentheist position entails.[257]

There are two angles that are important in this regard: First, to see how some basic human experiences can be related to panentheist concerns. An analysis of those may help us see more of how human experience is intrinsically related to what we can say about God. Some of the features in this analysis will also pave the way for the next main chapter of this book. Second, there are

---

[256] Ibid., 332.
[257] The following section is a reworking of some elements previously presented in Jan-Olav Henriksen, "The Experience of God and the World: Christianity's Reasons for Considering Panentheism a Viable Option," *Zygon* 52, no. 4 (2017).

elements in Christian Trinitarian reflection, and especially related to Christology, which may also be of relevance for the articulation of a panentheist position. Both these approaches are related to how God and the world interact – and they do so in ways that are captured by a *sacramental* understanding of the world.

The position I will argue for takes its point of departure in two distinct experiences that are both pre-scientific and pre-theological, both of which relates to material we have already touched upon: The experience of love and the experience of the existing world as conditioned by a power to be that transcends the actual entities of the world. In this transcending character, that is rooted in the experience of the "immanent," we can distinguish what I suggest calling a sacramental quality.

If God reveals Godself in our reality, it means that the reality we partake in mediates God. This view builds on what has been said so far about both representation and semiotics. Hence, a sacramental view of the world entails that God mediates Godself by means of the created world, a topic that classical theology articulated as the way in which God gives Godself *in, with, and under* the created means – in, with, and under something that is distinguishable from Godself, but still intrinsically related to God, and conditioned by God.

Thinking about God in this way makes God's sacramental mediation of Godself dependent on the created world. In this way, dependence goes both ways: The world as a sacramental reality is dependent on God as creator and as the one who brings forth the promise of the world's fulfillment and consummation in the creative and loving community with God. On the other hand, God is dependent on the created world in order to mediate this promise, and God is also dependent on the world's response to God's communication of the call to community. This response would not be possible unless there was already issued a graceful calling to such community. Against this backdrop, it is possible to say with Niels Gregersen, in his definition of "Qualified Christian panentheism," that "it is by divine grace that the world is codetermining God, so that temporal events may influence God and creatures share the life of God; all that is redeemed participates in divine life."[258]

One significant contribution from a sacramental approach is that by understanding the world as a gift and a promise, one does not have to accept the world as it presently exists as the final articulation of the reality of God. The world

---

[258] Niels Gregersen, "Three Varieties of Panentheism" in Philip Clayton and A. R. Peacocke, *In Whom We Live and Move and Have Our Being : Panentheistic Reflections on God's Presence in a Scientific World* (Grand Rapids, Mich.: William B. Eerdmans Pub., 2004), 23.

may still be acknowledged as in becoming, and therefore, as what I have repeatedly called "unfinished business." Therefore, not all that happens take on a
qualified sacramental character.[259] Unlike pantheism, which identifies God and
the world, panentheism maintains a difference between God and the world that
does not require us to take the present state of affairs to be one in which the
reality of God is fully displayed. The notion of promise and open-endedness
captures the still outstanding, the still-becoming, the still future reality of God
towards which the world is called. It enables a vision that captures basic conditions for human life orientation and for visions about (necessary) transformations. To see the world as a sacrament in which God mediates the reality of
Godself therefore also entails a *dynamic* approach to the world, where one is
guided by the contents of the promise as well as by the knowledge about what
is at present.

As indicated, the semiotic character of the world is the fundamental condition for seeing the world as a sacrament. Semiotic processes constitute, connect,
transform, and engage signs in order to exchange information within and between different living beings at all levels of reality. This semiotic character also
means that life mainly consists of such processes. Humans need to interpret the
experiences they have as signs of something in order to be able to *orient* themselves. This is the reason why it is so important to develop an understanding of
what in the world that is crucial to link to the concept of God. The content of
the concept of God, which is explicated in human thinking (cf. Hegel) not only
determines how we understand God but from a pragmatic point of view, it also
offers the basic resources for how we orient ourselves in the world. When it
works according to its purpose, the concept and the conceptions of God mediate
that which we find it important to care about.[260] Accordingly, sacraments as
mediations of God are closely linked to what I defined in the chapter on religion
as practices of orientation. They are signs that provide points of orientation.

Accordingly, the reasons contemporary Christian theology has for considering panentheism a viable option can be articulated as related to theological
concerns on different levels. On the level of both creation and redemption,
panentheism articulates the close, intimate, and reciprocal relationship between
God and the world, in which the two are dependent on each other in order to
realize themselves fully, once God has created the world. This close, intimate,
and reciprocal relationship between God and the world is the most important

---

[259] Accordingly, the sacramental approach developed here does not identify panentheism with a
pan-sacramental approach.
[260] Cf. the last chapter and its constructive reading of H. Frankfurt, 236ff.

concern articulated in panentheism. However, a panentheist position is based on specific features of human experience and is not only a position formulated in order to articulate a theoretical solution to the problem about the relationship between God and the world.

God's power: Presence and transcendence

Because the main concern of a panentheist position on the level of *creation* is to articulate the perpetual and continuous presence of God in the world, or, the presence of the world in God, one has to ask at what level one should take the point of departure for this concern. Danish philosopher of religion Knud E. Løgstrup defines God as "the power to be *in* all that exists." This is an ontological statement that points to God as the condition for what is (ontologically), but it can also be seen as a *transcendental* statement that implies that God is the condition for our experience of the world as we now know it. In his phenomenological philosophy of religion, he argues that our experience of this power to be emerges out of our experience of the familiarity of the existing world. We are familiar with the fact that something exists. This familiarity, however, also means that we know that all that is disappears and eventually becomes annihilated. This experience of the perishable character of the world, in turn, gives rise to the thought that no existing entity possesses its own power to be.[261] We are unable to *experience* the power to be in all that exists, he claims, because this power is not in itself an experience, but a condition for experience. Løgstrup can therefore also say that this power is *transcendent* – but transcendent not in the sense of being beyond and "outside" the realm of existence, but rather because it is closer to us than we are to ourselves (it is not "other-worldly" but "this-worldly." He writes (in my translation):

We can experience ourselves in our mental and embodied condition because we can distance ourselves from ourselves in an external perception of our body and in retrospection of what has happened to our mind. However, the power to be in all we are, and all we do is something from which we cannot distance ourselves in a similar manner. No matter how close we are to ourselves, the power to be is even closer to us, and we cannot relate to it as an experience. This is so even though we are not ourselves possessing this power.[262]

---

[261] K. E. Løgstrup, *Skabelse og tilintetgørelse: Religionsfilosofiske betragtninger*, Metafysik (Copenhagen: Gyldendal, 1978), 96; *Metaphysics*, 2 vols., Marquette Studies in Philosophy (Milwaukee: Marquette University Press, 1995).

[262] Løgstrup, *Skabelse Og Tilintetgørelse: Religionsfilosofiske Betragtninger*, 96.

Løgstrup here holds that human experience is conditioned by a certain distance with regard to its content. However, as human beings, we are unable "to look behind our own backs" or to relate to something in creation from beyond creation. All we can do is to investigate something from a scientific point of view with regard to *how* it is, whereas we cannot establish a position that can tell us *why* it is what it is.[263] The ultimate horizon of meaning or significance escapes us. If we relate this to Peirce's notion of quality, which we presented above, it implies that the quality of the experience is a given, which we experience as immediately given with a significance that cannot be fully grasped from a scientific point of view. It is present as quality from a first-person perspective.

The power to be in all that exists has a twofold character, according to Løgstrup. On the one hand, it is present in our experience, but as hidden. It is so present that without this power, everything would disappear. However, it is also so hidden or absent that it cannot be observed. The power that allows existing beings to exist is, in the Jewish-Christian interpretation of reality, simultaneously beyond and within this world,[264] or both transcendent and immanent. This approach allows Løgstrup to develop a specific notion of the transcendence. If this power is God's power, it means that God's transcendence does not consist in God's distance from the world, but that this transcendence is always present and manifest within the world as that which allows it to be. At the same time, it cannot be identified fully with the existing beings, as this creating power is also something that is beyond the present state of beings.

I will argue that Løgstrup helps us develop in more detail how God can be thought of as being in, with and under the features of this world, as already suggested. However, it has to be admitted that much of what he writes in this regard seems to be articulating God's immanence in the world – a point that is also articulated in theistic positions, and which does not need to imply any form of panentheism. So, why does Løgstrup fit for the panentheist approach? The main reason is that the way he develops his ideas about God as the power to be in all that is implies that he sees God as an *internal* condition of the world. God is not merely a transcendental power that sets everything in motion and separates Godself from creation, as in deism or theism. For Løgstrup, the idea of God's indwelling in creation is based on the experience of the power to be. Thus, he maintains the classical Christian position that God is ever-present in, with, and under God's creation.

---

[263] Cf. the basic metaphysical question, "Why is there something rather than nothing?"
[264] Løgstrup, *Skabelse Og Tilintetgørelse: Religionsfilosofiske Betragtninger*, 97.

Furthermore, Løgstrup argues that contrary to common assumptions, the idea that this power to be is beyond this world and simultaneously within this world is not a contradiction in terms. Instead, these features condition each other mutually: "As within this world, the power is omnipresent. As omnipresent, the power is hidden, and as hidden, it is beyond the world." [265] Therefore, if we weaken the idea about the power as something transcendent or beyond the world, we weaken the idea about the divine power's omnipresent this-worldliness also. Hence, these two features in the divine power contribute to the strengthening of each other.

As indicated above, one could characterize Løgstrup's mode of reasoning as transcendental: what he says about this power points to the conditions for the possibility of our concrete experience of the world. It is so because the idea about this power to be seems to presuppose a kind of transcendental deduction that leads to a conclusion similar to the ones we have suggested previously: *there are transcendental features involved in all human experience that cannot be taken simply as "facts" among other "facts of the world."* Our experience of this power presupposes that we can experience the world as more than what is in front of us. Such experience constitutes the sources of religion and is the reasons why humans may find it necessary to talk about God.

God as love: a transcendental condition for experience

In Christian theology, God's basic character is identified as love. Love displays itself in goodness and care. A viable claim about the love, goodness, and care that God displays in the world needs a reference to an experiential dimension. If not, talk about God as love remains empty. In human life, love, care, and goodness mostly take on an embodied character, and this is the fundamental reason why these can appear in human experience. From a theological point of view, this means that humans and God are so closely related in these experiences that humans are actually participating in the reality of God when they partake in events that allow loving phenomena to come to the fore. God works in human love and is experienced in goodness. This captures the essence of the Christian panentheist position. As God is not the world, and love is not God, the world nevertheless is in God and manifests God in instances of love, care, goodness, and creativity. *Love is the theme that relates God and the world most distinctively.*

---

[265] Ibid.

I argue that love is one of the fundamental conditions for concrete human experience. Love determines us, conditions us, both in its concrete and positive forms, and in its absence, and in our desire for it. Love is behind many of our quests for fulfillment, relationships, and flourishing. Our relation to love, both in the positive and the negative, determine how we experience and relate to the world.

The promise of Christian faith is eternal life as participation in God as love. We experience some of the content of what God is and what this promise might imply when we experience love. God is nevertheless always more than what our experiences contain – God is *semper major*. The share we have in the eternity of God we have by love and grace, a grace that is also present in the natural conditions we live on, and from, and of which we all partake in the presence of God. These natural conditions are something that God uses in God's sacramental presence in the world. We are the hands, the feet, and the bodies through, and by which, God can manifest God's love concretely in this world. Love is something that arises out of relations between beings, but it is not something that we can decide should be there – we can only be open to it – or not. Thus, to be open to God is to be open to love – and vice versa.

The main reason for approaching the theme of God and love from the panentheist position is that the human experience of love is always embodied. This basic feature of the experience of love means that God's love is mediated by a body or bodies. This is necessarily so. There is no experience of love without a body. However, when speaking of God's love as embodied through human love, we must take care not to conflate the two fully. As Werner Jeanrond writes, "any identification between human forms of love and divine love, however well intended, are in danger of not respecting and not loving God as God and the human being as a human being."[266] So, although human love is fundamentally conditioned by a loving and creative God, it also belongs to a human subject that relates to others. Love on the side of both humans and God is affirmed, enhanced, and consummated in the best way in networks of loving relationships where these differences are intertwined, but not dissolved. The main example for understanding this close relationship experientially is in God's incarnation as Jesus of Nazareth – a point we will return to shortly.

In the experience of love is a tacit *promise* about eternity, as well:[267] Hence, love itself appears in the mode of "unfinished business," as one does not engage

---

[266] Werner G. Jeanrond, *A Theology of Love* (London: T. & T. Clark, 2010), 243.
[267] This point is hinted at in Jean-Luc Marion, *The Erotic Phenomenon* (Chicago: University of Chicago Press, 2007), 110, but he does not develop its theological potential.

in loving relationships for a limited amount of time. We do not love within temporal limits, and say, "I will love you for some time now." "I love you" is an open-ended statement without temporal restrictions. We can see this point illustrated in the fact that we can have a love for others also after their death. Even a love that ends for specific reasons, once held the promise of continuity and endurance, and its disappearance establishes an experience of loss. This loss is due to the promise that love holds. When I am loved, the presence of this love in my experience is something I hope for and count on that will last – and the assumption that this will be the case is included in the promise that is present in love. This promise, in turn, shapes and influences my experiences of myself, the other, and the world. Thus, love also has a sacramental character, not only in being relational and manifesting the presence of the other (God) in me, but in its promise about being present in the future and become even more ful-filled.[268]

For Christian theology, the *incarnation* reveals God's intimate relationship to God's creation as a concrete expression of our deepest human desires: Love and community. The human longing for love and community reflects how deeply we are embedded in the process whereby God realizes Godself in the very same features. However, one can also say that the incarnation is an expression of how God uses God's creation to express who and what God is as love in full measure. The fact that God becomes human in order to realize God's intentions in the world points to how God makes Godself dependent on creation as the means for expressing Godself fully. The main point here is not God's power, but God's *vulnerability*. Thus, the incarnation is not only the key to un-derstanding nature from a theological point of view, but also a key to under-standing the ways of God in the world, and why God is affected by what goes on in the world. God works, in, with, and under the processes of nature, includ-ing evolution, not by intervening in ways that are opposite to nature's poten-tial.[269] Niels Henrik Gregersen sheds light on this idea in his proposal for *deep incarnation*, which I will draw on in the following.

---

[268] Cf. on the future element of love in the relation between God and the world, also Gregersen, "Three Varieties…", 27, where he writes: "In this temporal world, however, we are not yet there. Only that which is born out of love is attuned to the love that God eternally is, and only that which is attuned to divine love can dwell in God. While the prologue of John spoke of the world as participating in the life and light of the Logos, elements of the world are here said to be present in God in the qualitative mode of an indwelling."

[269] This is a point recognized even in Kevin Vanhoozer's fairly critical discussion of panenthe-ism, where he writes: "Panentheists consider the classical theist response – that God intervenes in the world as a substance outside it – to be a dead end. If God were external to the world, his

Deep incarnation (Gregersen)

So far, I have discussed the interaction and mediating sacramental presence of God in the creation and in love as part of the conditions of this world. As Chris Southgate rightly points out, this can – up to a point – be described as God's immanence in the world.[270] However, when we speak about incarnation, we speak about "the astonishing, gracious, humble gift of the Son's taking flesh for the salvation of all."[271] Incarnation means, accordingly, that the power and love of God as immanent and manifest in all of creation are *materially present in a specific way in Jesus of Nazareth.* In the present section, I will, as does Southgate, look into how the notion of incarnation has been extended beyond thinking about God as present in human flesh. Niels Henrik Gregersen has developed the notion of *deep incarnation* in order to articulate how the eternal Logos not only takes on human flesh but takes on nature more generally: "Jesus of Nazareth was not just a man but a human animal, an evolved human animal. More than that, he was the victim of the evolutionary process, both in the sense of dying without issue [....] but also in the sense of dying at the hands of the cruelty and violence in defense of self-interest that is utterly unsurprising in evolved animals."[272]

Gregersen himself uses the concept of *deep incarnation* to argue that "it is not sufficient to say that God – as a nude God without material connections – is pervasively present in the world of creation. God conjoins *with* and *for* the material world at large *as* a concretely embodied divine-human person who is experiencing perplexity and anguish from within. Deep incarnation thus urges us to reflect upon what kind of God we presume to be present in and for all creatures."[273] Thereby, he relates the language of deep incarnation quite closely to the language that panentheists usually employ. Of special interest here is that he expands the language of "in, with, and under" with another preposition, namely, "for": God is *for* us – therefore, God relates and engages with the world in a way that makes it impossible to conceive God as unaffected by what takes

---

actions in the world would necessarily be interventions and hence unintelligible in terms of this-worldly explanations, assuming that the world is a closed causal nexus." See Kevin J. Vanhoozer, *Remythologizing Theology : Divine Action, Passion, and Authorship*, Cambridge Studies in Christian Doctrine, 134.

[270] C. Southgate. "Depth, Sign and Destiny: 'Thoughts on Incarnation'" in Niels Henrik Gregersen, ed. *Incarnation : On the Scope and Depth of Christology* (Minneapolis: Fortress Press, 2015), 207.

[271] Ibid.

[272] Ibid., 208.

[273] Niels Henrik Gregersen, "The Emotional Christ: Bonaventure and Deep Incarnation," *Dialog* Fall 2016, 255.

place in the world. I argue that Trinitarian thinking is aimed at exactly that: to state that God relates to the world in such a way that what happens in the world (as God's creation), with God in the world (as the world's power to be and possibility for expressing itself as love) and as deeply incarnated in the world (as *taking the world up in Godself*) – all these features cannot leave God *unaffected* by the world.

Gregersen holds that God as the incarnated *Logos* actually is *"sharing* the conditions of materiality to such extent that the world is continuously embodied in Jesus the Christ (the *Logos ensarkos*)." Therefore, the earthy character of Jesus can properly be said to reveal the eternal character or identity of God.[274] Or, to put it in other words: It is as this human that Jesus is God, when and if God is a human.[275]

Furthermore, Gregersen sees deep incarnation as a notion that suggests "that God does not only enter material existence but also brings it back into a divine embrace." Of specific interest to us, as we are looking for elements that are of relevance to Trinitarian panentheism, is the concomitant claim that "there is no material world in which the embodied Christ is not actively present." Here, he builds on the ancient thought about the assumption – which he develops as a reciprocal relationship; a *two-fold assumption*: The assumption of the flesh by the divine word, as well as an assumption of the flesh into the divine life. The incarnate Christ thus "exemplifies God's own willingness to enter the material and imperfect realm of creation, including aspects of suffering and anxiety."[276] The incarnation understood thus implies that God meets the world of creatures where they actually are – in states of complexity and perplexity, disarray, and impurity. To assume the flesh of the whole of creation means more for Gregersen than "just tolerating the material world. It also means God's embracing and incorporating the cosmic aspects of the world in order to renew God's own world of creation from the inside out."[277]

Gregersen also points to how already in the Franciscan tradition the view was promoted that the incarnation of the divine Logos was a result of eternal predestination to come to the world of creation.[278] Thus, the Trinitarian God is

---

[274] Ibid.
[275] See Henriksen, *Desire, Gift, and Recognition : Christology and Postmodern Philosophy*, 333.
[276] Gregersen. "The Emotional Christ," 255–256. Here, Gregersen refers to the Athanasian Creed, which speaks about *adsumptio humanitatis in Deo* (§ 33). However, his position expands this assumption to creation in general. The point is further developed in Niels Henrik Gregersen, "The Twofold Assumption: A Response to Cole-Turner, Moritz, Peters and Peterson," *Theology and Science* 11, no 4 (November 2013), 455–468.
[277] Gregersen, "The Emotional Christ," 255.
[278] Ibid., 259.

from "the outset" determined to unite Godself fully with creation – a point he formulates as incarnation being "genuine" or "perfect" union is only possible if Christ embraces the entire mishmash of created existence, and not only its ideal forms." Therefore, "Divine perfection does here not mean staying aloof in simplicity but entering into the complex realities of creation in order to bring the manifold world back to God."[279] Restoration is only possible if the God of the heights goes deep into the full gamut of human existence – in order for God to be known by people living in a world of flesh.

The mediated or sacramental presence of God in the incarnation is, therefore, contributing to the concrete conditions on which human can experience the power and the love of God through Christ. This is possible in different realms of human existence. Gregersen writes: "The natural realm of flesh also becomes the social realm of powerlessness and humiliation. Birth and cross, deep incarnation and deep suffering, belong together. Similarly, the story of the incarnation is one that reaches into the body of Jesus no less than into his soul."[280] The fact that Christ can experience the world in all realms, and that we can experience God through Christ as one who takes an active part in all these realms, means that incarnation is about more than humanity. God, as incarnated in Christ, can be a human only because the whole of evolution has made it possible – and Christ is possible as incarnated only because God has worked in, with, and through evolution. Interestingly, Gregersen develops this by pointing to Bonaventure's Christology. In his (Bonaventure's) theology, "the bond between Christ and cosmos is rooted both in his cosmic exemplarism and in his understanding of the humanity of Christ as a fulfilled microcosm." Christ is "encapsulating the material realm of creation as well as the noetic orders of reality in his body and soul."[281] Deep incarnation thus has a cosmic scope: Christ is "the chief exemplification God's active embrace of the material configurations of the universe, from sand and rocks to living, sentient and cognitive life-forms."[282] Hence, Gregersen can claim that "Christ the Wisdom is operative in the whole nexus of creation."[283]

Gregersen asks if these considerations have any traction to today's worldview, and he answers in the affirmative. A physical perspective implies that "we are all made out of the same stuff as the stars." Furthermore, "we no

---

[279] Ibid.
[280] Ibid., 252.
[281] Ibid., 253.
[282] Ibid.,
[283] Ibid., 254.

longer speak of matter and the material as something dead to be vivified by an additional world-soul. Rather Matter-Energy forms a unity endowed with In-formation as its structuring principle."[284] Moreover, evolutionary genetics have taught us how we belong to an ecological community and are embedded in eco-logical networks as ceaselessly active niche-constructors, "and with a deep his-tory behind us and in us which we share with our forebears."[285] As a conclusion, then, Gregersen summarizes his notion of Deep incarnation as follows:

'Deep incarnation' is the view that God's own Logos (Wisdom or Word) was made flesh in Jesus the Christ in such a comprehensive manner that God, by assuming the particular life-story of Jesus the Jew from Nazareth, also conjoined the material conditions of creaturely existence ("all flesh"), shared and ennobled the fate of all biological life-forms ("grass" and "lilies"), and expe-rienced the pains of sensitive creatures ("sparrows" and "foxes") from within. Deep incarnation thus presupposes a radical embodiment that reaches into the roots (radices) of material and bio-logical existence as well as into the darker sides of creation: the *tenebra creationis*. Incarnation is thus about a radical divine self-embodiment that reaches into in the whole system of the ma-terial world (Mass/Energy/Information), including biological life forms from growth to decay, from cooperation to competition.[286]

The notion of deep incarnation makes it impossible to understand the world in a manner where God remains unaffected by what happens there. It means, first, that God is active in the world in order to create, and thus creates the specific conditions for incarnation as well, as they are part of the evolutionary process. But second, the notion also entails that if we take seriously the deeply reciprocal relationship between the divine persons, and therefore also between God and Christ as an example of the relationship between God and the world, then God cannot be unaffected. Christ is a sign and a reality, and as such, he is manifest-ing a real promise about the possible future of the world. This sign displays itself as vulnerable power and love.

Summing up, we can say that the notion of deep incarnation provides a means for articulating the integral relationship between creation and redemp-tion, between God and the world, and between the present and the promised state of the world. In Christ, the fulfillment of the world is manifest as a promise

---

[284] Ibid., 253. This is a point possible to relate not only to recent theory about information, but also to the semiotic character of the world as suggested above, and to recent philosophical criti-cism of a "dead-matter"-approach to nature as can be found, e.g., in Arne Johan Vetlesen, *The Denial of Nature : Environmental Philosophy in the Era of Global Capitalism*, Ontological Explorations (London: Routledge, 2015). 195–203. Vetlesen argues strongly for experience as a basic access to nature, instead of the objectifying and commodification-oriented approach to it.
[285] Gregersen, "The Emotional Christ," 253.
[286] Ibid., 255.

about the fulfilled future relationship that God will have with the world, and which is anticipated in faith, hope, and love in the present. Thus, incarnational panentheism is not only a statement about present affairs, but from a soteriological point of view also a promise.[287] It points to the world, God's intention for it, and our experience of all that is, as unfinished business.

Further on panentheism: A Trinitarian vision

Above, I have suggested that panentheism is closely related to experiential elements such as semiosis, the power to be, love, and the historical event of the incarnation. The latter, historical incarnation testifies to the promise inherent in all of creation, and the loving power that can be detected as working in, with, and under creation. Thus, panentheism articulates main concerns in classical Christian theology in ways that manifest the close relationship between God and the world in a far more interactive way than theism does.

This does not mean that all ambiguity with regard to the experience of the world is dissolved. To the contrary. As long as the world stands, there is a choice as to which vision of it we should engage, and thus realize. This is a choice about in what ways the world should be interpreted as a sign (used pragmatically), and as a sign of *what* (pointing towards content). As long as the world remains ambiguous, the faith in God as a loving creator remains a vision for the world that also implies a challenge to articulate faith, hope, and love as the best conditions for human flourishing, and for creation in general. When Christians worship the triune God, they give themselves over to, rest in, and glorify this God by manifesting the glory of God as the creating and redeeming power that brings the world forth from chaos, delivers it from evil, and who in the future will consummate everything in love. Accordingly, the previous analyses can be developed further into an articulate Trinitarian panentheist conception of reality that safeguards the intimate relationship between God and the world without compromising their respective integrity or conflating them. Furthermore, this articulation of the God–reality relationship offers good reasons

---

[287] Here, I also want to point to the relationship between the creation-based and the sacramental element in a Trinitarian panentheism. The need for maintaining the soteriological dimension is, as Niels Gregersen argues, that "the world's being 'in God' is not taken as a given, but as a gift. It is only by the redeeming grace of God that the world can dwell in God; not everything shares automatically in divine life. Wickedness and sin, for example, have no place in the reign of God. Thus in a classic Christian perspective the world's being 'in God' does not so much state a general matter of fact, but is predicated only about those aspects of created reality that have become godlike, while they still remain a created reality. Only in the eschatological consummation of creation shall God finally be 'all in all' (I Cor. 15:28)." Gregersen, "Three Varieties of Panentheism," 21.

for rejecting the *supernatural* as a category for making sense of the relationship between God and the world. Whatever there is to say about the relationship-between God and the world can be said only on the basis of how God manifests Godself in, with, and under human experiences of the world and on the conditions of creation.[288]

Among the backdrops to the concerns and aims here are also the contemporary discourses about "natural explanations of religion," in which the ideas about "supernatural beings" or simply the "supernatural" are under attack.[289] Here, one easily gets the impression that a rejection of the supernatural implies a rejection of religious belief in general, and that religious belief relies on assumptions about a supernatural realm or reality. The presumed "battle" between science and religion thus seems to suggest that if one rejects the supernatural, one also rejects any idea of God. However, with few exceptions, there is little elaboration offered on what the notion 'supernatural' means. Even among these exceptions, however, many of those who reject the "supernatural explanations," etc., are either attacking a straw man or are ignorant about what the supernatural has meant in most of the history of theology.

I argue that a panentheistic position, rooted in the incarnation, makes it possible for theology to leave supernaturalism behind. As suggested above, God reveals Godself as working with, in, and under nature and thereby partakes in reality. Furthermore, I argue that the best theological model for maintaining this close relationship between God and nature is a Trinitarian model of God that builds on God's incarnation in reality as a whole. This Trinitarian model endeavors to move beyond the dichotomy supernaturalism versus atheistic naturalism, which has shaped so much of the discussion concerning panentheism.[290]

Accordingly, my claim in the following is that the supernatural as a category by which to explain events in the experienced world is of no more use to the discipline of theology than it is to science. Instead, theology and philosophy of religion should be able to express the relationship between God and actual

---

[288] The following section is a reworking of elements in Jan-Olav Henriksen, "Panentheism without the Supernatural? On a Perichoretic Trinitarian Conception of Reality," *Philosophy, Theology and the Sciences* 3, no. 1 (2016).

[289] Recent examples are, e.g., F. LeRon Shults, *Theology after the Birth of God: Atheist Conceptions in Cognition and Culture* (New York: Palgrave Macmillian 2014), and Ilkka Pyysiäinen, *Supernatural Agents: Why We Believe in Souls, Gods, and Buddhas* (Oxford ; New York: Oxford University Press, 2009).

[290] On this, see Philip Clayton, "Panentheism Today: A Constructive Systematic Evaluation" in *In Whom We Live and Move and Have Our Being: Panentheistic Reflections on God's Presence in a Scientific World*, ed. Philip Clayton and A. R. Peacocke (Grand Rapids, Mich.: William B. Eerdmans Pub., 2004), 255.

human experience without relying on empty concepts (supernatural) or theoretical abstractions (nature as formalized in natural science). Because theology seeks to interpret the experienced world and its conditions, it needs to develop these interpretations based on the world as it appears to us from a phenomenological point of view.

Supernaturalism revisited

As many have pointed out, there seems to be four possible positions with respect to belief in God: Atheism (God does not exist), deism (God exists as a totally separate entity and does not engage with the world), pantheism (there is identity between God and the world) or panentheism (the world exists as finite within the infinite God). In the present context, the distinction between the latter two is the most important to consider, because they are the only ones that include the possibility of articulating the human experience of the world with reference to a supernatural realm.[291]

In a panentheistic approach, distinctions are constitutive: God and creation are distinct from each other but remain closely connected. The same goes for the infinite and the finite since the infinite encompasses all finite, which is a major point in Hegel. Panentheism assumes that "the Being of God includes and penetrates the whole universe, so that every part exists in God, but (as against pantheism) that God's Being is more than, and is not exhausted by, the universe."[292] The panentheistic position defers to a set of prepositions that articulates this distinction: We can speak of God as being with and by the world, or of the world as being in God. Furthermore, we can speak of the reality of God as in, with, and under the world, as opposed to a (deistic) notion of God as outside, by, over, or prior to the world. The choice of prepositions is significant for developing an understanding of panentheism but also shows how our use of language mediates the way we relate to and experience the world. It makes clear that these relations are important for conceiving of reality in a panentheist vision, as we cannot articulate the whatness (*to ti einai,* or Quality in the Peircean sense) of something without also relating it to what it is not. In panentheism, the whatness or Quality of something is determined by its relation to the other. The world is a creature because it is created by God, and God is Creator because

---

[291] See Gregersen, "Three Varieties of Panentheism," 19ff.

[292] The definition is taken from F. L. Cross and Elizabeth A. Livingstone, *The Oxford Dictionary of the Christian Church* (London; New York: Oxford University Press, 1974). Here as quoted by A. Peacocke, "Introduction," xviii., and modified by me for gender-neutral language.

God is related to the world. This constitutive relational element suggests that the most basic condition for something's being is *difference-in-relation*. Panentheism upholds and articulates the difference between God and the world, while simultaneously also affirming their deep interrelation. The world would not be if it were not in God. God would not be God, as we know God unless God created the world.

It follows from these considerations that the world would not be what it is if God were not distinct from it. That God makes the world possible could thus be seen as an expression of the whatness of God (God's identity), which makes God different from the world. There is unity in this distinction, so we can see the world as a unified system which is an expression of God.[293] From the beginning of the world, the ongoing process of creation not only makes the world possible, but it also manifests God as the one who is different. Through this difference, the world itself expresses who God is. Therefore, any notion of transcendence can only be articulated with respect to this differentiation.

One may see the semiotic character of the world as intimately related to the above formulation of relation-in-difference. The world has God as its ground, and any experience of the world is thus inherently a sign of God / by God / from God. However, God is not someone we can experience directly in the external world, and therefore, God is not "part" of our experience of the external world. So all experience of God must be indirect and mediated by some finite element that represents God. This mediation of God by means of the finite world highlights the radical implications of incarnation as the instance in which God reveals Godself and allows Godself to be represented in Christ. It also establishes the argument that we need not presuppose any supernatural intervention in order to understand this world. When the finite and natural world is the only world, and the only means by which God reveals Godself, the supernatural becomes

---

[293] The notion of system here echoes Bracken, but need not be taken as a subscription to his explicitly process approach. I see no need for elaborating it in order to make my basic argument here. See Joseph A. Bracken, *The World in the Trinity: Open-Ended Systems in Science and Religion* (Minneapolis, Minn.: Fortress Press, 2014). I do want to emphasize, though, that I share with Bracken the conviction that the relational is at the basis of this world and is the primary point of orientation for interpreting human experience. Writes Bracken: "[W]e human beings and all other creatures of this world do not first exist and then act according to our predetermined nature or essence, as in classical metaphysics (*agere sequitur esse*). Instead, from moment to moment we find ourselves already involved in various kinds of activities and only over time reflexively understand what that means in terms of our ongoing self-identity, what makes us different from others." Ibid., 3. Note here how the process of time contributes to the articulation of identity as being in relation to the world.

irrelevant. Since every experience of God must be mediated by means of symbols that also order our perception of ourselves, we cannot make sense of the word "God" without saying something about ourselves.[294] The symbol "God" may be articulated in different ways, but its primary function is not in what it is as such, but in how it works with regard to the way we experience the finite world. It has pragmatic relevance to the world rather than serving as a signifier for the supernatural.

God's articulation of Godself through difference is nevertheless an expression of God's unity with the world. Thus, we can infer that experiences of God change as the world changes. This is also a central point in process theology as opposed to the theology of Greek metaphysics. Philosophically, an unchangeable God is problematic if the world is seen as an ongoing articulation of God. Nevertheless, from this theological perspective, we encounter a reliable and trustworthy God who is faithful to the world God created.

Accordingly, the perspective of panentheism includes both distinction and relation between God and the world. The world's semiotic character requires linguistic articulation for expressing who God is because God expresses Godself through and in the basic conditions of creation. Panentheism arrives at these insights without presupposing any involvement of some additional, supernatural reality.

Against the backdrop of the above considerations, we have good reasons to reconsider the idea that a Christian vision of reality requires a category for the supernatural. In order to consider this claim in detail, we first need a clear idea of what the supernatural means. It is not always made clear or explicit in the literature, and particularly not so in the literature that problematizes the supernatural as a way to develop a conception of reality.

Nicholas Lash points out that until the seventeenth century, the term 'supernatural' was only used adjectively or adverbially.[295] Furthermore, the term had exactly the function of indicating difference, a point highly relevant in light of our reflections above. It was used "to indicate the difference that is made when someone is enabled to behave in ways above their ordinary station."[296] His most relevant example from a theological point of view is how so-called

---

[294] Cf. Ingolf U. Dalferth, *Die Wirklichkeit des Möglichen: hermeneutische Religionsphilosophie* (Tübingen: Mohr Siebeck, 2003).

[295] Nicholas Lash, *The Beginning and the End of 'Religion'* (Cambridge; New York: Cambridge University Press, 1996), 168.

[296] Ibid.

supernatural gifts (like grace) enable someone to be able to do something contrary to one's nature. Therefore, he follows this historical analysis by presenting an example, in which he is comparing a rabbit playing Mozart with a human being behaving generously, justly, and truthfully. Both are beneficiaries of supernatural gifts. However, the comparison is problematic on several levels. Most prominently, it disregards the notion of nature. It is not within the scope of the rabbit's nature to have the potential for playing Mozart. Conversely, a human acting honestly and selflessly can do so because his/her nature is renewed or elevated by God's grace, not in a way that is contrary to nature but working with and within it. The second problem follows from a lack of clarity and has to do with an understanding of the "natural" potential or capacities that humans have for doing good and acting according to God's will.[297]

The main point in Lash's analysis of nature, as opposed to the supernatural, is that in "the seventeenth century, for the first time, 'supernatural,' the substantive, began to connote a realm of being, a territory of existence, 'outside' the world we know. With 'nature' now deemed single, homogeneous and self-contained, we labeled 'supernatural' that 'other' world inhabited (some said) by ghosts and poltergeists, by demons, angels and suchlike extraterrestrials – and by God."[298] Hence, it moved from being an adjective or adverb to becoming something that described a realm or a substantive – a being or beings. Whereas the use of 'supernatural' already in the first sense took place in order to make a difference between ordinary and elevated ability or behavior, after the shift in the seventeenth century, another difference was established by using this word – the difference between different realms. Lash points to how this newly established difference is deeply related to "the spatialization of knowledge," a shift he rightly says is almost impossible to overestimate. It leads to "a transformation of the way in which relations with the Holy One, Creator and Redeemer of the world, were understood."[299] God is assigned to another realm, a realm remote from us, and is not close to us. God is no longer in, with, and under the reality that we experience, but belongs to another "realm." Consequently, one needs another model in order to reestablish a close understanding of the relationship between God and the world. Specifically, this model would provide the

---

[297] I leave aside here a discussion about the rather gloomy understanding of the human condition Lash seems to presuppose here, as it is not necessary in order to develop my argument. See, however, the suggestions about nature and grace below.
[298] Lash, ibid.
[299] Ibid., 168.

means for experiencing the relationship to God differently than what is possible within the framework of the "spatialization model."

In Lash' analysis, the supernatural is identified as a category in contrast to the "natural." Leaving aside for a while a discussion of what it means that something is natural, we can identify the purpose of the distinction in theological, ontological, and/or epistemological terms, all of which are implicit in his examples above.

Historically, the epistemological function for the category of the supernatural has been to depict occurrences and events that cannot be explained by known laws of nature or which are contrary to our expectations based on our previous experience. However, on the contemporary scene, this epistemological use of the supernatural typically serves one of two causes: either a naturalist rejection or as some kind of apologetics for religion.[300] Within the cause of a naturalist epistemology and/or methodology, its function is predominantly negative. The naturalist rejection of the supernatural has ontological implications, especially if it is employed in order to exclude any notion of things that are beyond what can be explained by laws of nature. The outcome of this use is the claim that "as no event or occurrence can in principle remain unexplained by laws of nature, there are no events that can occur contrary to such laws." Therefore, the very idea of a reality possible to describe by natural laws implies that there are no supernatural causes for the events that take place in the world. It is also hard to see what "supernatural causes" should mean if our only basis for identifying or determining them is our experiences of this world.[301] From the

---

[300] For examples of the former kind, see the treatment of scientism in Mikael Stenmark, *Scientism: Science, Ethics, and Religion* (Aldershot; Burlington: Ashgate, 2001). For a rather undefined use of "supernatural" within a more apologetic frame, see Craig S. Keener, *Miracles: The Credibility of the New Testament Accounts*, 2 vols. (Grand Rapids, Mich.: Baker Academic, 2011).

[301] The reference here to "this world" identifies the sphere from which we develop our knowledge as an intersubjectively accessible realm. If we had some public or common access to a supernatural realm, this would not, in itself, validate a claim about this realm as a basis for supernatural explanations. In order to do so, we would also need a specific epistemology that could establish intersubjective knowledge about this realm, and a methodology that could produce data and predictions from it. However, as these qualifiers suggest, it would then appear strange to call the realm in question supernatural anymore, it would just be another realm or dimension of human reality, like the different realms now described by natural science, social science, or psychology. For a careful and extensive discussion of explanations that also refer to the supernatural but address it more broadly from the point of view of possible so-called theistic explanations, see Gregory W. Dawes, *Theism and Explanation*, (New York: Routledge, 2009), 9–11, et passim. Dawes' careful analysis concludes that one cannot exclude such explanations in principle, but that those presented until now cannot claim to be scientific (cf. 146). However, given the necessary qualifiers suggested above, it is hard to see in what way such explanations would count as supernatural anymore, and in a way that makes it necessary to speak of separate realms.

perspective of philosophy of science, resorting to supernatural causes to explain the hitherto unexplained seems too hastily established. The elements of contingency and complexity in the actual world of human experience suggest that we should not employ the category of the supernatural as a catch-all for everything we cannot (yet) give a suitable explanation for.

The above suggestions are significant for theology because they imply that all we can experience, and all conditions for our experience, are within the realm of the natural world (theologically speaking, we should speak of the created world). The created world functions according to regularities and principles that are articulated in, or are possible to articulate as laws. However, it is problematic to see such laws as absolute; rather, they are dependent upon the "system" or relational matrix within which they work. Given the many (although, strictly speaking, not infinite) possible forms the world might take as it evolves, we cannot assume that we will be able to formulate laws for all events and circumstances. Instead, we can assume that all our experiences are part of the created world and conditioned by creation. This means that even if we experience something we refer to as God, God will have to manifest (or reveal) Godself on the basis of the conditions of creation. We cannot know anything about God that is not part of, in, with, or under the conditions of this creation and manifest in some type of representation. Hence, we have to assume that some type of law applies, even when we are unable to specify which one. Recently, Niels Gregersen has argued that "the actual transition of contemporary scientific interest from basic laws of nature to the investigation of the various capacities of complex systems implies a change of emphasis from seeing nature as passively subjugated to laws of nature to a new understanding of nature as affording local centers of activity, with only a relatively loose coupling to the fundamental laws of physics."[302] For theology, this means that events such as creation, new creation, or even "special divine action" "may come into the foreground of theological interest, without needing to violate the naturalistic principle that whatever will be formed in the course of evolution will be based on

---

[302] See N.H. Gregersen: "From Laws of Nature to Natural Capacities: A Theological Thought Experiment," in *Essays in Naturalism & Christian Semantics*, ed. Troels Engberg Pedersen and Niels Henrik Gregersen (Copenhagen University, 2010) 167–199, here 169. Among the advantages of Gregersen's view for the present context is that this enables him to develop a notion of God's creativity as being internal to creation, and not as separate from it, and furthermore, that it is able to develop this understanding in relation to the biblical material (cf. 190).

the physical and chemical substructures that are studied by the respective physical sciences."[303] So even when we talk of God as manifesting Godself in creation, we have to see God's manifestations as taking place on the basis of the regularities of the system, although not exclusively determined by them (which would leave out the possibility for God to act in new ways within God's creation). God manifests the potentialities of the created world in their concrete actualization, but as God does so, God also adds to this potential and enhances it. If this is the case, we do not require the concept of the supernatural in order to understand and relate to the reality of God because it is right in front of us.

The spatialization model for understanding the supernatural underpins the idea of orders of beings, some natural and some supernatural. This ontological idea we can leave behind without much discussion: All that is, is created by God. God, on the other hand, is not a being, but the condition for being. To speak of God as a supernatural being, in contrast to the natural, is problematic for two reasons: First, it makes God a being instead of seeing God as something that is the condition for being. Second, this distinction separates God from the natural in a way that suggests distance instead of community and interaction. From a Trinitarian point of view, this is deeply problematic. God, in Christian theology, is acting in, with, and under creation as its very ground. The Spirit gives all creation life and is present in the full range of human experience, guiding us to fullness through participation in the community with God and the world. Christ's fully human nature is the actualization of the possibilities of evolution, and as a human being, he does not belong to a supernatural realm exempted from the workings of this process. Finally, God as Creator is the power to be in all being. To speak of God's presence in creation as supernatural would suggest that there is something of God which we can experience separated from what takes place in the natural world. Contrary to this, a Trinitarian panentheist view suggests that we experience God in, with, and under what takes place in this world. The incarnation of God in Christ is the primary example for this point, but there are others as well, e.g., the manifestation of grace in unexpected acts of mercy, or the sudden illumination of human insight, made possible by the Spirit. These all happen by means of our actual, embodied mode of being in the world. As one can see, this perspective diverges significantly from the idea of "supernatural" which is under attack on the contemporary scene, namely supernatural explanations for that which science does not yet have an understanding. Instead, similar to the arguments developed in medieval

---

[303] Ibid, 169.

theology in order to discern the relationship between grace and free will, it offers an interpretation of that which enables humans to fulfill their capacities beyond the *expected*. Hence, open-endedness manifests itself in this way, as well.

As a conclusion, there is no need to employ the concept of the natural in order to safeguard theological concerns. A theological notion of the world and of transcendence needs not operate with an "outside" of the world in order to conceptualize the world itself as conditioned by and manifesting God as the creator. This perspective implies that the reality of God is transcendent and immanent simultaneously, and transcendence is not to be considered as spatial or supernatural, but as that which is beyond the scope of our immediate experience – that which has hitherto been designated as transcendental. A theologically relevant concept of nature is thus not conditioned by contrast to the supernatural, but by openness towards new and unexpected manifestations of God in the world, mediated by representations that may lead to further development of the concept of nature itself.[304]

Before proceeding to the theological implications of this understanding, one more epistemological factor should be added. By manifesting Godself as Trinity in, with, and under the conditions of the created world, God reveals Godself in the concrete world we can experience. This point implies that a theology of revelation that claims that God reveals Godself only in the Holy Scriptures is false.[305] To make the Scriptures the focal point of divine revelation contributes to the impression that it is not the world that reveals God, but a piece of human culture. Of course, human culture is also an articulation of God's creativity, but to identify God's revelation with Scripture considerably restricts what it means that God is revealed. It also ignores the fact that we always understand the Scriptures against the backdrop of our existing experience of the world and categories for perceiving reality. Our experience and knowledge of

---

[304] This conclusion is also in accordance with Dominic D. P. Johnson,, Hillary L. Lenfesty, and Jeffrey P. Schloss, 2014, "The Elephant in the Room: Do Evolutionary Accounts of Religion Entail the Falsity of Religious Belief?" *Philosophy, Theology and the Sciences,* 1 (2): 200–231, which state that, "We are not suggesting that supernatural causes (whether or not they exist) be employed in scientific explanations. Indeed, we are suggesting that our construal of what constitutes the natural is always tentative, ambiguous, and malleable. Real world events are open to empirical scrutiny, and novel proposals that seem to involve the supernatural, if evidentially supported, do not mandate inclusion of the supernatural but may expand construal of the natural" (225).

[305] Cf. e.g., Bracken, *The World in the Trinity,* 154 *et passim.* I return to the topic of Scripture as revealing / representing God at the end of the next chapter.

God are related to all of reality, not limited to specific, delineated realms or sectors of it.

The Triune incarnated God

Christian theology determines the basic character of God as love. In principle, this decision is what shapes, orients, and transforms Christians in their practices and their relation towards the world. Love displays itself in goodness and care. A viable claim about the love, goodness, and care that God displays in the world needs a reference to an experiential dimension, which means that God needs to be represented in ways that make this display possible. In human life, love, care, and goodness mostly take on an embodied character, and this is the fundamental reason why these can appear in human experience. From a theological point of view, this means that humans and God are so closely related in these experiences that humans are actually participating in the reality of God when they partake in events that allow these phenomena to appear. God works in human love and is experienced in goodness. This captures the essence of the panentheist position. As God is not the world, and love is not God, the world nevertheless is in God and manifests God in instances of love, care, goodness, and creativity. Love is the theme that relates God and the world most distinctively. Furthermore, as Michael Brierley has pointed out, "the difference between classical theism and panentheism comes back to a difference of human experience, namely, which of these loves experienced by humanity, agape or agape-eros, is the deeper symbol of the love of God; and this conforms *human experience* as the prompt for the rise in panentheist doctrine."[306] Love is then the starting point for any human experience that can give us access to an understanding of the relationship between God and the world. In this context, love is not supernatural or otherworldly; instead, it is the very condition for human being, becoming, and flourishing.[307]

Since love is at work in creation, it must, therefore, be enabled by the process of evolution and developed throughout the history of the world. Love is

---

[306] Brierley, "Naming a Quiet Revolution: The Panentheistic Turn in Modern Theology," in Clayton and Peacocke, *In whom we live and move and have our being*, 14. My italics.

[307] Niels Gregersen points to how an expressivist view of divine love, from a historical point of view, "emerged in a situation where philosophical theologians attempted to find a third way between pantheism and supernaturalism." A main challenge in this regard was Spinoza. See Gregersen, "Three Varieties of Panentheism," in Clayton and Peacocke, *In Whom We Live and Move and Have Our Being*, 28.

evolving as the spiritual and embodied character of the world comes increasingly to its fruition. Accordingly, love is understood neither by an approach articulated in mechanistic materialism nor from some claim to supernatural influence. Rather, love is conditioned by the increasing multilevel differentiation of the world and the different modes of concrete community that surpasses mere materialist or supernatural positions.

Christian theology is built on (and contributes to) the experiences of life, love, and hope that have been present in history and indicate that reality must be understood as still implying some unfinished business. These features that point to the not-yet-finished are deeply embedded in human life, yet they have the power to transcend our familiarity and contentment with our present conditions. Within this framework, the Christian vision of human life makes sense. However, when asking which moments or events mediate God's power, "the answer can only be potentially *all* experience, the whole world. There is no exclusive zone, no special realm, which alone may be called religious."[308] Panentheist theology is nevertheless well advised not to underplay the ambiguities related to the development of the world and of human life. The interaction between God and the world goes both ways, which is underscored by the fact that the incarnation takes place for the sake of the salvation of the world. The fact that God creates, and that creation also makes God dependent on what takes place, makes God vulnerable and exposed as creator. Creation changes God. As Gregersen writes, "Redescribed theologically, evolution is not a risk-free thing but includes the labor of nature. The groaning and suffering of creation are thus not to be seen as specifically designed by a malicious, all-determining God. Setbacks and suffering are part of the package deal of participating in a yet-unfinished creation. However, there is also a principle of grace built into the whole process." Gregersen also suggests that this grace is closely related to God's promises for the future: "There is, taken on a whole, a surplus of life-

---

[308] Elizabeth A. Johnson, *She Who Is: The Mystery of God in Feminist Theological Discourse* (New York: Crossroad, 2002), 124. She continues: "The breadth and depth of experience that may mediate holy mystery is genuinely inclusive. It embraces not only, and in many instances even primarily, events associated with explicitly religious meaning such as church, word, sacraments, and prayer, although these are obviously intended as mediations of the divine. But since the mystery of God undergirds the whole world, the wide range of what is considered secular or just plain ordinary human life can be grist for the mill of experience of Spirit-Sophia, drawing near and passing by" (125).

intensity promised to those who take up the chances of collaboration."[309] To put it otherwise: Nature will be fulfilled in and through grace.

As an elaboration on these ideas, we may turn to the doctrine of the Trinity. In order to explicate this doctrine, one has developed the idea of *perichoresis*. It aims to articulate the close relationship between that which is different, without separation and without confusion. Here, I use it not only as a metaphor for the relationship between the three persons of the Trinity as they interact with creation (the economic Trinity), but also to reflect the close relationship between the Trinity and the world.

God is three persons in Unity: Father, Son, and Spirit. Each of the three divine persons is distinguishable through and because of their relation to the other persons. The unity of the Trinity does not dissolve the distinctions between the divine persons; instead this unity "established those distinctions by showing that it is precisely through their reciprocal relations with one another, and in virtue of their incommunicable characteristics as Father, Son, and Holy Spirit, that the three divine Persons constitute the very Communion, which the one God eternally is, or which they eternally are," as Thomas Torrance writes.[310]

Perichoresis thus signifies a cyclical movement and "evokes the coinherence of the three divine persons, an encircling of each around the others."[311] As Elizabeth Johnson points out, the term may have both static and dynamic meaning: it may mean to dwell or rest within another, or that things interweave, permeate, or encompass each other. These dual meanings have relevance both to Trinitarian relations and to the relationship between God and the world.

Because the world is a manifestation of the Triune God, we must see the divine community as allowing humankind to develop and articulate itself through expressions of love and community, which have their origin in God. Such a Trinitarian vision of God and the world stands in contrast to an abstract, philosophical form of theism (or deism[312]) that allows the possibility for the world to be fully experienced and understood apart from the constant activity of God. Instead, this Trinitarian vision of God and the world is experientially

---

[309] Gregersen, "From Anthropic Design to Self-Organized Complexity," in *From complexity to life: on the emergence of life and meaning*, ed. Gregersen (New York: Oxford University Press, 2003), 228.

[310] Thomas F. Torrance, *The Christian doctrine of God, one being three persons* (Edinburgh; New York: T&T Clark, 2001), 175.

[311] Johnson, *She who is*, 220.

[312] See Dalferth, *Becoming present: an inquiry into the Christian sense of the presence of God*, 157f.

related to the development and evolution of the world. The close relation of the world to the work of God throughout the past, the present, and the future of the world can only come into full expression by means of a symbol of God that is the origin of life, embodied and participating in the world, in which the future is present as an effective promise. In all of this, love is the *telos*. As Johnson says: "Perichoretic movement summons up the idea of all three distinct persons existing in each other in an exuberant movement of equal relations: an excellent model for human interaction in freedom and other regards. *Precisely as community in diversity Holy Wisdom has the capacity to be the ground of the turning world*."[313]

As the core interactional reality of both the Trinitarian God in Godself and God and the world, *perichoresis* underscores how the essence of God (and the world) is to be in relation. God's relational character points towards a dynamic understanding of God in unity, whereby God's essence is defined as not independent of God's relations (as they are realized in the unifying reality of the Trinitarian persons). It also points to how the fullness of human experience is realized in relation, especially in relations shaped and marked by love.

Human beings are what they are because of the works of God, in and through nature and grace. Separated from God, we are not properly or fully ourselves, as Kathryn Tanner underscores.[314] Therefore, the presence of God in our lives also generates a desire for God and for participation in the divine reality – a point that we will see developed further in the next chapter. Grace and God's freedom are related: "Desire for God is the product, in short, not of our nature but of grace understood as a strong form of participation in God." This desire is not due to a lack in human nature, but from our gratuitous participation in the reality of God.[315]

---

[313] Johnson, *She who is,* 221. My italics. It is worth noting "Holy wisdom" is the name that she chooses for God in this context.

[314] Cf. Kathryn Tanner, *Christ the Key* (Cambridge: Cambridge University Press, 2010), 107ff.

[315] Ibid., 126f. She summarizes this idea on p. 129 in a way that adds depth to the *gratia non tollit*: "If not ours by nature, the gift of God's own life is still, however, naturally ours or natural to us; and in this way any naturalistic claim of self-containment for the human creature apart from grace is countered. Despite the fact that desire for it is not solicited by our nature independently of grace, grace in the form of God's presence to us remains natural to us in that our nature has not been made to exist on its own apart from it. The grace of strong participation in God is natural to us because our nature is such that we exist well only with it. The gift of strong participation in God shows itself to be natural to us in this sense in that its loss does us fundamental harm; in some significant sense we lose ourselves in losing God. Life without it must be an unnatural condition, a condition contrary to the character of our created nature, given the wretchedness and suffering that ensue."

Tanner adds that "because existing with the grace of God is the normal condition that God created us to be in, this understanding of the relationship between nature and grace gives one no reason to imagine what human nature would be like apart from the gift of grace and then to identify that with our original created state. But it makes no sense to speculate [...] about what human beings would have been like if they had not been given grace." Thus, she rejects the position that humans would have been able to become what we are without God's grace.[316] God's grace is what we experience as the power that enables us to realize our full nature – what we are destined to become.

In a similar vein, Irenaeus reasoned that God's glory increases in direct proportion to human flourishing (*Gloria Dei vivens homo*).[317] In his view, "the glory of God is a human being fully alive, and the life of humanity consists in the vision of God."[318] Humans do not flourish unless they are given access to all the realms of experience that we have developed the capacity to partake in through our own evolutionary history. If our access to any of these realms is impeded, it directly restricts our participation in the fullness of the reality of God. This, in turn, is the mode in which God reveals Godself as love.

From a distinct theological point of view that transcends the philosophical theology developed so far, we can see that this interrelation between God's glory and human flourishing fleshes out a perichoretic understanding of Trinitarian relations. God as Father becomes known as the loving Creator through the Son's witness concerning the caring and loving Father who offers the gifts of life, love, and hope to everyone. Because of God's great love, God is incarnated in the world which the Son shared with the Father in creating. And the Son witnesses about the Father, thereby creating faith that orients the world in the direction of love. Simultaneously, the work of the Spirit is to create faith and community which anticipates the future of humankind and creation and which shapes the hope and the orientation of those that want to serve God. None of the three divine persons could do their work without reference to the person and work of the others, as they each bring to completion the world that they share with the other persons in loving it and repeatedly offering it chances for life.

---

[316] Ibid., 131f.

[317] I owe this point to Cherith Fee Nordling, *Knowing God by name: a conversation between Elizabeth A. Johnson and Karl Barth* (New York: Peter Lang, 2010), 117.

[318] Irenaeus and James R. Payton, *Irenaeus on the Christian faith: a condensation of Against heresies* (Eugene, Or.: Pickwick Publications, 2011), 4. 34. 5–7.

God is always in movement, as is the world. The world's movement and direction reflect the influences of God and God's attempts to lure and inspire the world to fulfill its destiny in God. Thus, the perichoretic interaction between God and the world implies that the world would not be if not for God. The world needs God in order to move beyond itself toward a community of love in the full sense. God's interaction with the world can be interpreted as the generous expansion of divine *perichoresis* in order to include more than God in God.[319] God does not need the world in order to be God or to have community, but God freely chooses to indwell in and partake in the world for the sake of love for the world. Since God chooses to relate to the world to this degree, the perichoretic mutuality goes both ways. The world exposes and explicates externally to God what it means for the three triune persons to interact, mutually refer to each other, and participate in the triune community without inequality or separation. Thus, God achieves God's goal, not only in cooperation with creation but by enabling creation's potential for agency in a world where one can experience love and goodness as basic features of orientation. These goals are not yet fulfilled, but they begin to be realized in the world and in the incarnation.

God – Conclusion

Why does God matter? God matters as the instance that orients and transforms human life. From a substantial point of view, God matters because love matters – and the very notion of God allows humans to imagine a reality beyond the immediate present, in which love can come more to fulfillment than is the case in the actual situation. Hence, God is not only the source of everything one can experience but also the source of what may be.

The transcendental mode of reasoning I have presented in this chapter suggests that reality is not easy to comprehend in this manner without God. God is the one who works all in all. If this fact is not recognized, the fundamental relationship between God and the world is compromised. When God works all in all, then God is the sovereign source of reality, of goodness, and to God

---

[319] There is no reason, however, to see the so-called immanent and economic Trinity as conceptually identical. They are identical in terms of who is acting, but the immanent Trinity is prior to the world, and is the one that is known as the economic Trinity because of the works with, in, and under the world. In order to have a notion of the economic Trinity, we need to have an understanding of the relationship between God and the history of creation and salvation, whereas we do not need that for a notion of the immanent Trinity. Having said that, though, I underscore that the relations of the immanent Trinity are only accessible to us as relations between the three distinct persons insofar as they are realizing their community through their work in and for the world.

alone, all honor is due. God can be God only if God is the fundamental source of goodness.

God's power is infinite and, therefore, ubiquitous. Furthermore, it is present in all that is, even "the tiniest leaf."[320] "…God creates, effects and preserves all things through his almighty power and right hand, as our Creed confesses."[321] God's omnipresence means that God is present in the innermost and outermost of all beings, yes, God is truly present in everything.[322] God is thus the first or principal cause of all that is,[323] and all beings in the created world must be seen as originating from God's work, and as dependent on God. In turn, it means that God uses creation for God's own purposes and that God can hide Godself under the mask of God's creatures. Thus, when God governs the world, God is not appearing directly but uses masks "under which he conceals himself and so marvelously exercises dominion and introduces disorder in the world."[324] This idea of God as being both active and concealed is present in different forms throughout Luther's writing. This is also in consonance with our previous analysis of God as the power to be in Løgstrup.

Against this backdrop, it also makes sense to speak about God as the one who not only offers God's gifts, but who offers Godself as the main gift: "What God gives is not an effect of a cause, but himself, and the preached word is the way he bestows this gift upon creatures."[325] This gift allows humans to find a basis for their lives, a point that is articulated well in one of the most quoted texts Luther offers on God, namely the explanation of the first commandment in the *Large Catechism*. It reads:

What is to have a god? What is God? Answer: A god is that to which we look for all good and in which we find refuge in every time of need. To have a god is nothing else than to trust and believe him with our whole heart. As I have often said, the trust and faith of the heart alone make both God and an idol. If your faith and trust are right, then your God is the true God. On the other hand, if your trust is false and wrong, then you have not the true God. For these two belong

---

[320] Jaroslav Pelikan, ed. *Luther's Works* (St. Louis: Concordia Publishing House, 1955), Vol 37, 57.

[321] Ibid., 57f.

[322] Cf. ibid., 59. This is a point that Luther develops in relation to the real presence of God in the sacraments, as well.

[323] Paul Althaus, *The Theology of Martin Luther* (Philadelphia: Fortress Press, 1996), 107.

[324] Pelikan, *Luther's Works*, Vol 45, 331.The notion of God's masks is used also in other contexts, such as in Vol. 26, 95 (On Galatians), 95. Further on the topic of *Larvae Dei*, see A.J. Steinbronn, *The masks of God: the significance of larvae Dei in Luther's theology* (Diss. Concordia Theological Seminary, 1991).

[325] S. Paulson, "Luther's doctrine of God," in Kolb, Dingel, Batka (Eds): *The Oxford Handbook of Martin Luther's Theology* (Oxford: Oxford University Press, 2014), 188.

together, faith and God. That to which your heart clings and entrusts itself is, I say, really your God.[326]

Here, Luther offers a formal and universal definition of God that simultaneously opens up to several different layers of meaning. How a human being orients herself in the world by means of faith is the decisive element.[327] Thus, to speak about God is to speak about the instance from which one governs and orients one's own life. Hence, it all hangs on believing in a true God, i.e., a God who deserves to be called God, and who *can* be God.[328] One main contribution in Luther's understanding of God is accordingly that it directs the human being away from a focus on herself and her own achievements, and towards the basis for justification *extra nos*. By directing the human being outside herself, towards the works of God instead of herself, Luther indicates that the only reliable God is a god who is *extra nos*, i.e., one who is not ourselves and the achievements of human agency. When Luther introduces the basic distinction between God and humans, between God's works and the works of humans as a governing distinction in his *theo*logy, it is because he recognizes the fact that we have been developing throughout this chapter: That God's agency and presence is the condition for human existence, experience, and agency, and that one gets it wrong if this fact is not recognized.

Luther's definition of God opens up to an understanding of God that engages the human being in a critical self-assessment: Whom do you trust? From what do we orient ourselves? This is not an approach meant to bring about a basic lack of trust in oneself, but it aims at directing one's trust towards God when it comes to the question about justification and the basis for it.

A further element in the considerations in the explanation of the first commandment is that it *relates God and the good to each other,* as we already have

---

[326] Luther, *Large Catechism*, I, 1.

[327] Gunther Wenz, *Gott*, Studium Systematische Theologie Bd. 4. Bd. 4 (Göttingen: Vandenhoeck und Ruprecht, 2007), 20, identifies this usage in Luther as pointing to an anthropological condition, and interprets Luther as seeing the topic God as something that is not uniquely Christian, but an "anthropological universal." Therefore, everything depends on in which God the human puts her trust. Accordingly, Luther is not concerned with atheism as an option, but with true and false worship (However, it is necessary to add to Wenz' point here that it is only in true worship that God can be God as God wants to be God).

[328] Cf. Paulson, "Luther's Doctrine of God," who points to how it is "the faith of the heart [that] makes its God from the law, and so misidentifies God. If God is not grasped as he wants to be grasped in the preached word of promise apart from the law, then necessarily God will be your God unpreached as wrath and death" (193). Accordingly, the only chance for humans is to trust in the preached word that offers us God's gifts *extra nos*, and not as something derived analytically from human works.

indicated above. Thus, Luther links the human *expectation for goodness* intimately to the notion of God. God is trustworthy because this God is the source
of goodness, the one who provides human life with what humans need and for
which they strive. This understanding allows humans to see the experienced
goodness as something that is not originating from themselves and their own
work but from the abundance offered by the generous God. Accordingly, the
meaning of the first commandment is that it directs the human being (outwards)
towards the only reliable source from which he or she is to expect the good:

> [...] we are to trust in God alone and look to Him and expect from Him naught but good, as from
> one who gives us body, life, food, drink, nourishment, health, protection, peace, and all neces-
> saries of both temporal and eternal things. He also preserves us from misfortune, and if any evil
> befalls us, delivers and rescues us, so that it is God alone (as has been sufficiently said) from
> whom we receive all good, and by whom we are delivered from all evil. Hence also, I think, we
> Germans from ancient times call God (more elegantly and appropriately than any other language)
> by that name from the word Good, as being an eternal fountain which gushes forth abundantly
> nothing but what is good, and from which flows forth all that is and is called good.[329]

We can then close the circle – the eternal quest that follows from the close link
between God and goodness: God's gifts can be expressed in the understanding
of God as *love*. It is because God loves the human being that God bestows God's
gifts on them. Thus, God's nature is love, a point that also comes to full expression in how God gives humans the eternal goods in his Son as God's representative – and thus Godself as well.[330] The fact that this loving God is the one and
only *summum bonum* constitutes, in turn, the creature's obligation to let God,
and nothing else, be God. The flipside of this understanding is that only when
humans allow God to be God can humans realize their full humanity.

---

[329] Luther, *Large Catechism*, I, 1.
[330] Cf. Althaus, *The Theology of Martin Luther*, 115–16.

Desire and vulnerability: The human condition

Introduction

This chapter builds on two, interrelated, premises. The first is that the resources the Christian tradition stewards provide rich opportunities for reflecting on the human condition, and about what matters in human life. The second premise is that we need to consider these resources as not fixed formulas that present fixed and ready recipes for dealing with every aspect of human life. The resources are means for continuing the unfinished business of religion and theology, and not means for closing debates, impeding the search for new answers to difficult questions and challenges, or for avoiding to consider earlier solutions to problems from a critical angle. Moreover, these reflective resources contribute to guiding human practices. That Christianity as a religion sees humans as part of an ongoing history suggests that our being, as conditioned by ever-occurring changes, entails that we need to do more than repeat former solutions in order to solve contemporary problems. This point may be hard to realize for those who think that a return to so-called "classical Christianity" is the recipe for whatever religious problem we are facing – but that cannot mean that we can ignore the challenges we face in the contemporary world. Some of these were not foreseen in the tradition hitherto. An obvious example of this is the Christian practice of forgiveness: is it unconditional – or is it morally offensive in a world that has seen atrocities like the Holocaust, The Cambodian Killing Fields, the Gulags, Rwanda, or Srebrenica?

In the previous chapter on God, we put considerable emphasis on the point that God, as the reality that is only accessible by means of representation, reveals Godself through these representations, among which the primary one is Jesus Christ, as the *true image of God* – a designation that all humans are called to realize. For humans to realize this, however, it is necessary to acknowledge and appropriate for oneself what it means *in practical terms* to be the image of God – and that can be done only in life led as faith, hope, and love. To realize true humanity is to find an adequate shape for how one practices the realities of the human condition. This point, however, needs not be understood in the Feuerbachean way, as if the true content of religion is about humanity, and nothing else.[331] It should be read as an expression of the point Hegel repeatedly makes, that God realizes Godself in the relationship with humanity, just as humanity realizes itself in the relationship with God. From this point of view, then, the meaning of religion in all its forms and modes, as narrative, ritual, doctrine, sacraments, symbols, artwork, buildings and sites, and belief, have one thing in common: to mediate this relationship so that it can manifest its close and non-dissolvable character in the best way possible through practices that are shaped by the resources for orientation and transformation.[332] The point is not that this is always already the case – the very fact that human beings repeatedly are called to come to terms with what this relationship entails and find the most adequate ways to express it means that religion, in its pragmatic character as the mediator between God and humanity always implies unfinished business. Moreover, it also entails the constant risk of misapprehension and failure, due to lack of faith and trust in the reality of God as the best condition for fulfilling human life and for providing the best opportunities for flourishing.

In the following, I will argue that the task of finding a good way to live a human life requires that humans come to terms with two basic features: desire and vulnerability. These features do not exist in opposition to each other, but they present us with the constant challenge of figuring out how to deal with them – be it in terms of balance, complementarity, or negotiation. None of them is better than the other: both present us with challenges by and for themselves, and both also represent challenges to the other. Unchecked desire may lead to hurting others in their vulnerability. However, the attempt to shield oneself from vulnerability may also lead to an unhealthy negation of desires, and a rigid rejection of life qualities that contribute to flourishing. Furthermore, the denial of both desire and vulnerability may cause problems for human fulfillment. One

---

[331] Cf. Feuerbach, *The Essence of Christianity*.

[332] Even Nietzsche, the most ardent critic of Christianity, realized this from early on: "Christianity is essentially a matter of the heart; not until it is incorporated in us, when it has become our very nature, is a human being a true Christian. The principal teachings of Christianity express merely the basic truths of the human heart; they are symbols, just as the highest must always be merely a symbol of something still higher. To be blessed by belief means no more than the old truth, that only the heart, not knowledge, can make us happy. That God became human merely indicates that the human being should not seek blessedness in the infinite but ground its heaven on earth; the illusion of the supernatural has placed the human spirit in a false relationship to the earthly world: this was a consequence of the childhood of peoples. The glowing youthful soul of humanity accepts these ideas eagerly and darkly pronounces the secret that roots itself in both past and future, that God became human. Humanity will become manly through arduous doubts and battles; it recognizes in itself 'the beginning, the middle, the end of religion.'" Here quoted from Daniel Blue, *The Making of Friedrich Nietzsche : The Quest for Identity, 1844–1869* (Cambridge, United Kingdom: Cambridge University Press, 2016), 140.

can interpret the meaning of religious representations as helping to deal with these tasks, through practices of orientation (What is the best thing to do or be?), transformation (Should I transform the object of my desires or my way of dealing with vulnerability?), and reflection (How do I live and relate in the best way possible to others and to God?). Hence, the relevance of religious practices can be identified in how they mediate semiotic resources that shape human lives in ways that allow desire and vulnerability to be an integral part of a good life in community with others.

Desires present humans with the need for orientation (what should I desire?) and transformation (I need to desire something else). One can learn about what one may have good reasons to desire, and why something is not worth desiring within communities and their spaces of learning, communication, and discourse. The Christian communities, and religious communities in general, are such spaces, in which one learns to offer reasons for one's choices and preferences with regard to the desires one seeks to realize. Contrary to this position, the Nietzschean individualist "has deliberately excluded himself from and invited others to exclude themselves from just those types of practice and just those types relationship in and through which we learn how to become practically rational agents and how to exercise those virtues without which rational deliberation is not possible. But to exclude oneself from those practices and relationships is, by impoverishing one's moral experience, to deny oneself the possibility of understanding what it is to be such a rational agent."[333]

Because one can approach the human condition and its relationship with religious faith from different angles, the focus on desire and vulnerability as the main starting points for Christian practice provides us with experiential content that is not constituted by a specific religious doctrine. They are important for everyone to come to terms with in order to secure flourishing. When religious representations and imaginaries provide resources for doing so, community, human growth, moral insight, and profound human relationships marked by care and love, interdependence and trust can be developed. This does not imply, however, that trust and hope cannot be misplaced or go astray. However, "in one way or another the foundational importance of trust for the process of personal formation shows that [...] the person lives by the future in which its trust is placed."[334] Misguided desire, or lack of recognition of vulnerability, may

---

[333] Alasdair C. MacIntyre, *Ethics in the Conflicts of Modernity : An Essay on Desire, Practical Reasoning, and Narrative* (New York: Cambridge University Press, 2016), 58.
[334] Wolfhart Pannenberg, *Anthropology in Theological Perspective* (Edinburgh: T. & T. Clark, 1985), 527.

close off from true relationships with others, and result in the neglect of community, lack of recognition of one's own finite condition, and impeded personal growth and profound interrelations with others, as well as trust in something or someone external to oneself. This last option is what theology calls *sin*. In other words: Religion(s) addresses and interprets the human condition as it appears and offers means for coming to terms with it. Religion does not start in belief or doctrine, but in the experienced conditions of human life, which calls for a context of interpretation and significance.

This semiotic character of religion as mediation of the God-Human relationship is not possible unless one can also articulate the semiotic dimension by means of language. Language allows us to articulate the world and express its different realms and dimensions. It is *constitutive* of our ability to experience and express the rich world in which we live. Language is itself relational, it is practiced, and it makes it possible for us to point to God as the one both beyond and within the world. From a Christian point of view, by equipping us with the capacity for language, God made it possible for Godself, by way of God's representatives (which are, in principle, every human being) to address us by means of created language. The implication of the human ability to comprehend and express the world through language is that the semiotic dimension is no additional part to a world already experienced as such-and-such. Instead, our experience of the world is fundamentally semiotic, and the fact that the world can be expressed in language is a structural dimension that shapes its character in our experience of it. Therefore, language is one of the ways in which the world is present for us, and we in it, just as value is also part of the world. This pragmatist and semiotic perspective implies that "expressibility is a factor fundamental to the structurality of Beings and of Being."[335] Expressibility by language is one of the basic and intrinsic characteristics of the world. In essence, the world exists as expressible.

Accordingly, human identity is the result of a historical process in which the individual experiences contexts of meaning and significance and can apprehend their continuity. When he makes this point, Wolfhart Pannenberg also argues that this fact makes it possible to see experience as having priority over action. He goes on:

Unlike experience, action presupposes the identity of the acting subject. Not only must agents grasp in advance the connection between means and ends, as well as the possible side effects of

---

[335] Lorenz B. Puntel and Alan White, *Structure and Being: A Theoretical Framework for a Systematic Philosophy* (University Park, Pa.: Pennsylvania State University Press, 2008), 371.

their action; in addition, they themselves establish the connection between means and ends by actually using the means in order to achieve their purposes. The unity of the connection is based on the identity of the acting subject through time. But the identity of the subject itself is constituted by a process of identity formation that takes the form of a history in which the particularity of the individual's existence is grasped in the context of more inclusive continuities of meaning and in the medium of linguistic articulation and communication.[336]

The implication of the above from the point of view of Christianity is that the world, therefore, constantly must be made expressible as the reality in which God reveals Godself. Against this backdrop, it is possible to understand the whole struggle about theodicies: they appear because of the basic human intuition that the world is not what it should be – and the reality of God is the basic reality against which we measure the present condition of things. When people say that they cannot believe in God because of the evils and atrocities of this world, in one way, they are right: as long as the world contains such elements, it is, indeed, hard to experience the world as the reality of God. But if God and the reality that religion mediates visions of as God's reality did not exist or was not articulated at all, it would be harder to articulate the protest against the present state of things by means for practices that oppose these contradictions of God's reality. Then the present state could just as easily be interpreted as the normal state, with which we should have to comply ourselves. The Christian vision of humanity as created in God's image, and therefore called to represent and realize who God is by living in faith, hope, and love, makes the world itself God's unfinished business – whereas simultaneously presenting human beings with a still unfinished task in their quest for goodness.

Desire, flourishing, goodness[337]

As suggested above, desire constitutes the need for orientation, transformation, and reflection if it is to provide us with the content of a life led well. Hence, desire is an open and dynamic phenomenon. This is the reason why the unfinished business of religion and humanity expresses itself primarily in the deeply rooted human desire for goodness. Although part of this unfinished business is

---

[336] Pannenberg, *Anthropology in Theological Perspective*, 513.

[337] Much of the present section is based on an earlier work on the topic of desire, some of which has been presented lectures given in different contexts: at the Nordic Conference on Philosophy of Religion in Iceland in June 2011, for the Swedish Theological Academy, Uppsala 13.5.2003, and at the Richardson Lecture at the University of Durham in December 2000. Some elements are also previously published in my article "Creation and construction. On the theological appropriation of post-modern theory", in *Modern Theology* 18, no. 2 (2002).

to find out if, and to what extent, our desires are actually able to realize goodness and provide for flourishing, it is nevertheless beyond question that desire
is always a desire for what we assume is good – at least for us personally.[338]

According to Maurice Merleau-Ponty, desire is not adequately understood
if seen only as a primitive biological event. It is neither the result of an invol-
untary biological impulse nor a phenomenon apparent to a lucid mind. Humans
cannot produce their own desire. Humans cannot and do not say that "I want to
desire X" and thus force desire to appear. Desire exists in another type of structure, linked to our way of relating to the world. It expresses itself in intentionality that conditions human existence[339] and in the wills and wants that we articulate. Desire is thus an integral element in the embodied direction toward the
world and toward oneself; a moment in the human being-in-the-world. Desire
emerges spontaneously in the experience of the world as the other, and out of
the pre-thematic emotional being-in-the-world. Hence, it is not primarily an element in consciousness, to be appropriated intellectually, but in the world as
this world is given with the body and its perception. This is the reason why we
say that it is the other who stirs my desire. Hence, humans do not only desire
actively; desire is what happens to humans in passivity as well. Desire is a relational phenomenon.

Given that Merleau-Ponty is right, it is possible to see desire as something
that is prior to, but also informs faith in different ways. Desire guides and in-
teracts with faith. It is an interplay between the desire for goodness and flourishing on the one hand, and faith and in what we put our trust, on the other hand.
It is not recommendable to ignore this relationship, because it is against the pre-
subjective experience of desire, and its more or less articulated content in faith,
that it becomes possible to see religious beliefs as rooted in, informed by, and
shedding light on the contents of human experience.

Merleau-Ponty sees desire as a motivating force for our choice of experiences. It opens up the individual to a dimension of value and preferences in its
actualization of being-in-the-world. Some relationships, imaginaries, actions,
and experiences are preferred over others. These preferences come with desire,

---

[338] For an analysis of the diverse meanings of 'good' and their relationship to desires, see Macintyre,
Ethics in the Conflicts of Modernity, 13–16, 24–31. An important element in Macintyre's contribution is how he links his constructive understanding of the neo-Aristotelean connection of desire and
the good to human flourishing, and thereby to all human capacities, not only to the immediate desire, but also to rational contemplation. Hence, he also underscores the partly contextual element in
the conditions for (the realization of) the good/goodness.
[339] Cf. Maurice Merleau-Ponty, *Phenomenology of Perception* (London: Routledge, 1994), Part
I, Ch. 5 (178ff.).

and thus, desire directs us toward that which is considered or perceived as valuable, as desirable, and it thereby becomes a constitutive part of human action.[340] Accordingly, desire is not only important in erotic moments, but is poured out into the whole of human existence. Only in this way can it also be said to define the human being-in-the-world. Accordingly, desire should not only be defined as sexual desire in a narrow sense, but as something that shapes one's directedness toward the other, or others, in a variety of different ways.

Because desire is always personal, and something related not only to the object but also to the embodied self, it exists in a dialectical structure, in the movement or oscillation between the relationship with the other and one's relationship with oneself. Hence, desire is of crucial importance for a relationship with the other. Yet, it is also vital for the ways in which one is able to perceive oneself, namely through the opportunities which desire opens up by relating to imaginaries, contexts of understanding, and belief. The dialectical structure in desire implies a movement from subjectivity to intersubjectivity and vice versa. Although desire emerges out of the relation with the other, out of intersubjectivity, its motivating force is always providing the individual with a direction in which one is placed in a specific, definitive situation by desire. Desire demands that one takes on this situation in a specific manner – and thereby realizes a specific mode of being-in-the-world. Thus, desire defines subjectivity and shapes the concrete situation by bringing the individual into relation with that which is exterior to its immediate self.[341] Against this background, it becomes important to understand desire as a pre-subjective phenomenon, prior to the subjectivity that emerges out of inter-subjectivity, which in turn allows one to become a subject.

We cannot ignore the implications that these phenomenological features of desire have for how humans engage religious imaginaries and representations in their quest for self-fulfillment and flourishing. Such representations of God and imaginaries of the world provide ample opportunities for perceiving oneself and one's desires in a certain light: sometimes affirming them positively, sometimes making them appear as problematic and in need of adjustment, correction, or negation.[342]

---

[340] Cf. Ulla Thøgersen, *Krop Og Fænomenologi : En Introduktion Til Maurice Merleau-Pontys Filosofi* (Århus: Systime, 2003), 168–69.

[341] Cf. ibid., 170–1.

[342] Cf. MacIntyre, *Ethics in the Conflicts of Modernity : An Essay on Desire, Practical Reasoning, and Narrative*, Chapter One, on how the understandings and depth of human flourishing are different in an emotivist (individualist) and a community-based (communitarian) approach to desire, goodness, and flourishing.

However, to repress and ignore desire has severe consequences. If one is to negate desires, they nevertheless should be recognized as being present, first. Only then can one assess desire adequately. Furthermore, to ignore the desire for the other (whatever it may be) implies not only losing a specific mode of possibility for self-transcendence (since one then also loses the other, which presents itself as the other, the one able to open up one's world in a certain respect). One is then also losing a specific chance for self-relation, for relating to oneself in the modus of desire, i.e., as an individual who directs oneself towards someone or something outside of oneself. The crucial consequence here is that one thereby ends up in a situation (or better: lack of situation) that could be described as absolutizing finitude, namely a finite mode of existence in which the other that is present in desire fails to play any significant role with regard to who one is able to become. Ignorance or repression prevents desire from functioning as an instrument for self-transcendence and genuine other-relatedness. The potential severity of this situation is expressed not only in the fact that one may lose the relation to the other constituted by desire. It is also expressed, e.g., in the repression of erotic desire or the desire manifested in creativity, as such repression entails that we may lose our relationship to ourselves as a body, or as a spontaneous or creative agent.

Erotic desire illustrates this possible opportunity and loss in this regard: One can take the situation seriously that this desire constitutes, and realize that the desire in question requires an expression, its own fulfillment in an erotic situation where we not only focus on our own desire as such but rather hand ourselves over to the other. In this act of "handing ourselves over to" is implied an openness to the radical otherness of the situation, an openness to a situation different from the one which was previously there, and a moment where control is lacking.[343] Or we can do the opposite. If we ignore the desire emerging in this situation, we lose the chance for the expression of that desire, but also lose the chance for being open in a manner that may give us a possibility for truly experiencing the other. Hence, to recognize desire is to recognize oneself as a being who is open to what lies beyond the immediate presence of the situation and beyond one's own clearly defined projects.

Against this backdrop, religious faith can be understood in analogy with desire. One has to engage in faith in order to realize the specific type of subjectivity it entails. This follows from what we have already said in the first chapter of this book about the necessity of a first-person perspective. So also in the first

---

[343] Cf. Thøgersen, *Krop Og Fænomenologi*, 169.

instances of an erotic situation: one must express desire if that moment is to become an erotic situation at all. If I do not express my outwardly directed desire to her, she will neither know me in this respect nor the openness that I am inviting her to participate in. Merleau-Ponty states that desire without any expression is closed, captured, and cannot breathe. When desire constitutes the presence of the other as an erotic partner, it is thus only in the expression of desire that the situation can be realized as what it is – as erotic. But his point can be applied to other types of relationship with others, as well – including the relationship with God.

At this point, it seems apt to consider a point in Hegel's analysis of desire in *Phänomenologie des Geistes*.[344] His analysis suggests that desire must be understood as that which negates the desired by integrating it into the horizon of the active subject. However, given our discussion above, this understanding of desire appears one-sided and lacking in nuance. Embodied desire is not, as he claims, only the function of a curious mind eager to know and to integrate the other into the "sameness" of rationality. Rather desire may serve to open up the self in ways that are both emotionally, perceptively, and rationally unpredictable. The ethical thrust of this openness, as developed in Lévinas' understanding of what he calls metaphysical desire,[345] safeguards the other from being negated; instead, it allows for the other to break in on and crack open the self-encumbered, finite, or absolutized self.

A possible positive function of enjoying desire beyond its mere gratification, appears when we are able to recognize that unfulfilled desire is an insurmountable constituent of human life. This is an enjoyment in which desire nevertheless relates the subject to a reality where its own finitude is affirmed and appreciated as part of what it is to be a human open to the other. Then, desire also serves to remind oneself of one's own finitude. It reveals a being who is more than a self-sufficient self. Desire is, therefore, that which disrupts subjectivity without abandoning it, that which transcends what is conceived in the rational subject's already given understanding of the world. It reminds the self about its origin in the other who gives content to its world, and about that which creates fissures and disturbances in its complacencies. Desire is not only negating and negative, it does not necessarily destroy the other but makes something

---

[344] Cf. Hegel: *Phänomenologie des Geistes*, in Hegel: Werke – Theorieausgabe Vol 3), esp.139ff. See also Scott Jenkins: "Hegel's concept of Desire" *Journal of the History of Philosophy* 47 (2014), 103–130.

[345] Cf. Emmanuel Lévinas, *Totality and Infinity. An Essay on Exteriority* (Pittsburg: Duquesne UP, 1969), 33.

new appear: the reality of self-consciousness and subjectivity[346] where the other may appear as a constitutive part and where I am called to appropriate desire in the way I want to lead my life. Hence, desire is not only pre-subjective, but it also has important bearings on how subjectivity is constituted.

Moreover, desire also points to a self that is vulnerable, open, unfinished, exposed to what happens in her passivity, and pursuing the quest for goodness in her activity. Thus, one can see these features also expressed in the desire for God – God as a composite symbol, implying goodness, justice, love, community, safety, and fulfillment. The analysis above must, therefore, be seen in close connection with what the later analysis will develop about the desire for God. Here, however, I want to point to the anthropological point that desire exposes the human subject as vulnerable, in a precarious situation where it always lives under the risk of lack, misfortune, or the consequences of being misguided in her desires.

If desire is not guided by some form of moral intentionality or insight, a possible result is the subject's internal fragmentation and personal failure. Contemporary interpreters of Hegel's concept of desire have begun to understand him as increasingly pointing to the impossibility of a coherent subject, in contrast to models that operate with the assumption of a harmonious relationship between reason and desire. One reason for preferring the latter interpretation is that desire, as an instantiation of the other in consciousness, is what enables the subject to grow, develop, and reflect.[347] The otherness of desire thus suggests that it is not reason alone that constitutes the subject, but it also suggests that the subject of desire is involved in a project with itself, in order to develop a subjectivity that comprises both reason and desire. This is further testimony for the unfinished character of human existence.

The theologically fruitful result is that reason alone, and the self-conscious subject, can no longer be seen as the principle which establishes human identity. Human identity is dependent upon elements exterior to the subject that operate

---

[346] Cf. Thøgersen, *Krop Og Fænomenologi*, 172–73.

[347] Cf. Judith Butler, *Subjects of Desire. Hegelian Reflection in the Twentieth-Century France* (NY: Columbia University Press, 1999), 33: "[W]e learn that human desire is distinguished from animal desire in virtue of its reflexivity, its tacit philosophical project, and its rhetorical possibilities. At this point, however, we are equipped only with the insights that Force and Explanation have provided us; we understand movement as the play of Forces, and Explanation as the necessary alterity of consciousness itself. Predictably enough, the experience of desire initially appears as a synthesis of movement and alterity."

within and beyond (as well as behind) desire, but which can never be overtaken or fully integrated into rationality.[348]

Ricœur's analysis of desire seems to move in a similar direction, further developing the above analysis. Ricœur locates desire in the "between": between opening and closing, between the vision of the world and a point of view.[349] Ricœur's emphasis is not primarily on the possibility of the self to become aware of itself (i.e., of subjectivity), but on how desire places the subject outside itself, in the world. His description here is accordingly not very different from the one offered by Merleau-Ponty:

Desire does not show me my way of being affected, nor does it shut me up within my desiring self. It does not speak to me at first of myself because it is not at first a way of being aware of myself, even less an "internal sensation." It is an experienced lack of ..., an impulse oriented toward.... In desire, I am outside myself; I am with the desirable in the world. In short, in desire, I am open to all the affective tones of things that attract or repel me. It is this attraction, grasped on the thing itself, over there, elsewhere, or nowhere, which makes desire an openness onto ... and not a presence to the self closed on itself.[350]

This is as far as Ricœur follows Merleau-Ponty. In the next steps of his analysis, he views the functions of desire in relation to the self and the body. Here, he underscores the role of the self as the mediator between the body and the world. The body as "the flesh of desire, does not manifest itself as a closed figure but as a practical mediation, in other words as a projecting body in the same sense that we were able to speak of the perceiving body."[351] The parallel he suggests here between desire and perception is noteworthy. It suggests that both perception and desire, though intertwined as bodily conditioned functions of the self, are both similar in that they are not only anchored in finitude but are also that which allow us to transcend finitude: "My flesh of desire is wholly anticipation, that is, a prefigured grasp or hold, over there, elsewhere, nowhere, outside myself. The desiring body steals away in advance, proffering the élan of its flesh to the projecting self."[352]

---

[348] In Pannenberg's theological anthropology, this testifies not only to the hubris of a philosophy of mind but also, more positively, to the way in which divine providence guides the processes that establishes human identity in a manner that is still open to the future, and never self-enclosed. Cf. Wolfhart Pannenberg, *Anthropology in Theological Perspective* (Philadelphia: Westminister Press, 1985).

[349] Paul Ricœur, *Fallible Man*. Rev. ed. (New York: Fordham University Press, 1986), 53.

[350] Ibid.

[351] Ibid.

[352] Ibid.

To understand desire as an integral part of the self's being-in-the-world sheds important light on the role of human finitude in relation to desire. The same finite perspective that shapes the content of the perceiving body engenders an affective equivalent in a desire that may obscure its content. Desire may have a certain type of clarity, but the function of the affections may also obscure and darken it. Hence, desire is linked to the emotional confusion to which it may give rise.[353] Ricœur's intentions in pointing out this are related to his understanding of the relationship between intentionality and desire. The "clarity of desire" can be found in intentionality. Without intentionality, desire may lead us into darkness. However, Ricœur speaks here of an intentionality that – in spite of being fully anchored in the perceptive and desiring body – allows us to relate the object to the anticipated states of the self, given in our hermeneutically constituted understanding of the world:

Desire is a lack of ... a drive toward.... The "of" and the "toward" indicate the oriented and elective character of desire. This specific aspect of desire, taken as desire of "this" or of "that," is susceptible of being elucidated – in the precise sense of the word – by the light of its representation. Human desire illuminates its aim through the *representation* of the absent thing, of how it may be reached, and the obstacles which block its attainment. These imaging forms direct desire upon the world; I take pleasure in them; in them I am out of myself. The image is even more; not only does it anticipate the perceptual outlines of gestual behavior, but it also anticipates pleasure and pain, the joy and sadness of being joined to or separated from the desired object. This imaging affectivity, held in pledge by the affective effigy or by the representative or analogue of future pleasure, ends by bringing me in imagination to the goal of desire. Here the image is nothing other than desire. The image informs desire, lays it open, and illuminates it.[354]

I have italicized the word *representation* in this quote in order to make visible how desire is linked to representations constituted by the imaginations that guide it. Representations and desire work in tandem. Hence, one can say that the desired is worked over by intentionality in order to overcome the immediate character of the presence of the desired object in the consciousness. This also suggests that it is the self, by constituting the image of desire in a representation, which opens up to desire as that which enters into its field of motivation. The self's motivation is not given with the desired object alone, but with its relation to the self – *because of what it represents to the self in question*. This is why desire must be appropriated in subjectivity. Representation is the instance that makes it possible. Hence, desire can achieve clarity only from intentions as they

---

[353] Ibid.
[354] Ibid., 53—54.

are linked to representations. These intentions are shaped by values and prefer-ences that orient the self. "From the standpoint of value, desire may be com-pared to other motives and thereby sacrificed or privileged, approved or re-proved."[355] It is in this sense, then, that we can say, with some qualifications, that desire relates us to the good. Without the clarity established by intention-ality, it is not necessarily so. Here, desire is not relinquished but rather refined, in terms of the contribution given with its relation to the good.

Religious representations can contribute to shaping the intentions that clar-ify desire and guide its realization and eventual gratification. However, if this is the case, one immediately faces the question if religions represent no more than imagined representations of gratification, which have their origin in human lack. Is religious imagery simply the result of perceived lacks in the human condition? At this point, we need to move beyond Ricœur's analysis towards what Lévinas calls *metaphysical desire*. Such metaphysical desire does not orig-inate from lack, but rather out of the openness for the absolute other, which is not under the control of the subject's intentionality. "The metaphysical desire does not long for return, for it is desire for a land not of our birth, for a land foreign to every nature, which has not been our fatherland and to which we shall never betake ourselves," Lévinas writes.[356] Desire defined in relation to the 'I,' as its lack or need, is desire determined from the position of the same, or from absolutized finitude, to put it otherwise. However, the goodness that emerges from desire must emerge from a context and from a desire shaped not by the self alone. Hence, the above understanding of the clarity of desire in Ricœur appears apt only if we see that the other who constitutes the self, shapes these intentions also – this other who is never there only to fulfill the need, want or lack of the desiring self. Thus, metaphysical desire is the strongest possible ex-pression for the basic, non-satisfied character of the human struggle to gratify desire: it is in this form that desire keeps ourselves open to, and deepen our relationship to, goodness, and does so in a way that allows us to transcend the immediately given content of life by remaining open continuously to that which is to come – that which is still open-ended, unfinished, without closure.

The desires one can satisfy resemble metaphysical desire only in the deceptions of satisfaction or in the exasperation of non-satisfaction and desire which constitutes voluptuosity itself. The metaphysical desire has another intention; it desires beyond everything that can simply complete it. It is like goodness – the Desired does not fulfill it, but deepens it.[357]

[355] Ibid., 54.
[356] Lévinas, *Totality and Infinity*, 33.
[357] Ibid., 34.

It is worth noting that Lévinas here points to how the intention behind meta-physical desire extends beyond everything that can complete it. Only a self that understands itself as more than a mere finite embodied being, self-enclosed and independent, can harbor such desire. This is exactly the mode of self-under-standing that religious consciousness mediates. Hence, metaphysical desire abolishes the totality given with the finite self. It opens the finite self to the infinite beyond itself. Here Lévinas' phenomenology offers a religiously neu-tral, although still highly potent, description of the desire for God that we find in early Christian theology (see below).

According to Lévinas, desire can help us attain a more concrete notion of the infinite. This is an interesting position since desire is always given with a self that exists in the tension between the finite and the infinite, as indicated in our analysis of Hegel in the first chapter. This claim testifies to the fact that, from a phenomenological point of view, the only way to make sense of the infinite is to develop an analysis of how it affects and shapes specific human phenomena and allows us to see them more clearly. From the outset, we should remind ourselves here that the phenomenon in question is *goodness*: Goodness can only prevail if the desire is constituted as metaphysical, as a desire for something that is more than an object to possess. Lévinas' analysis describes how desire opens up totality to infinity:

The infinite in the finite, the more in the less, which is accomplished by the idea of Infinity, is produced as Desire – not a Desire that the possession of the Desirable slakes, but the Desire for the Infinite, which the desirable arouses rather than satisfies. A Desire perfectly disinterested – goodness. But Desire and goodness concretely presuppose a relationship in which the Desirable arrests the "negativity" of the I that holds sway in the Same – puts an end to power and emprise. This is positively produced as the possession of a world I can bestow as a gift on the Other – that is, as a presence before a face.[358]

Lévinas here also anticipates an important element in more recent phenomenol-ogy (not least as developed by Derrida and Marion), namely, that of the gift. A gift is not determined by a symmetrical relation, rather it is, in their understand-ing, outside economy, outside calculation.[359] As a gift, I offer myself to the other in a way that places my power on hold. In a specific and profound way, this is an expression of my desire for the other, not as a possible asset in my

---

[358] Ibid., 50.
[359] For an extensive analysis of this understanding of gift, cf. Jan-Olav Henriksen, *Desire, Gift and Recognition: Christology and Postmodern Philosophy* (Grand Rapids: Eerdmans, 2009).

possession, but for the other as an other, not determined or controlled by me. Thus, this desire is the opposite of the desire for control, for shielding myself from being vulnerable (see below). Instead, it is a desire where the I is not in control since this desire is in no way determined by the content of the I – the same. Paradoxically, this also implies that in offering oneself and one's world as a gift to the other, and thereby exposing oneself to the vulnerable position of possible rejection, one is also able to *receive* a gift, to receive something that was not there previously and un-determined by oneself, and which enriches and expands one's experienced world. As a result of this desire, the face of the other manifests a surplus compared to all that pre-exists in one's ideas of that other; thus, it destroys one's totality:

For the presence before a face, my orientation toward the Other, can lose the avidity proper to the gaze only by turning into generosity, incapable of approaching the other with empty hands. This relationship established over the things henceforth possibly common, that is, susceptible of being said, is the relationship of conversation. The way in which the other presents himself, exceeding the idea of the other in me, we here name face. This mode does not consist in figuring as a theme under my gaze, in spreading itself forth as a set of qualities forming an image. The face of the Other at each moment destroys and overflows the plastic image it leaves me, the idea existing to my own measure and to the measure of its *ideatum* – the adequate idea. It does not manifest itself by these qualities, but καθ' αυτό. It expresses itself.[360]

Thus, the presence of the other is not to open up an abstract possibility for the expansion of my world, but to allow me to show generosity. When I am only in me, in my totality, gifts and giving cannot be an issue. However, as soon as the other appears and presents me with the opportunity to desire metaphysically, to desire goodness in a way that is not extinguished in a certain number of acts, the infinity contained in this metaphysical desire shapes my concrete subjectivity and overflows it. By giving, I transcend the borders of the finite self; I engage with the other for the sake of the other, and not exclusively for my own sake (even though I do also act for my own sake: for the sake of not being self-enclosed but rather open, desiring, and participating in goodness). This positive relation to goodness, opened up by desire, provides us with a fruitful approach to desire that can help us understand further the role of representation in the Christian religion.

---

[360] Lévinas, *Totality and Infinity,* 50–51.

Representation, desire, and the order of the created world

The above analyses of desire provide a contrast to presentations that see it as something that urges the subject, the person, to grasp something, to occupy it for the subject's own sake. This approach is probably expressed most clearly in views that conflate desire with covetousness or greed. While this description suggests the active, cognitive, and simultaneously relational elements of desire (as there can be no desire without an object of desire), it also indicates a fundamental relation between desire and agency, more specifically a type of agency which (more or less consciously) strives for the occupation and appropriation of a particular object. However, as suggested above, this is a misleading description. It sees desire's origin in the active agent, who has the possibility of agency and the ability to follow his or her intentional desires, moreover, this understanding focuses on agency in a way that masks the presuppositions underlying the conditions for such agency, and thus ignores questions of gender, political, economic or other types of social status. Such an understanding of the desiring subject also ignores the way in which desire is fundamental (in the literal sense) to the becoming of an individual, and to becoming a conscious and reflexive subject. Hence, it ignores the pre-subjective level on which desire emerges, and the role it plays both in, and prior to, the constitution of human subjectivity. From this, it follows that to understand desire primarily as the subject's intention to appropriate or occupy the object of desire omits an understanding of desire as something that both individuates the person (making him or her aware of individual desires, and hence providing a condition for agency) and occupies or appropriates that individual. This understanding of desire has been dominant in Christian criticism of desire since the apostle Paul (cf. Rom 7,7), and it needs critical scrutiny.

In the alternative view, which I advocate here, desire is not only prior to subjectivity or agency, but emerges from, or within, a state of *passivity,* in which the subject is occupied with desire before he or she, by means of such desire, reaches out to occupy the other, the object of desire. Hence, the individual becomes what he or she is because desire – as the other of consciousness or reflectivity – makes the subject aware of who he or she is as a desiring subject. It is in the recognition and awareness of oneself as a desiring subject that one becomes aware of oneself as a self with potential for agency.

By being prior to subjectivity, desire is also structurally prior to all instances of order and normativity. Such order and the ideals that it provides the chances for recognizing, represents a given (a gift) implied in the social and inter-relational dimension of human life and socially constituted subjectivity.

As such, order and ideals emerge from an understanding of the good as human persons, under the conditions of the social and cultural world, shape it. Hence, the pre-existing presence of order and ideals provides the individual with a deeper and more fundamental understanding of the good than the one immediately present in desire. This deeper, and sometimes alternative, understanding of the good is the precondition for adjustment, correction, and assessment of desire. It opens up desire to the communal dimension of human life and the social order. Thus, the goodness here is also part of what constitutes the understanding of human representations of God as good.

The first name of this dimension of the good is *justice*. Justice emerges when the subjects of the human community realize their common vision of (and thus a representation that guides their desire for) the good. Against this backdrop, one need not see visions of order and the sharing of ideals and norms as a means to repress or negate the desire for goodness; rather it opens up new dimensions of this desire. In this sense, the new understandings of those desires that are harbored by the subject are developed, as well. It is only when desires are not rooted in, or able to be integrated into the common vision for justice and the good, that the normative dimension of order aptly manifests itself in dedicated efforts to control and delimit desire. Hence, desire may also emerge in consciousness with and over against the law, a point made both by Paul and Foucault.[361] One could even say that it is in the presence of and in response to desire that the law emerges – as the instance that contradicts and rejects a common vision for the benefit of the individual's (mistaken) desire. Normativity thus exists in an ambiguous relationship with desire: It can serve the desire for the good, or it can be used against those desires that close us off from the good and from justice. This point is not totally lost on Paul. Thus, notions of justice represent conditions that may serve to both orient and transform human agency.

However, an inherent problem in the Christian tradition is that it often starts with an understanding of the human being as related to the law, and not with the pre-existing, and pre-given, elements of relationality that comes to the fore in desire and feeling in general. This makes the agency the starting-point for theological reflection – and it makes the rational and active subject the main

---

[361] For Paul on this point, cf. Rom 7:8, a verse on which Foucault offers an interesting comment: "One should not think that desire is repressed, for the simple reason that the law is what constitutes desire and the lack on which it is predicated. Where there is desire, the power-relation is already present: an illusion, then, to denounce this relation for a repression exerted after the event; but vanity as well, to go questing after a desire that is beyond the reach of power." *History of Sexuality*, 81, quoted from Judith Butler, *Subjects of Desire: Hegelian Reflections in Twentieth-Century France* (New York: Columbia University Press, 1999), 221.

instance of consideration. Of course, one cannot ignore the role of agency and human conduct for the shaping of human life and its content, but the normative dimension in human life is not constituted by human agency, but given prior to it, and inherent in the interpersonal character of human interaction. If the human relationship with God is determined primarily from the point of view of human agency, then it is what humans do, and not what God has provided as the gifts for enabling human life, goodness, and flourishing, that becomes the center of attention.

Agency implies control, choice, and deliberation. From a theological point of view, this point is not without importance since one of the basic characteristics of sin is the act of placing one's point of departure in one's own agency and in one's own ability to control the world. A subject that understands herself from the perspective of agency will always perceive desire as the other of consciousness, the other of law, the impetus on which one must (or must not) act. Hence, desire becomes subjected to the subject as agent. In this process, desire and the preconditions that are not under human control appears inevitably as a threat against agency, as potentially uncontrollable, and as signs of that which determines reality prior to the agency. In this perspective, neither desire nor the order that justice expresses is seen as the gifts that may jointly enable the subject to realize that good is given prior to the subject and independent of its agency.

It is the threat to the personal agency as the starting point for the individual's self-relation that makes desire ambiguous in theological terms. It suggests something potentially uncontrollable that transcends the human person but nevertheless influences him or her.[362] Moreover, it reminds that individual that subjectivity is the product of something other than the conscious and acting human being, something that can be positively related to God, or implies a disruption of the order that the subject attempts to establish in order to conform to that which he or she believes to be the will of God. The more emphasis is placed upon the law as posited over against agency, the more subjects attempt to avoid recognizing the way in which their desire makes them vulnerable and dependent upon something given prior to their own agency.

For the person who wishes to start with his or her own agency when relating to the world, desire is thus not only an indication of the good prior to agency

---

[362] This uncontrollable element is probably also the reason why many mystics see desire as something that relates them to God: The uncontrollable opens up to the mystical – that which is not secure and secured, and as that to which one nevertheless has to give oneself over.

(present in desire, and not constituted by agency), but holds a message regarding the fact that agency is rooted in ambiguous elements prior to subjectivity. Hence, for those wishing to start with themselves, with control, the initial passivity in which the good appears with and in desire confronts them with the limits of agency and subjectivity both. Desire thus becomes a sign to those individuals that they do not constitute the world. Theologically speaking, this is a possible sign of transcendence, of the good desired, and thus, the reality of God is the origin. However, it is also a reminder that the law by which one understands and controls desire cannot allow desire to be totally suppressed, subjected, or controlled, since desire is the condition for the individuated, desiring, and conscious self. To give up desire is to give up oneself.

The analysis above may potentially shed some light on the reasons why desire has a complex relationship with religious subjectivity. Yet it also says something about why desire is so important to guide and to relate to from the point of view of this subjectivity. Religion is a way of ordering human life, and any kind of desire which is not in some way integrated within that order threatens to disrupt it. Almost by necessity, the law then becomes contrary to desire. Positive religious employment of the law serves to transform, shape, and control desire. Thus, the law makes desire appear as under control. This may, in turn, give rise to the illusion that desire can be controlled fully. The subsequent view is that the law can control everything and be a means for establishing righteousness (as that which is the result of the human desire for justice and the good). However, when the law is used in this way by conscious human beings, not only is the pre-subjective element of desire ignored, but the presumed good to which that desire relates prior to the law is also ignored. So are the pre-existing gifts that are presented independent of human agency, and the insight into the fact that that the law cannot control everything, and that human agency is not the main source of goodness: grace and love is.

Consequently, to understand human agency as the initial means by which we can access God-given goods makes God's gift-giving activity secondary. A notion of righteousness that leaves out or ignores the fundamental role of desire for the gift of goodness in human life is doomed to make human agency its central element. Furthermore, desire for control and apprehension that expresses the need for safeguarding oneself against the vulnerable character of human life is a feature of human subjectivity that erodes subjectivity's own foundation in life and goodness (desired) as a gift. Here we find one reason why human attempts to become righteous and safe by means of obeying the law is bound to fail: It ignores the way in which desire is related to God's gifting of the good through grace, love, and care. These are the initial conditions that make goodness present in desire.

Eschatological desire for God

Against the backdrop of the previous analysis, God can be seen as the fundamental origin of human desire, and as the gifting instance that humans relate to thematically or non-thematically.[363] As suggested, the notion 'God' is composite – with all its inherent implications for love, justice, community, restoration, and hope – and it is understood thus, so we can say that language about God can stir the desire for God. Given this situation, the desire for God is principally and fundamentally defined as something that cannot be fully reduced to a lack or need, although it may also be rooted in experiences of such kind. Rather, God adds a surplus to the concrete, bodily experience of goodness. Consequently, we can see faith as a desire for God. However, faith must be understood as an opening desire, a desire where one accepts that this desire can never be fully satisfied in the present, a point already made by Gregory of Nyssa.[364] Desire – as that which opens, as that by which we place ourselves in the hands of another, implies trust, a vital element in faith. Hence, the path from an opening desire to trust and then faith is not at all a very long one.

Because desire may imply lack, God can easily become a name for what I miss or lack, what is not manifest, not present here. Hence, desire and God belong together due to the present human condition. However, this relation is one of negativity. This negativity is complex, for several reasons: First, a desire that makes God a function of human need constitutes the absence of God because it, taken in its *prima facie* form, is something that is not able to relate to God as God – as something that transcends my needs, my desire. God is encapsulated in the sameness of the self. Hence, where we think that we have grasped God thus, as the realization of our want, in reality, it is God's absence, God's

---

[363] This is the basic point that was developed theologically in Wolfhart Pannenberg's anthropology. See Wolfhart Pannenberg, *Anthropology in Theological Perspective* (Philadelphia: Westminster Press, 1985).

[364] For Gregory, faith is closely linked to the process of learning, through which the believer enters into an eternal process of searching for and never ceasing to ascend to God. The believer is the one whose desire is awakened by God's love, so that such believing desire is stirred by God's desire for that believer. Whenever that believer's desire is fulfilled, it produces further desire for the transcendent, for God. On this point, cf. Martin Laird, *Gregory of Nyssa and the Grasp of Faith : Union, Knowledge and Divine Presence* (Oxford: Oxford University Press, 2014), 97.

not-yet-here, to which we relate. Second, there is no means for a final overcoming desire as long as we live. We will continue to desire for as long as we live. Hence, desire striving for fulfillment by means of God negates God – and thereby, God appears in the consciousness in the mode of negativity, because that which is not here is not fulfilled. Where desire is present, God is absent, or present in his absence – i.e., in consciousness. In this way, we can say that when God "appears" as absent, desire based on lack or want constitutes this very absence. Absence does not constitute desire, as we would normally think.

However, popular religion sometimes plays on a simple relation between God and desire by claiming that God is the answer to your desire, the fulfillment of all your needs. This is the very oversimplification that negates God as god. In Neville's words: Then God is not someone we relate to as the ultimate. This is a lesser god, a god created for and determined by my desire. Such a god is no god – it is only a subtle version of myself, my needs, my reality, my urge for harmony, and demand for closure. If desire becomes extinct in the presence of such a god, you remain content; with no further need. You do not develop further, you remain satisfied. Desire is gratified, there is no more unfinished business.

In contradiction to such a position, I argue for a position that keeps desire alive, thereby also keeping the consciousness of the coming God, the not-present God awake. The aim is to secure an understanding that allows for maintaining that God remains a true God and not an idol for our desire, our consciousness, and faith, as well as to keep open, alive, and alert the critical consciousness about the lacks and injustices in reality that can constitute desire for something else. Moreover, thereby, we can also continue to be aware of the incomprehensible, contingent, and mysterious that can let me remain open for something I am not, and that which I do not know yet.

Behind all attempts to transcend ourselves is the recognition of lack, and thus, desire. In every perception, confrontation, or meeting with the other, desire is present. In this sense, desire is what connects us with the *world*. In the desire directed towards others, there is the chance of transcending oneself and what is already given. But there is also, as indicated, the risk of reducing the world and the other to the same, to that from which desire arises. In the latter case, the world as constituted by desire always risks being reduced to a function of the narcissistic mirror of the desiring ego. This is probably one of the main reasons why theological treatises that deal with desire see it as a danger: desire establishes the present, and my lack, in the center – and not God. Thus, the orientation of my world is based on my desire, and not on the reality of that which is desired (the object). If this is the case, then every possible fulfillment of my desire excludes God as God – since God becomes a mere instrument of gratification. Hence it is not because desire is filthy, sinful, or indecent that it is perceived as problematic, but because it implies a restriction to transcendence and otherness, and a possible threat to the other that is not I: desire might imply reduction.

All this notwithstanding, theology and religion also keep desire alive, by telling stories of possibilities of life not yet fulfilled, and by engaging in different kinds of practices that that imply transformation and transcendence. However, this cannot hide the fact that our desire for God, or for understanding God, can never become satisfied or receive gratification in this world. The negativity in theology that maintains the lack of God as a full presence but simultaneously as a condition for living in reality determined by God will concern us in the following.

There is no doubt about the fact that God can be the "object" of our desire. God can also transform it by letting us realize what it implies, and letting us become aware of what is not present where desire is. Or to put it otherwise: desire proves a good starting point for discussing some features in recent religion that points in the direction of a *theologia negativa*, while at the same time letting us learn more about ourselves and how we relate to *the world* in our desire.

However, before presenting a further analysis, Richard Kearney's fruitful distinction of different types of desire can be put to use and contribute to a further deepening of the previous. Kearney distinguishes between onto-theological and eschatological desire: "First, what I refer to as the *onto-theological* paradigm construes desire as lack – that is, as a striving for fulfillment in a plenitude of presence. Here desire expresses itself as a drive to be and to know absolutely. *Conatus essendi et cogniscendi.*"[365] He rightly sees the Bible as full of warnings against such desire. But these warnings are by no means reducible to a rejection of desire *per se*. Nevertheless, if such desire constitutes the fullness of human life, it is good advice to seek for its negation. This negation is, in turn, what opens for another kind of desire: "[T]he destruction of onto-theological desire might be more properly conceived as a spur to transcend our captivation by all that is (*ta onto*) for another kind of desire – a desire for something that eye has never seen nor ear heard. That is to say, eschatological desire."[366]

---

[365] See R. Kearney, "Desire of God," in John D. Caputo; Michael J. Scanlon, *God, the Gift, and Postmodernism* (Bloomington, IN: Indiana Univ. Press, 2006), 112f.
[366] Ibid., 113.

Kearney summarizes his understanding of this desire thus: "This desire beyond desire I call eschatological to the extent that it alludes to an alterity that already summons me yet is not yet, that is already present yet always absent (Philippians 2:12), a *deus adventurus* who seeks me yet is still to come, unpredictably and unexpectedly, "in the twinkling of an eye" (I Corinthians 15:52). "Like a thief in the night" (I Thessalonians 5:2)."[367]

In other words, eschatological desire is a desire for that which is not determined by lack, and which transcends lack and no-lack. It is a desire for the infinite, for that which supersedes all finitude. In this respect, *this desire is not for something in the world* – it is for the impossible, for that not even perceived as a possibility for the subject. The desire for God framed in this context – if we can call it a context – emerges from the realization that a god that is a possible gratification of my desire is a lesser God. Hence, a gratifying god is no god, and what I should desire is exactly a God that is not determined by my desire for gratification.

Kearney builds upon Lévinas in his development of this position. In Lévinas, he says, "the desired of eschatological desire exists before memory and beyond anticipation. It is immemorial and unimaginable, exceeding the horizons of historical time. But if the desired good gives itself thus from 'beyond' history, it is nonetheless inscribed, as vigilance and summons, in each instant of our existence. It is incoming at all times."[368] However, I argue that this is merely the basis for a negative identification of God, as it can only take place insofar as this desired maintains its position as unimaginable, and as infinite. Hence, desire, as Kearney suggests, is not guided by representation. He insists, and rightly so, that the exteriority of the desired cannot be understood in terms of horizontal questioning – "as an endless restlessness that satiates itself in some dialectical infinity."[369] Instead, it is to be understood as an ethical relation to the infinite as verticality. In Lévinas the alternative is thus that "the good *beyond* finds itself inscribed *between* one and another. Desire here again reveals itself not as deficiency but as positivity."[370] In other words: it is in the representation of the divine as it confronts me in the concrete face of the other that it becomes possible for myself to also act as a representation of God – on the horizontal level. The relationship with God as the infinite constitutes all relations as being

---

[367] Ibid., 114.
[368] Ibid., 116f.
[369] Ibid., 117.
[370] Ibid.

beyond control and not conditions by human systems of reciprocity and retribution. Nevertheless, the phenomena that can open up to this way of representing, manifesting, or revealing God in the world as *imago Dei* have to do with grace, gratuity, openness, hospitality, surplus, and surprise. Strangely enough, this is what characterizes the triune God who Christians see as revealed in the history and preaching of Jesus Christ. When we desire to represent God, we do not desire something in order for us to return to ourselves – but in order to be moved beyond, behind knowledge, beyond ourselves, into a world constituted by the Other.

Rowan Williams has developed further insights into how the construction of the given or created desire is most fruitful when it does not imply an instant gratification of full unity with the desired object – in this case, the *final self of a human being*. For him, the existence and maintenance of desire keep the individual on the track, allows for further development, further promotion of reflexivity about what one can and should be. This point corresponds to the theological insight into how one's identity as a human being and as *imago Dei* is not yet fully realized, still in the future. This state, holds Williams, should not be considered negatively as a flaw, but as something that makes it possible for us to be liberated from our own instantly self-seeking selves – and also, e.g., to seek justice for others.

When the human being seeks himself or herself in a not yet fulfilled destiny, realizing that this cannot be wholly appropriated or fulfilled at present, it safeguards the possibility of living here and now in a way that recognizes the vulnerability of both others and oneself. We are not perfect, and to realize this is to be confronted with the vulnerability that is given with the fact that we are dependent upon others, and live exposed to the power of others. Writes Williams:

> The self becomes adult and truthful in being faced with the incurable character of its desire: the world is such that no thing will bestow on the self a rounded and finished identity. Thus there is in reality no self – and no possibility of recognising what one is as a self – without the presence of the other. But that other must precisely *be* other – not the fulfillment of what I think I want, the answer to my lack.[371]

Thus, the human being acquires a more true identity and self-understanding by realizing, or being confronted with what it is – and what it cannot yet be – as

---

[371] Rowan Williams, *Lost Icons : Reflections on Cultural Bereavement* (London: Continuum, 2000), 153.

imago Dei. Hence, Williams spells out the positive function that God as the Other can have in the development of human identity. God represents the stability that no human can have in him/herself, and the relationship of humans with God offers the human being a possibility to grasp him/herself as an unfinished and problematic project and to live with the impact of that insight. To see God as the Other thus underlines how every attempt to try to make God a function of one's own gratification of desires not only implies the attempt to overcome God's otherness, and makes God less than God. It also implies that by doing so, the human being loses its chances for becoming a true self, its soul, writes Williams.[372]

Williams' analysis is modelled on the relationship between psychoanalyst and patient in a therapeutic setting. However, it can be argued that he thereby also illuminates how human beings can be seen as images of God, as well as some aspects of the relationship between humans and God. The reason for this claim is the assumption that a religious configuration of self-reflection or subjectivity makes possible a specific form of self-relation and sense of self.

It follows that the self-relation configured in the presence of God as *the Other as a non-gratifying ultimate* is a condition for avoiding the temptations of idolatry. Idolatry is here to be taken as the worship of oneself or of someone or something in the world (generally: the created), and hence, as not ultimate. The self-relation in the presence of the Ultimate Other is the form of life that secures the basis for an authentic and sustainable life in the most profound way. How can we say that? We can point here to the experience of how therapies function in which there is a *distinct and realized representation (but not presence!) of otherness.* Williams points to how different forms of therapy (and thus, self-relations) can be developed on the basis of either an embodying or reification of otherness *or* on the basis of otherness as *represented.* I suggest that this idea of representation, offered by Williams, can be understood as a constructive means for signifying the presence-absence of God that was suggested above. God, when being absent, remains in and with and working through consciousness, without becoming identified with it, when it is realized that God is only present by such representations. This point also corresponds well with Kearney's idea of eschatological desire, as presented above.

The distinction between representation and embodiment is crucial here and helps us to see how the presence of what is desired can be understood in two distinct ways, and thus contributes to two quite different functions for the self.

---

[372] Ibid.

Embodying or reification of otherness can be perceived as presence, and thus open to idolatry, as the actual presence of the other is assumed to offer some kind of (provisional or illusory) gratification for the self. Such reification captures the human in a position of lack of identity instead of liberating its self to further development and quest. Williams writes in the continuation of the quotation given above:

> The therapy that releases or constructs the viable, truthful sense of self that is needed for a life without crippling misperception is a therapy that represents such otherness. And (here is a further twist of paradox) it must represent and not claim to *embody* it; if it slips into the latter, it becomes a new slavery and illusion. The claim to embody the Other says, in effect, that the Other is *here*, an answer, a gratification, a terminus of desire, so that the other is reduced to the dimension of my lack and ceases to be Other.[373]

To be aware that neither God nor my own self is something that I can acquire, possess, and make present myself, is also to ralize that these "objects" are not controllable or can be reduced to something I know or can handle. This awareness is liberating to the extent that it lets me give up the search for constituting my own self by my own agency and instead must live in trust and faith in God. It is also to realize that life cannot be now what it shall be. But it also means that every attempt to embody or reify God by deifying something manageable, be it by putting my trust in other humans, money, sex, power, or ecstatic experiences, implies a human failure, theologically speaking. It is the result of misguided or derailed desire. I only acquire myself when I am able to live with the awareness of an otherness that cannot be embodied in any kind of object, an otherness that is – exactly – represented, but not fully embodied in my reality.

Accordingly, this idea of, and the ability to live with, representations instead of embodied substitutes for gratification excludes the options of idolatry as well as closure. It provides insight into the fact that human existence in general and human flourishing more specifically depend on being lived as an unfinished project. This, as well, can be seen as a parallel to what Kearney means when he speaks of eschatological desire as the desire for that which is impossible, for that which cannot be seen as a fulfillment of my longing or desire.

God is thus only able to make us into those we are to become if God is not embodied in the world but represented there. This is the psychological wisdom behind the representation of God in the incarnation and the sacraments, but it is also a way of manifesting how God can work and promote God's reality through

---

[373] Ibid., 153.

and by our relationships with other people and the rest of creation. Moreover, it is also the religious *motivation* for any type of critique of religion directed against the reification and finite embodying of the divine. Simultaneously, it is the reason behind the rejection of every form of critique of religion that claims that religion is nothing else than symbolic constructions and extrapolations of the wishes and desires of humanity that has their origin in lack or need. Religion functions according to its aim exactly when it does *not* contribute to such fulfillment – when otherness is safeguarded in a way that lets both God and human identity remain something still to come, not to be fully acquired by human controlling powers.

If human self-relation is configured along the lines here described, something more than a meeting between two human persons is taking place in therapy or in a conversation that contributes to the formation of human identity. It follows from the above that a meeting of two who represent God, who bear God's image, involves a third party, who can be present in the representation, but not embodied, and who contributes to developing the selves in question. Although Williams himself describes this in non-theological terms, the following quotation shows how God in paradoxical absent presence is constitutive for the content in the human soul or self:

> [This] is not just a skilled invitation to the life-giving contradiction or frustration of desire; it works as such by doing something significantly more, by invoking the necessarily absent, non-particular ('non-existent') Other. It is a three-cornered relation, not only a dialogue, in which the presence of the absent third makes possible some kind of liberation from the net of ideas and projections that binds us in the fantasy that some specific other can supplement our lack, once and for all, and end our desire.[374]

The presence of the Other opens up new access to our own lives, and a new way of relating to oneself, determined neither by the past and its actions nor by the desire or the longing that is deeply situated in our own person and its experiences. Thus, the presence of the Other gives rise to new possibilities of experience, but these are only realizable when the individual is able to transcend his or her present self – and appropriate the resources made available by the Other.

The presence of the other human person as an image of God, *God's representative*, can thus help me realize and come to grips with my present situation. God, as the present-absent third party, can become represented by an Other. What God wants to give – as a gift of life, experience, and identity – to a human

---

[374] Ibid., 154.

being, can be carried out in our meeting with another person, if we are able to realize her/his otherness, and not only see him/her as something we can turn into controllable sameness on the basis of who and what we already are. This is a point that can be developed in a more Christological direction, but it also has implications for understanding what it means to function as an image of God. In this respect, the Other contributes to the clarification and transparency of who I am and what I am to become, and thus to my understanding of the given relationships in which I am challenged to live my life.

…the absent 'non-existent' third is manifest as the condition for the truthful recognition of my own limits, of the persistence of my incompleteness, because it is not itself *a* point of view, mirroring or competing with mine; it is not another system of desiring, any more than it is something being fitted into the system of *my* desiring. Its otherness is radical enough to allow me to be other – to be distinctive, to be this-and-not-that of temporal particularity. And the finite other who 'holds' this perspective does so only out of the same awareness of the permission given by the 'third' to be a finite self; if this is not so, I remain trapped.[375]

Thus, Williams gives a detailed and profound account of what it means to be guided with the desire for God and to maintain that God can be at work also when God is absent in the presence of desire. His analysis provides an excellent opportunity to develop a religious understanding of the human condition that can enter into a fruitful and constructive dialogue with psychological theory in order to become more informed about how desire works in the attempts humans make to fulfill their lives. Accordingly, desire it not to be understood as a blunt negation of God. It is a chance for conceiving of God's distinct otherness, and at the same time, to see that such a God is larger than the one who gratifies my desire, or is interwoven with some kind of onto-theological conception of reality. Thereby, paradoxically, the presence of God manifests God as the infinite or ultimate Other – in the presence of human desire.

Vulnerability

Human life has a tragic dimension. Practices shaped by misguided, corrupted, and distorted desire may cause great evil. So may tragic events that befall us, but which nevertheless do not have their origin in human agency (and are therefore not caused by sin, as theologians would say).[376] Illness, disease, accidents,

---

[375] Ibid.

[376] Criticism of the Augustinian interpretation of all evils as caused by human sin has recently been launched in a comprehensive study by David Tracy, see David Tracy, "Augustine Our Contemporary," in *Augustine Our Contemporary : Examining the Self in Past and Present*, ed.

earthquakes, fire, and different types of loss, including the death of close ones, are part of this tragic dimension. Some of the latter can be remedied by human action, whereas other tragedies seem inevitable in the way they cause suffering.

The resources for reflection in theological anthropology serve to interpret human experience, including that which has to do with tragedy. At its best, they offer human orientation in relation to the question: what does it mean to live a good life? How can human flourishing be possible when we are so vulnerable to misfortune? However, as Heike Springhart writes, "While vulnerability as a phenomenon is not controversial, the question of whether and in which respect vulnerability is a value?"[377] Vulnerability seems to be at the center of what makes the tragic elements in our lives. All the above negativities are what they are because of the vulnerable character of human existence. Without vulnerability, no tragedy. Because vulnerability is a deeply ambiguous element in this existence, it constantly sparks the need for orientation, transformation, and reflection with regard to the how to cope with the conditions on which human beings live. This is unavoidable because to be human is to be vulnerable. Already before being born, the conditions of infants are dependent on their mothers, and the way mothers take care of themselves, their bodies, and their health. What mothers do affect their children. Later, children are dependent on the responsive care of parents, siblings, teachers, and peers. How the people around them react, respond, and interact with children have an impact on their development and their experience of themselves and others. Dependency and vulnerability go hand in hand. It affects the embodied human, and the psychological and social dimensions of being human, as well.[378]

Although cultural ideals in contemporary Western culture stress the need to be independent of others (a point which will be addressed below), there is nothing problematic in being dependent on others as such. Furthermore, to be dependent is a fundamental part of what it means to be human for most of life. In the first 20 and the last 20 years of a normal life span, even in the Western world, humans will usually have to rely on others for some tasks and challenges. Moreover, due to the fact that we do not all the time live in, and participate in,

---

Willemien Otten; Susan Elizabeth Schreiner (Notre Dame, Indiana: University of Notre Dame Press, 2018), esp. 51f.

[377] Heike Springhart, "Vulnerable Creation: Vulnerable Human Life between Risk and Tragedy," *Dialog* 56, no. 4 (2017), 383. As will be obvious, I am much indebted to her analysis of vulnerability in the present section.

[378] For psychological dimensions of vulnerability, and the relationship to a theological interpretation, see W. Paul Jones, "Suffering into Wholeness: Vulnerability and the Imprisoned Child Within," *Quarterly Review* 15, no. 3 (1995).

relationships that are symmetric and shaped by equality, we constantly find ourselves in positions where we are either better off than those who depend on us, or worse off than those on whom we are dependent. Relationality involves being affected by how others live and what they do, or that we are affecting others by what we do and how we live. The exposure to asymmetry, no matter how it is shaped, means that we constantly must consider how to deal with our own vulnerability or that of others.

Of course, one could try to imagine that it would be possible to be dependent without being vulnerable. That is not the case: to be dependent as a human, exposes us to vulnerability because we are not self-enclosed and unaffected by our environment and those with whom we interact. Humans are receptive, responsive, and susceptible to what others do to them – and to be susceptible have positive and negative elements alike. On the positive side, it means that we can empathize with others, participate in their experiences of joy and suffering, and hence, share a common world shaped by emotions, mutual recognition, common tasks, and values. Vulnerability is also related to elements like love and trust – because such phenomena expose us to the care and safeguarding of others. If my love is not recognized, and my trust not met by someone who deserves my trust, I am broken, hurt, or frustrated.

Accordingly, instead of starting out by seeing *sin* as a basic element in the human condition, this section will argue that the finite character of human life, and more specifically, the vulnerability it implies, is the backdrop against which it is possible to understand a theological designation as sin. Finitude implies that there are limits to human life and the practices in which we partake, and some of these limits are actually conditions for a good life, for flourishing and thriving.[379] To describe human life as finite and vulnerable does not only imply that there are endangering aspects to it. As Springhart writes,

Created human life is finite life. It is limited in terms of (life) time, resources, power, and possibilities, and it exists in a limited framework. Talking about finitude means talking about limits, which either may be valuable or threatening. Vulnerability characterizes life as susceptible to harm and transformation, and generally open to others and to the environment and social factors.[380]

---

[379] This is a point I have argued extensively in *Finitude and Theological Anthropology : An Interdisciplinary Exploration into Theological Dimensions of Finitude*.
[380] See Springhart, "Vulnerable Creation: Vulnerable Human Life between Risk and Tragedy," 382.

There are two important elements in this quote that are significant in my perspective, and which Springhart links together: the fact that human life is seen as created, i.e., as having its origin in something other than itself, and that created life, as finite and vulnerable, is subject to transformation. The implication from this is that human life, as vulnerable in both positive and negative aspects, and therefore involved in processes of change, cannot be adequately described as fixed and as something that should be shielded from transformation. When the vulnerability is seen as a feature of the created world, it moreover means that it is designated as positive. To the extent that this is the case, we can be transformed by being affected by our relationships with others and the world around us, and they can be affected positively by us. Hence, vulnerability is represented in religious symbols like "created," which makes it possible for us to recognize human life as a processual and unfinished business.

Accordingly, when we recognize our finitude and our vulnerability, humans can live better with themselves, and in community with others. Acceptance of vulnerability is crucial for a wise way of engaging in practices with others. But as we shall see, this is by no means an argument for idealizing vulnerability as such. As mentioned, it is a deeply ambiguous phenomenon.

Ontological and situational vulnerability

In her thorough analysis of different aspects of vulnerability, Heike Springhart suggests a distinction between situated and ontological vulnerability. The ontological vulnerability she defines as follows:

[It] addresses vulnerability as the human condition. Birth and death mark vulnerable transitions in which the interrelated dependency, fragility, and the bundle of possibilities ahead and behind become real. Human life is susceptible to harm and to love, to transformation and violence, to disease and decay. As an ontological dimension, vulnerability names the potentiality of being harmed, wounded, and affected.[381]

We see here, as well, the point that was already made above, about how the ontological dimension in vulnerability is marked by elements of transformation. Ontological vulnerability is part of what makes human existence an unfinished process – and it is hard to see how humans can grow, adapt, and face challenges that do not in some way also imply vulnerability. One cannot ever do away with

---

[381] Ibid., 384.

this type of vulnerability – even though one can fall for the temptation to imagine that it is possible and that one can control and limit it.

On the other hand, the notion of *situated* vulnerability identifies the different levels of vulnerability as they are realized under social, cultural, and environmental conditions. Here, it is possible to speak about increased or decreased vulnerability, as well as about to what extent vulnerability is life-threatening and endangering.[382] This vulnerability can, therefore, be under our control, to some extent.

Springhart argues that both types of vulnerability make it possible to experience life as holding threatening as well as enriching aspects. She speaks of the need to realize a broad range of vulnerabilities, "which in some cases manifest as pure threat and endangerment, in others as pure joy or trust, and in still others as all of the above."[383] Hence, the nuances in the vulnerable character of human life present themselves as an important element for the orientation of human practices – and vulnerability will therefore also be one of the features of this life that calls for expression in religious symbols and representations.

From the perspective of the present book, among the important elements in Springhart's analysis is that she argues that ontological and situated vulnerability must be kept together for the sake of *transformation*. Springhart argues that a reduction of vulnerability to its ontological dimensions implies that one loses sight of its transformative power. On the other hand, an exclusive focus on the situated dimensions of vulnerability runs the risk of identifying social groups as deficient, weak, or even not fully accountable for life. However, she holds that by keeping the two dimensions together, vulnerability can have a critical, counter-cultural function against "attempts to describe humanity primarily or even exclusively as autonomous, independent, strong, and powerful."[384] All humans are vulnerable, not only those who find themselves subject to unfortunate circumstances.[385]

Sarah Coakley has also emphasized the transformative power in vulnerability. She holds that true empowerment requires vulnerability, and she therefore uses the phrase "power-in-vulnerability." The impact of this "power-in-vulnerability" as a practice can lead to the overturning of oppressive structures, among which she is especially concerned about the patriarchal ones. "Here, if I

---

[382] Ibid.
[383] Ibid., 385.
[384] Ibid., 384.
[385] Cf. the following reflection: "Instead of using vulnerability as a criterion for social discrimination, emphasizing the ontological character makes clear that vulnerability is the shared human condition, regardless of gender, health status, race, or religion." Ibid.

am right, is 'power-in-vulnerability,' the willed effacement to a gentle omnip-
otence which, far from 'contemplating' masculinism, acts as its undoing." Accordingly, she, as well, sees vulnerability as counter-cultural, and as the tool
that will reverse structures of domination and oppression.[386]

The negative aspects of vulnerability appear in how it is being threatened
by sin and shame, guilt, and destruction.[387] This point, which Springhart makes
almost in passing, is nevertheless worth pondering somewhat further because it
illustrates well how exposure to vulnerability not only can make humans afflicted by the actions of others but also is connected closely to how we are dealing with the conditions of our existence.

As for sin and shame, both can affect our vulnerability due to others or
ourselves. One example is how others can sin against us in ways that hurt us
(e.g., in abuse), and they can inflict us with shame due to that (since shame is
often the result of being affected by abuse).[388] But we can also deny our own
vulnerability in ways that indicate that we are ashamed of how it shapes our
lives,[389] and in sinful ways that imply that we make false images of who we are
and what we are able to do – in ways that, from a theological point of view,
imply that we do not recognize ourselves as finite beings created by God (hence:
sin). We can also act in ways that make us guilty in relation to others. Moreover,
destruction is something that we can cause in the lives of others, and which
others can cause in our own lives. In any case, vulnerability is in play.[390]

---

[386] See the analysis of Coakley in Annie Selak, "Orthodoxy, Orthopraxis, and Orthopathy: Evaluating the Feminist Kenosis Debate Orthodoxy, Orthopraxis, and Orthopathy," *Modern Theology* (2017), 534. She builds this analysis on Coakley's contribution in Margaret Daphne Hampson, *Swallowing a Fishbone? : Feminist Theologians Debate Christianity* (London: SPCK, 1996). "Kenosis and Subversion: On the Repression of 'Vulnerability' in Christian Feminist Writing," 110.

[387] Cf. Springhart, "Vulnerable Creation: Vulnerable Human Life between Risk and Tragedy," 385.

[388] Cf. Alistair I. McFadyen, *Bound to Sin : Abuse, Holocaust, and the Christian Doctrine of Sin* (Cambridge: Cambridge University Press, 2000).

[389] Shame as the result of denial of vulnerability is a central motif in Brené Brown's widely acclaimed TED-talks, as in her Brené Brown, *I Thought It Was Just Me (but It Isn't) : Making the Journey from "What Will People Think?" To "I Am Enough"* (New York: Avery (Penguin Random House), 2008).

[390] Cf. also for further elaboration on this point Springhart's analysis of sin and self-endanger-ment, which is fully in accordance with what I have developed here: "This is related to the real-ization of human self-endangerment as a consequence and expression of sin. Human beings are not only vulnerable with regard to potential violations through other people and other circum-stances, they also are vulnerable with regard to their own actions. Following the distinction of ontological and situated vulnerability, I argue for a notion of sin that is related to the ontological dimension of humanity. This means that sin is not reducible to morals and to sinful deeds, but that sin describes the separation of God and humankind. In terms of anthropological realism, the

A major advantage in Springhart's distinction between an ontological and situated vulnerability is that it allows for transcending the hamartiological approach that Tracy criticizes in dealing with tragedy. As part of the created human condition, it makes no sense to see the human experience of vulnerability in the negative elements of life as a consequence of sin. She writes:

> This hamartiological approach insinuates a causal understanding of suffering, disease, and dying that leads to problematic shortcuts. That is, it claims that human sin is the "cause" of the vulnerabilities that are constitutive of human existence. Vulnerability, I argue, here helps to do what Luther found crucial for a theology of the cross: taking a sharp and close look at reality and naming things as they are. The threatening and the enriching vulnerable dimensions of human lives are described with such a sharp look, even as they are framed and reframed into a theological framework, which makes clear that theology is not only about simple solutions. It also avoids the causal structure of hamartiologically oriented concepts.[391]

Hence, just as the finite character of human life cannot be a consequence of sin but is the inherent consequence of being a created being, so also with vulnerability. I argue that the identification of vulnerability within the sphere of the positively affirmed created world provides us with a religious notion that allows for fuller recognition of its ambiguities. Furthermore, it can provide a resource for theological efforts that run counter to mistaken religious ideas about how a truly religious life implies that one can do away with its vulnerable character. To speak about the human condition in this way is not true.

Springhart sees sin as the fundamental brokenness of humanity. It is related to ontological vulnerability as the unavoidable human condition. "If sin becomes real in deeds of guilt, we may connect it with situated vulnerability. In terms of sin, the distinction between sin and guilt is crucial for a hamartiology that avoids moralistic short-circuits as well as hamartiological blindness."[392] To interpret sin as correlated to vulnerability allows for the ability to "grasp the destructive and threatening forms of sin in Creation but also sharpens sensitivity to the reality that there are powers of sin and structural dimensions of sin, which we cannot use to explain threatening aspects of life."[393] Hence, a theological

---

notion of sin grasps the unavoidable vulnerability of human life, but it is not the reason for it."
Springhart, "Vulnerable Creation: Vulnerable Human Life between Risk and Tragedy," 388.
[391] Ibid., 383.
[392] Springhart, "Exploring Life's Vulnerability: Vulnerability in Vitality," in *Exploring Vulnerability*, ed. Heike Springhart, Günter Thomas (Gottingen: Vandenhoeck & Ruprecht, 2017), 25.
[393] Ibid.

identification of these features can acknowledge that "the basic value of vulnerability implies a challenge, sometimes a threat for human life, but it does not destroy the fundamental worth and dignity of it."[394]

Accordingly, vulnerability can be recognized as a *value* of human life when ontological and situated vulnerability are complementing each other. Ontological vulnerability is "the precondition of trust, love, communication and mutual affection, and also the finitude and fragility of human life." Situated vulnerability points to actual conditions and factors and can be decreased and increased by means of human practice and political decisions. Springhart, therefore, can claim that,

In both perspectives, ontological and situated, vulnerability is a risk and a resource of human life. On the fundamental or ontological level, we can say that it is good to live a vulnerable life, while at the same time, vulnerable vitality exists under the threat of death and its finitude. On the situated level, we also may value the multifaceted vulnerability, but face at the same time the strife-filled and threatening dimensions that come with it. In other words: the full range of vulnerability makes it a value, not the particular situations of vulnerability, or at least not all of them.[395]

As we shall see below, the ambiguity suggested here have both anthropological and theological implications and calls for an interpretative context that allows for symbolic expressions.

Vulnerability and religious representation

It follows from the above analysis that a theological approach to vulnerability immediately can take up the notion of created being as its fundamental context of significance. Vulnerability is part of the created world, and hence, it can be considered as part of what constitutes the goodness of Creation. Accordingly, it is possible to agree with Springhart that vulnerability, finitude, and fragility are dimensions of God's good creation.[396] However, despite the forms of vulnerability that testify to God's good creation, there are also destructive forms of vulnerability that calls for human action and practices that can restrict their impact.[397] Against this backdrop, it makes sense to relate underscoring of God's good creation and God willing to redeem this creation, to the main representa-

---

[394] Ibid.
[395] Ibid., 24.
[396] Ibid.
[397] Cf. Ibid., 25.

tion of God in Christian theology: Jesus Christ. Because Jesus makes God appear as a human being, this representation provides the means for seeing God as related to and taking part in the vulnerable state of humanity. Accordingly, Springhart speaks of "divine vulnerability addressed in incarnational Christology and God's susceptibility to humanity."[398] The primary instance of this exposition of vulnerability is Christ's birth and his crucifixion, but she also points to the "risk of incarnation that God takes in Jesus Christ."[399] Furthermore, she points to how Paul interprets Christ's vulnerability as something that "has a direct impact on human vulnerability and vice versa" when he writes about how believers are "always carrying in the body the death of Jesus, so that the life of Jesus may also be made visible in our bodies" (2 Cor 4:10).[400] Hence, she sees physical vulnerability in humans in general, not as a defect of the created body. Within the framework of the semiotics that a Christian point of view represents, it is "the visualization of the life and death of Jesus." Moreover, this close connection between human and divine vulnerability takes vulnerability's cruelty seriously without ignoring its Christological significance.[401] And although "the stigmata of the resurrected Christ are traces of vulnerability and are the signs to prove God's humanity," she holds that "the stigmata lose their destructive character after the resurrection."[402]

The resurrection also opens up to an eschatological perspective that enables a focus on the transformative dimension inherent in the vulnerability: thus we can address the tension between the real world and the redeemed world, between creation and new creation, a theme that is closely linked to the Christian vision of an embodied community that transcends what is presently given. "This community is the church as the body of Christ, which is constituted by the awareness and recognition of one's own vulnerability and of the vulnerability of others as the community of the vulnerable, sanctified by the Spirit," writes Springhart. She continues:

By being the body of Christ, believers not only are vulnerable in an individual sense, but they also carry the stigmata of Jesus Christ. Those are the signs of the vulnerable God, which indicate the transformation of vulnerability in an eschatological sense. The Lord's Supper as the meal of vulnerable members of the vulnerable body of Christ is the remembrance of Christ's vulnerability and the eschatological outlook toward the transformation of vulnerability.[403]

---

[398] "Vulnerable Creation: Vulnerable Human Life between Risk and Tragedy," 385.
[399] Ibid., 388.
[400] Ibid.
[401] Ibid.
[402] Ibid., 385.
[403] Ibid., 389.

Whereas it is important to underscore from a theological point of view that vulnerability is a risk, it must also be recognized that it is a resource for a truly human life: "it is the precondition and the expression of trust, mutual respect, and responsibility, and a salutary limitation on the illusion of the feasibility of a successful and perfect life. Vulnerability characterizes human life between risk and tragedy and keeps it open to transformation."[404] Again, we see how there is an inbuilt element of openness and unfinished tasks in human life, that suggests that one has to counter the tendencies that lead to stagnation or petrification by idealizing the *status quo*.

Given the acknowledgment of vulnerability as a resource, it is important to address the desire to overcome or ignore it by struggling for independence from others or to develop resilience in the face of it. However, not to acknowledge it as a basic and unavoidable feature implies that relationships that only thrive if they build care, trust, empathy, and love are impeded. Western individualism is possible to interpret as one way to try to overcome vulnerability. Other ways to cope with it can be identified in attempts to increase resilience or to embrace it without reserve.[405] However, the two latter approaches appear as one-sided, and they "fail to come to a sufficiently complex and realistic concept of vulnerability" that takes the ambiguity of vulnerability sufficiently into consideration.[406] Each of them contributes to "a static and isolationist understanding of the human life."[407] They do not offer enough room for the processual element in life and for the mutual character in social life. "Unlike resilience, vulnerability implies both the acceptance of given vulnerable situations and the need to enhance life and deal with risky parts of vulnerability."[408]

What about other attempts to achieve *invulnerability*? The first thing to be said about such attempts is that if they are to be successful to any degree, they must relate to situated vulnerability. It is only in specific situations and under conditions that are not ontological that one can have any chance for achieving some sort of invulnerable state. Moreover, as already indicated, to establish oneself as invulnerable is also a way of closing oneself off from others and from participation in a community that can provide chances for human growth and flourishing.

---

[404] Ibid.
[405] Ibid., 385.
[406] Ibid.
[407] Spinghart, "Exploring Life's Vulnerability: Vulnerability in Vitality," 20.
[408] Ibid., 23.

Springhart sees the advantage of accepting vulnerability in how it makes it possible to safeguard both "existential and conceptual aspects of calmness and an acceptance of the fundamental openness of life."[409] To embrace the vulnerable character of life is also a means to avoid the impact of surprise it entails. The effect of this is, as already suggested, increased opportunities for flourishing: "Paradoxically, it is not the struggle for invulnerability that enhances life and gives room for vitality, but the venture of vulnerability. The venture of vulnerability is not to be confused with a pure acceptance or embracing of vulnerability." It can imply the courage to weep, abandonment of pride, and openness to consolation. Thus, it can also strengthen the susceptibility to change and transformation.[410] "It takes the course of life and the ongoing transformation of life not only seriously, but considers it an essential part of life rather than an endangerment of a certain status of life."[411]

Vulnerability: Its different dimensions

Vulnerability has specific facets that come to the fore in its somatic, psychic, and social-systemic dimensions. These permeate and cause each other, but they can be differentiated. Furthermore, as we have seen, all these dimensions of vulnerability can be seen as something that either occurs from outside or is carried out from inside. Thus, on the one hand, vulnerability implies the *possibility* of being hurt or harmed and the awareness of this possibility. But it also "means concrete experiences of injury and harm that have happened. So, vulnerability as a phenomenon grasps three aspects: The *potentiality* of being wounded, harmed or injured, the *awareness* of this potentiality and the *experience* of concrete injury, harm, and affectability."[412]

In this sub-section, I will follow Springhart's analysis of some of the features of somatic and psychic vulnerability and therefore, I postpone the social dimension to a separate section below, which also allows us to address the political elements it entails. In *ontological* terms, somatic vulnerability means the fragility of the body as well as its affectability, its susceptibility to transformation and the possibility to intervene into the body. In terms of *situated* somatic vulnerability, concrete experiences of injury, harm, and affectability, such as disease, violence, but also sexuality come into play.[413]

---

[409] Ibid., 21.
[410] Ibid.
[411] Ibid., 22.
[412] Ibid., 26. My italics.
[413] Ibid., 28.

Somatic and psychic vulnerability are closely related to each other. Nevertheless, it is important to acknowledge that psychic vulnerability may reach beyond the somatic. Its ontological dimension is expressed in the affectability mentioned above, and by how mutual openness is a precondition for trust and sociality. Situated psychic vulnerability expresses itself in shame and trauma, but also in instances related to love and affection. "External psychic vulnerability describes the violation of the psychic integrity by interventions from outside, such as sexual abuse, mobbing, or other forms of shame and humiliation."[414] Moreover, as also indicated previously, shame and vulnerability are connected in a complicated manner: although shame "works as protection of the vulnerable person, it increases situated vulnerability at the same time."[415] The psychic integrity of the person is always under the risk of violation and endangerment, whereas on the other hand, the psychic aspects of vulnerability can be identified as the precondition of trust, empathy, and interpersonal relationships.[416]

Against the backdrop of her analysis so far, Springhart points to factors that connect the analysis of vulnerability with certain religious aspects. In a religious framework, appropriation of vulnerability that has implications for practice is related to how it is established via a self-symbol that recognizes the human being as existing in faith towards someone else, as well as being a sinner. She writes:

Faith is characterized by a general openness to the other, to the world and to God. It is based on the awareness of the need for salvation and on the assumption that there is always something beyond this life, be it in eschatological terms, be it in existential terms. The awareness of human finitude and potential failure is expressed exemplarily in the confession of sin. The ambiguous character of vulnerability as endangerment on the one hand and as trust oriented vulnerable sensitivity on the other hand, shapes faith in the classic trifold concept, that is faith as trust (*fiducia*), knowledge (*notitia*) and confession (*assensus*). This is related with the realization of human self-endangerment as a consequence and expression of sin. Human beings are not only vulnerable with regard to potential violations through other people and other circumstances, they are also vulnerable with regard to their own actions. In other words: Human beings are in danger to become an agent of vulnerability.[417]

It is this risk of becoming an agent of vulnerability, and our propensity to afflict harm on others, that makes humans responsible for others than themselves.

---

[414] Ibid.
[415] Ibid.
[416] Cf. Ibid.
[417] Ibid., 29.

Therefore, vulnerability has an unavoidable social and political dimension, which deserves its own section in order to be treated more extensively.

Vulnerability and the responsibility for justice

Understanding human life from the point of view of vulnerability roots the responsibility that humans have for each other in a phenomenon that is deeply relational and therefore has social and political dimensions. It makes it obvious that the moral obligation that humans have towards each other is rooted in vulnerability just as much as desire, which we addressed previously. Responsibility is not rooted in convention, will, or human decision. Poverty, lack of health, access to resources, and a safe environment can be identified as crucial and basic problems of humanity, not because of a scarcity of resources, but because of violence, injustice, unequal distribution, and lack of access to care. These are not ontological but situated conditions that are possible to address by means of human action and transformative practices of care and justice. This means taking up responsibility by transforming relationships and opening up to the situation of the other. Nico Koopman writes aptly about this when he points to how "True humanity is not defined by independence and rationality, but by the willingness to enter into relationships with others. [...] We receive our existence out of the relationship with the other, and my existence is meaningful because there are others who want to share their existence with me."[418] Like other authors who write on vulnerability, he is also pointing to the fundamental character of dependence and vulnerability in human existence.[419] Furthermore, Koopman suggests that significant elements for orientation and transformation in this regard can be found in the biblical narratives repeatedly pointing to God's identification with those who suffer.[420] This acknowledgment of vulnerability and suffering as something God actively relates to can thereby be articulated in religious discourse and by symbols in ways that provide chances for dealing with the features of vulnerability in terms of both orientation and transformation.

However, such transformations are not the task of the individual. As sociologist Bryan Turner points to, humans have established *institutions* in order to make sure that the vulnerable condition of humanity is taken care of. "In order

---

[418] Nico Koopman, "Vulnerable Church in a Vulnerable World? Towards an Ecclesiology of Vulnerability," *Journal of Reformed Theology* 2, no. 3 (2008), 245
[419] Ibid.
[420] Cf. Ibid., 238.

to protect themselves from the uncertainties of the everyday world, they must build social institutions (especially political, familial, and cultural institutions) that come to constitute what we call 'society.'"[421] He goes on, in a way that also points to how these institutions themselves must be seen as vulnerable and in need of protection:

We need trust in order to build companionship and friendship to provide us with means of mutual support. We need the creative force of ritual and the emotional ties of common festivals to renew social life and to build effective institutions, and we need the comforts of social institutions to fortify our individual existence. Because we are biologically vulnerable, we need to build political institutions to provide for our collective security. These institutions are themselves precarious, however, and cannot work without effective leadership, political wisdom, and good fortune to provide an enduring and reliable social environment. Rituals typically go wrong; social norms offer no firm blueprint for action. The guardians of social values – priests, academics, lawyers, and others – turn out to be open to corruption, mendacity, and self-interest.[422]

Moreover, Turner argues that when humans are aware of and share their experiences of vulnerability, "this shared world of risk and uncertainty results in sympathy, empathy, and trust, without which society would not possible."[423] Hence, "the experience of vulnerability provides a norm for the assertion of a human bond across generations and cultures, and this cross-cultural characteristic of vulnerability presupposes the embodiment of the human agent."[424] As Springhart points to in her analysis of the social-cultural dimension of vulnerability, it is not only a feature of individual human beings.[425]

The institutional aspect implies that juridical institutions, but also schools, hospitals, and police exist to address different aspects of vulnerability by taking care of humans in different situations or prepare them for living with vulnerability. The double-sided feature that Turner points to emerges in the inequality of power, asymmetry, unequal access to resources, and different modes of dependency. Springhart addresses this point: "Those who are in the more powerful

---

[421] Bryan S. Turner, *Vulnerability and Human Rights* (University Park, Pa.: Pennsylvania State University Press, 2006), 26.
[422] Ibid.
[423] Ibid.
[424] Ibid., 35. Cf. also Sturla Stålsett, who addresses the contemporary global situation with reference to "the precariat" thus: "Without experiencing ourselves as vulnerable, true empathy, ethical action or solidarity is impossible. That is why the common experience of the vulnerability or precariousness of the precariat could be seen as a resource for its common action, and not as something that necessarily should give reason to despair, nor, much less, make the precariat potentially dangerous." Sturla J. Stålsett, "Prayers of the Precariat? The Political Role of Religion in Precarious Times," *Estudos Teológicos* 58, no. 2 (2018), 421.
[425] Springhart, "Exploring Life's Vulnerability: Vulnerability in Vitality," 30.

position owe those who are in the less powerful position respect and responsible behavior given this vulnerable relationship."[426] This fact leads to the need for acknowledging the moral dimension for each individual along the lines of vulnerability, because, as Sturla Stålsett writes, "in any relation of dependency, there is power, and call for responsibility. Your dependency on me gives me power over you."[427] But the presence of vulnerability in such a situation makes one aware of that responsibility. Furthermore, "my own awareness of being a vulnerable person provides me with resources (knowledge, experiences, competence, fantasy, creativity...) in my effort to respond as properly as possible to the demand issued by the vulnerability of the other."[428]

Stålsett, however, moves on from the basis for ethics in vulnerability towards a theological proposal. He holds that "Christian faith in God provides resources to uphold and protect this vision of the value of human vulnerability." Nevertheless, this position is not uncontroversial. Traditionally, mainstream doctrinal Christianity sees God as immutable and impassible, and therefore as invulnerable.[429] But as we have already seen, a position that is qualified by a Christology that underscores God's own representative in the world as vulnerable provides an alternative to this notion of God. It provides the opportunity to see God "as affected by suffering – a vulnerable God (*Deus vulnerabilis*)." Stålsett argues – in my view correctly – that this approach provides a "more adequate interpretation of the normative Christian sources (identity) and takes better into account contemporary human experiences and knowledge (relevance)."[430]

In Stålsett's view, this is not an academic enterprise aimed at the change of a specific conception of God. The notion of a vulnerable God who relates to vulnerable humans is inherently related to how Christian faith *is practiced*: Accordingly, the symbol of a vulnerable God opens up to "a political theology that enhances human vulnerability as a value, thus promoting a different understanding of political power from the prevailing one, often informed and shaped by illusions of invulnerability."[431] This political theology he describes as follows:

Based on theological interpretations of human life as constitutively vulnerable, and of God as having chosen to be affected by vulnerability, a (cosmo-)political theology of vulnerability

---

[426] Cf. Ibid.
[427] Sturla J. Stålsett, "Towards a Political Theology of Vulnerability: Anthropological and Theological Propositions," *Political Theology* 16, no. 5 (2015), 469.
[428] Ibid.
[429] Ibid., 476.
[430] Ibid., 477.
[431] Ibid.

should provide resources for understanding and exercising political power in ways that enhance, protect, and promote human life in community as vulnerable and yet good. In short, if God's ways in this world are embracing and protecting vulnerability, this should influence the way in which we interpret the political field, and exercise political power.[432]

His approach to religious symbols implies that Stålsett also addresses critically versions of Christianity that do not take vulnerability sufficiently into consideration or only deal with it partly. On the one hand, religious fundamentalists seem to fear and even despise vulnerability, whereas "the charismatic movements often take peoples' vulnerability as their point of departure, offering a kind of religiosity which promises to overcome these challenges with help from spiritual resources, such as prayer, blessings, tithing, exorcism, healing, or the experience of community and mutual strength."[433] The only type of religiosity that takes vulnerability fully into account, claims Stålsett, is the ecumenical and liberation-oriented, which is critical of economic globalization and the "increased focus on wealth that creates social inequalities and environmental damage." "In contrast with the two other religiosity types, this one offers resources to acknowledge and recognize the religious and ethical value of vulnerability."[434] The political and social focus in this type of religiosity establishes a firm link between vulnerability and social justice that is backed by powerful symbols, such as God being vulnerable and marginalized.

Stålsett's contribution thereby highlights that we can identify quite different symbols that guide the practices related to vulnerability within the boundaries of Christianity. Hence, he underscores the need to approach these critically, in order for religious communities to engage in practices of orientation and transformation that take the ambiguous character of vulnerability fully into account.

Theological resources for critical approaches to vulnerability

Hardly anyone is strong enough to determine her own reality, independent of others. Therefore, some modern forms of individualism work under the illusion that we can find ourselves without having to stand in an affirming relation to others. Humans are fundamentally dependent on the recognition of others, and recognition is among the elements that make us vulnerable, since it may, or may not, be. To be susceptible to affirmation, acknowledgment, confirmation, and

---

[432] Ibid.
[433] Stålsett, "Prayers of the Precariat? The Political Role of Religion in Precarious Times," 422.
[434] Ibid.

being recognized as valuable is important. But in a society in which relationships are avoided because they remind us of our vulnerable condition, it can lead to a precarious situation, in which narcissism grows, and where the struggle for recognition directs and shapes desires in its closed mode – as an exclusive struggle for recognition of myself and not as openness to the other. Others appear only as a means for confirmation, and as expressers of signals that can tell me if I am worth anything. Isolde Karle points to how this creates a situation in which many are hungry for and seek recognition, but are not able to offer this to others. Others desire to liberate themselves fully from the need for recognition, in order to not experience themselves as dependent and vulnerable.[435]

Karle stresses that God's affirmation of humanity takes into account the ambiguous character of human life, including how it comes to the fore in vulnerability. God sees more in the human than what is present – and affirms not only the factual human but also what this human can become.[436] God's love is therefore not ignoring that humans try to avoid the creaturely existence as it is expressed in relationality and vulnerability, but nevertheless recognizes the human as loveable. A human being who can recognize itself from this perspective is, therefore, liberated to relate to others in modes that do not reflect the narcissistic orientation, and which allow for being vulnerable:

Wird Gott als eine transzendente Größe verstanden, die sich dem Menschen wohl- wollend (gnädig) zuwendet, dann verändert dies das Verhältnis des Menschen zu sich selbst und zu anderen und dies nicht zuletzt im Hinblick auf die Erfahrung von Schwäche und Fragmentarität. Erfährt der Mensch, "das eigene Leben von einer Macht und einem Sinn getragen, über die er nicht verfügt und den er seinem Leben selbst nicht beilegen kann – und auch nicht muss", wird er befreit von der Sorge um sich selbst. Als Geschöpf Gottes muss er nicht Garant des Lebens sein und dieses immer auf den eigenen Schultern tragen. Nicht immer stark, gesund, unfehlbar, unanfechtbar und allmächtig, kann er auch schwach, berührbar und gebrochen sein. Die Gabe der Anerkennung ereignet sich zwar vorrangig in der zwischenmenschlichen Erfahrung, aber sie geht, religiös gedacht, zugleich nicht darin auf. Das gilt auch für die Erfahrung der Verweigerung: Selbst wenn mir menschlich Anerkennung verweigert wird, kann ich vor Gott auf Anerkennung als sein Geschöpf hoffen. Gott hält mir die Treue, auch wenn es mir oder anderen Personen in meiner Umgebung schwerfällt, mir die Treue zu halten. Gott begründet eine Identität jenseits der Selbstbeschreibungen, die ein Mensch alltäglich herstellen kann und muss.[437]

The critical perspective this approach offers to a culture that focuses on health, beauty, and fitness as expressions of the ideal human is obvious. It is crucial to

---

[435] Isolde Karle, "Die Suche Nach Anerkennung – Und Die Religion," *Evangelische Theologie* 76 (2016), 408.
[436] Cf. Ibid., 410.
[437] Ibid., 412.

human development and survival that the conditions that emerge in vulnerability are possible to thematize and articulate in adequate symbols that encourage engaging with them. Without symbolic and linguistic capabilities – it is impossible to become aware of, understand, relate to, and transcend (to some extent) the restrictions to which vulnerability subjects life.

Ingolf Dalferth sees the situation in which religious believers bemoan God's absence or evoke God's presence as a way to express their experience of God's relation to them. Accordingly, he sees the terms 'present' and 'absent' as part of what he calls a scheme of orientation. Such schemes

provide us with a semiotic order of the world and help us to locate others and ourselves in that order…. In short, in schemes of orientation we employ specific differences or semiotic distinctions by which we orient ourselves in our world, in our relations with others, and in relation to God. These schemes are not fixed once and for all but vary according to the contrasts and distinctions that seem important and useful to us.[438]

Against this backdrop, we argue that a scheme of orientation that employs a distinction in which we can speak of the experience of God's presence or absence in human life offers an adequate tool for describing vulnerable elements in human experience, compared to those which are not able to do so.

We suggested above that vulnerability has a difficult place in the mind of modern humans,[439] and that a typical contemporary approach to vulnerability is to deny it or try to protect oneself from it. However, *the individual who is exposed to vulnerability is the one who comes closest to the undisguised experience of what human existence truly is: shaped by dependency, mortality, the frailty of relationships, and existential loneliness. Thus, the one who experiences herself as vulnerable is given an opportunity to come closer to what it means to really be a human.* Modern ideals of free, autonomous, and self-contained individuals who do not recognize their own vulnerability may actually develop into alienation from the very nature of being human.

As we saw that Karle points to, awareness of God manifests the constitutive relationality of all human beings (cf. dependence in Schleiermacher), and the external conditions on whom they rely. The act of praying is tantamount to acknowledging, at least tacitly, this dependence. Prayer opens up the one who

---

[438] See I.U. Dalferth, "God, Time, and Orientation," in Ingolf U. Dalferth, ed. *The Presence and Absence of God* (Tübingen: Mohr Siebeck), 3.

[439] The best contemporary analysis on the topic of vulnerability from a philosophical point of view is in Alasdair C. MacIntyre, *Dependent Rational Animals : Why Human Beings Need the Virtues* (Chicago: Open Court, 2006). The strength of MacIntyre's position is not least how he is able to connect his analysis of vulnerability with those of relationality and dependence.

prays to God but may also manifest an (implicit) acknowledgment of one's own vulnerable state, of being in need of assistance. Sincere prayer and vulnerability appear in tandem. Passionate prayers often voice desires and therefore amount to egoism – but they may also be a practice in which one is giving oneself over to God. Because the human needs for dependency, connection, and affirmation are never left behind, the desired relation expressed in prayer to God under the conditions of suffering is not an attempt to provide cheap and empty consolation, as critics of religion would argue. Instead, it is an expression of the inherent human condition of relatedness and the drive for those emotional resonances that sustain us as human beings. It also places the human in a vulnerable state.

This point about prayer can be developed further by some of Sarah Coakley's insights. She holds that contemplation in wordless prayer is a state in which discursive thought is reduced to the minimum. The aim of this conscious process is to make space for God and to cease to set an agenda. Thus, she suggests that prayer is a practice in which one opens one's desire to God instead of for one's own control. For Coakley, this has implications for her understanding of the power that resides in vulnerability: "Wordless prayer can enable one, paradoxically, to hold vulnerability and personal empowerment together, precisely by creating the 'space' in which non-coercive divine power manifests itself."[440] This she sees as crucial for her understanding of a specifically Christian form of feminism that can empower women in their fight against patriarchy. Such prayer also has implications for desire in other ways, as it implies the practice of askesis, or self-discipline. She sees askesis as "a crucial step in avoiding replication of the worldly power of patriarchal systems. Without askesis, one risks creating. new systems that mirror the patterns of domination which one is trying to subvert due to the fact that these abusive powers are often internalized."[441] Hence, Coakley argues for a positive assessment of vulnerability, in which it is not primarily representing an opportunity to objectify or oppress women, but rather seen as something that draws all people together through emphasizing interdependence.[442]

As indicated above, the human need for relationships and the emotional dimension of being human are what make us vulnerable. These features also make us truly human, as they are characteristic of us as God's creatures. In the

---

[440] See for Coakley here the analysis in Selak, "Orthodoxy, Orthopraxis, and Orthopathy: Evaluating the Feminist Kenosis Debate Orthodoxy, Orthopraxis, and Orthopathy," 534f. She builds her analysis here on Sarah Coakley, Powers and Submissions Spirituality, Philosophy and Gender, (Oxford, UK Malden, Mass.: Blackwell Publishers, 2002), 5; 35.

[441] Selak, "Orthodoxy, Orthopraxis, and Orthopathy", ibid.

[442] Cf. ibid., 535.

gospels, there are several stories that point to the existential "givens" of vulnerability and dependence, which can be said to culminate in the Gethsemane story: think of the *dependency* of the paralytic on his friends (Mark 2), the *vulnerability* of the woman suffering from hemorrhage (Mark 5), or the lepers who are marginalized or excluded from society (Mark 1); consider how *mortality* expresses itself in the stories about the resuscitation of the dead (Mark 5,21ff.), the *frailty of human relationships* as they are exhibited in the stories of Judas (betrayal) and Peter (denial), or the *existential loneliness* of the Samaritan woman who went in solitude to the well (John 4). In all these instances, Jesus addresses their conditions and improves them by taking into account that the persons he meets are something other – indeed, something more – than only afflicted by how these conditions manifest themselves in their lives. Jesus relates to these existential givens as recognized for what they are and takes them into account in his relationships with those who suffer. Moreover, the community to which Jesus invites them safeguards human relationships, protects members from being exposed to the negative risks of situated vulnerability, and compensates for existential loneliness as another existential "given." As for mortality, Jesus' message implies that mortality is not a given that is the definite and final element determining human life, although it cannot be avoided as part of the human condition.

The people Jesus heals and those with whom he associates are thus also vivid reminders of these existential givens, the disturbing character of which, for those unable to recognize them or who ignore or deny them, may explain why people took offense at Jesus. The givens experienced and exhibited in the company of Jesus were, in a word, reminders of human *finitude*. Theologically speaking, to recognize that one is the image of God and not God, means acknowledging this finitude. The opposite is to reject finitude and its associated feature vulnerability, and thereby one's calling to be an image of God. Based on that premise, we can then establish a connection between the rejection of the human vocation to be *imago Dei*, of human finitude, and a lack of faith, because faith implies that one accepts one's own standing in the eyes of God.

Paradoxically, it seems that when the human being seeks herself in an unfulfilled destiny while realizing that this cannot be wholly appropriated or fulfilled at present, this paves the way for living here and now in a way that recognizes the vulnerability of both others and oneself. We should note here how this is a corollary to the earlier analyses of desire. We are not perfect, and to realize this is to be confronted with the vulnerability that is given with the fact that we are dependent upon others and live exposed to the power of others.

Human beings mature and live more truthfully when facing the *incurable* character of their own desire for being perfect, complete, and without deficiency. Accordingly, the human being acquires a more well-grounded identity by realizing or being confronted with what she is – and what she cannot yet be. We are vulnerable, dependent, and mortal, while human life is imperfect and may always present us with dangers, suffering, and challenges. To think otherwise is a failure to accept human life as it is. However, the relation to God offers the possibility to grasp ourselves as an unfinished and problematic "project" and to live with the impact of that insight. To see God as the Other underlines how every attempt to make God a means of one's own gratification of desires not only implies the attempt to overcome God's otherness, but also makes God less than God.

We can read the Gethsemane story as one in which the true and vulnerable conditions of human existence are articulated in the life of Jesus. Thus, the story provides *validation* for all those to have a similar experience of vulnerability, the need for an affirming relation to God, and the concomitant experiences of lack of answers to their prayers, and of God's being absent. The one who suffers from vulnerability can see her situation as recognized in the biblical material without having to try to transcend, negate, or deny the boundaries and limits of her condition because they are not in accordance with religious ideals for how life should be. Thus, this text opens to a more profound and sound affirmation of the vulnerable givens of the human condition. The acknowledgment and recognition of these fundamental conditions of human life may, therefore, make life better.

Moreover, the passion story exhibits Jesus as exposed to a lack of relations, which he experiences as distressing when he is facing his suffering and death: his friends leave him, deny him, or betray him. This is severe, since togetherness, relationships, and the possibilities of orienting life, accordingly, are essential for human life. His vulnerability is expressed in his anguish, despair, and finally in his mortality. Moreover, the given of *existential loneliness* expresses itself in the Gethsemane statement, "He is gone!" as in his cry on the cross, "My God, why have you forsaken me?" Jesus had to face the givens of human life, in which existential loneliness is part. The conditions of human existence that Jesus shared with the rest of humanity could not be obliterated by his close relationship with God. His passion experience makes the real and vulnerable conditions of human life visible and manifest.

Love as the means for coming to terms with desire and vulnerability

In his theological anthropology, Wolfhart Pannenberg developed an under-standing of the human being as living in the tension between openness to the world, and what he called centricity. The first, the openness, he connected to the notion of being created in the image of God, whereas the latter he connected to sin.[443] Pannenberg is right in connecting the notion of the image of God to fundamental features in human existence. However, contrary to Pannenberg's approach, which builds on philosophical anthropology, I have tried to develop an understanding of human life from desire and vulnerability in order to develop a more substantial understanding of the motivations and drives behind human life and action, and the needs for coming to terms with basic elements that are rooted in our embodied existence. Moreover, the approach developed above avoids identifying some traits as positive, whereas others are defined as nega-tive. Instead, we have seen that both desire and vulnerability are ambiguous phenomena that require that we engage practices of orientation, transformation, and reflection. Both are also indications of how life is an unfinished process. At this point I share a concern of Pannenberg's: that life must be seen as oriented towards something it is not yet – and hence, the calling to be and become the image of God is not only a basic designation on which humans have to under-stand themselves, it also presents human life with a goal and an aim to be real-ized. The thesis of this section is that *humans realize their calling to be and become the image of God by living in faith, hope, and love – and among these, love is the most important element, because it is through the practice of love that desire and vulnerability can be handled in a way that represents and makes present the will of God in the world. Thus, God is represented by humans that are created in God's image, as they relate to the world in faith, hope, and love.* This thesis points to concrete practices in the community and for the community as the primary modes in which God's presence can be experienced. As should be apparent from this claim, the following corresponds with what was already said in the previous chapter about God as love and the interrelation of God and humans in concrete agency.

It follows from these initial remarks that it is not only advisable to orient one's life from the task of dealing with desire and vulnerability, but that such orientation also can direct oneself towards processes of transformation. The transformative power that contributes to shaping the way humans can handle these fundamental features in the best way possible is *love*. It is because humans

---

[443] Pannenberg, *Anthropology in Theological Perspective,* passim.

are created in the image of God that they not only are capable of loving (a created capacity), but this is also the reason why human beings are lovable: they
are the object of God's unconditional love – and hence, the symbol of God as
love point to an experiential element of ultimacy in the midst of human life.
Therefore, we can relate the notion of the image of God to the notion of love as
a transcendental condition for human experience.

As unconditional, love is spontaneous, not based on merit, achievement, or
specific capacities or religious status. It is like grace: spontaneous, impossible
to trace back to the conditioning causal elements. However, unconditional love
needs to be expressed or stated in ways that presuppose close relations of communication and affirmation. Unconditional love allows a person to experience
the love present at hand as something that is more and different than just a limited instance of something good – it is unlimited.

To see *love as basically unconditioned* has a profound impact on the establishment of God as a powerful symbol as well as for concrete experiences of
charity. In Christian theology, such love is often expressed by the notion *agape*.
Jean-Luc Marion points to a feature that may deepen our understanding of this
feature: He sees this unconditional love as something that, from a phenomenological point of view, is not part of ontology, but prior to ontology, as love is in
need of nothing to go on; it is not based on being, on reciprocity, or on a return
of investment. "The lover has the unmatched privilege of losing nothing, even
if he happens to find himself unloved because a love scorned remains a love
perfectly accomplished, just as a gift refused remains a perfectly given gift,"
Marion writes aptly.[444]

We have hardly any ability to know what it means that God is love without
the experience of the love of others. This is why it is so important that God is
represented by those who are called to be God's image. Although some people
have not had the chance to experience the love of others, they are still directed
towards love, desiring love, desiring both to receive love and to love others.
This underlying desire for love in human life seems to be a basic element in our
world-orientation. Love determines human life even when it has not been or is
not present. Theologically, it is due to our fundamental relationship with and
non-dissolvable participation in God, as Paul Fiddes so beautifully has spelled
out: "God is not the *object* of our desire, a thing to be desired, but the one *in*

---

[444] Marion, *The Erotic Phenomenon*, 71.

whom we desire the good. We are truly *in* love. God offers a movement of desire in which we can share."[445]

As indicated in the chapter on God as love, it is the experiences in our love stories that are the crucial experiential content that shapes our experience: not only our experience of the world, but of the world, and of ourselves as *all exist in relation.* This goes not only for our "successful" love stories, but also for those which were failures, and for the stories with parents, children, spouses, siblings, lovers, and other alike. Even when love is not there, it is the lack of love and the desire for love that may determine us – even if we do not know it, or even it takes place in distorted ways. Love is an (almost) all-determining occupation of ours, which also hides in the desire for success and recognition, or in the love of life which makes (some of us) health-freaks that want to shield ourselves from the negativities of vulnerability.

The love I am addressing here goes in several directions: It is love for God, for the Other, and for oneself (cf. Matthew 22; 37-39). When such love shapes the concrete experience of the world, it also shapes the distinct character of human life and human participation in the world as it is mediated by desire and vulnerability. Thereby, it may also help us to see how the one we call God is present in the other, and someone we participate in the life of through the experiences with them – in ways that are not guided by our immediate need for recognition or affirmation in relationships with others. Thereby, actual experience manifests religious content, and the contents of the everyday may point beyond the immediate present. The transcendental character of experiences claimed to be related to God, is tied to the immediate claim that God is manifested in experience (albeit then as mediated) – and as Other. As we developed in relation to Rowan Williams above – God is the not-present third party. Therefore, God's love surpasses our finite experience but can nevertheless be experienced in our concrete and finite experiences.

To recognize God in the other precludes us from focusing on God at the expense of the other human. This is a point that can be substantiated by Werner Jeanrond's critique of Augustine's concept of love. He argues that love in Augustine's view fundamentally is and can only be God's love or the love of God.[446] In this perspective, the other person is subjected to the risk of becoming

---

[445] Paul S. Fiddes, *Seeing the World and Knowing God : Hebrew Wisdom and Christian Doctrine in a Late-Modern Context*, First edition. ed. (Oxford, United Kingdom: Oxford University Press, 2013), 264.

[446] Jeanrond, *A Theology of Love*, 45–66, see esp. 52. Jeanrond here builds on the critique posited by Hannah Arendt in her work on Augustine.

instrumentalized as a means for displaying my love for God and may lose her status as a true object of love in and for herself.

Thus, to live as the image of God is to have faith in God as love. It is to live in a specific manner in the world – directed from a vision of love and oriented with love in mind. From this vision, God may be understood as the infinite source of that which is directing the world toward its future and its consummation in love.[447] The impact of the symbol "God as love" provides a vision for human life that may change the world, and not allow it to be a mere expression of self-interest and the struggle for survival – as a mere evolutionary account can be taken to imply. When we spell out the symbol 'God' like this, it becomes clear that who you believe in matters, and what is ultimate: If we orient ourselves from a vision determined by the symbol "God as love," it means that the basic features of human orientation and transformation relate to the transcendental conditions for specific experiences, and not to some arbitrary empirical elements: God is the fountain beyond life that we can understand as the source of all that is good in life. To speak of God as love is an adequate expression of why this goodness is either present or something we desire or struggle for. The vision of love keeps us open for the continuous gifts that we receive through life from others and from participating in the world.

To see God as love as the ultimate source and ground for life implies that God is not a contingent or arbitrary designation of what we mean when we speak of love: *love goes to the core of what faith means as a way of being in the world.* In a profound manner, this is expressed in an interview made with Emmanuel Lévinas. He says: "Faith is not the question of the existence or non-existence of God. It is believing that love without reward is valuable."[448] Against this background, it is also possible to say that there is a gospel in the statement, "God is the commandment to love."[449]

Faith is the insistent conviction that we lose ourselves and the world God has given us if we orient ourselves basically from another perspective than love. The risk of losing this way of life is linked to the vulnerable state of all life –

---

[447] There is also a Christological dimension to this point, that is well expressed by Paul Fiddes in a way that also points to the semiotic character of Christ's work and presence: "So Christ is the bodily text which gives the due to whole text and body of the world. This is not because he is a cosmic mediator, bridging a gap between two worlds, but because the pattern visible in the actions and words of Christ is the rhythm in which the world comes to its fullness." Fiddes, *Seeing the World and Knowing God : Hebrew Wisdom and Christian Doctrine in a Late-Modern Context,* 346.

[448] Lévinas, "The paradox of morality," in *The Provocation of Levinas: Rethinking the other*, ed. Robert Bernasconi and David Wood, 177.

[449] Ibid.

not only human life but life on this planet in general: Living truly in a world that is permeated with rich opportunities to love is a way of making the symbol of God change the world. The Christian understanding of God's realization of Godself through those who are created in God's image thus makes possible the strong claim that *to face and engage in reality from the perspective of love is the most rewarding way to lead a life.* Moreover, the creative and sustaining power of love that is present in all realms of reality, and which is struggling to come to the fore in them enables us to uphold a vision of the world and of life that constantly may manifest itself in new forms of community and creativity, and to positively shape desire and deal with vulnerability. With the perspective of love as a basis for living, it makes sense to keep on the quest for justice, goodness, and integrity of creation, without giving in to the powers that are threatening the efforts to achieve these aims. In short: to live as if love is the deepest meaning of it all is to lead a meaningful life. It requires faith and hope, but these two are made possible from the perspective of love (cf. 1 Cor 13,13).

In his work on vulnerability, Sturla Stålsett claims that "vulnerability is such a decisive phenomenon since it is an irreplaceable dimension of love."[450] It is worth noting here that it is love, and not vulnerability that is the fundamental notion, and vulnerability is a dimension in love. He holds that love requires vulnerability because it is only a vulnerable human who can love. Moreover, love *creates* vulnerability in the loving subject. Vulnerability also makes love a *sine qua non* for life. Stålsett also refers to Werner Jeanrond, who writes: "Love seeks the other. Love desires to relate to the other, to get to know the other, to experience the other's life, to spend time with the other." Stålsettt points to the tacit dimension of desire in relation to vulnerability as well, since there is a risk in love: "In this seeking, there is an opening up. There is receptivity; there is a need. There is a longing. All of this implies vulnerability."[451] Love creates vulnerability in the loving subject as one can never be sure if the desire it entails will be unrequited.

There is in love an invitation, and a proposal, which may be turned down. There is a trust that may be misused. And this is not just a vague possibility. It is something that happens often. Most people would know from their own life that the risk of having one's love turned down is part and parcel of the loving experience. It is part of its excitement, its bliss – and its possible sorrow.[452]

---

[450] Stålsett, "Towards a Political Theology of Vulnerability: Anthropological and Theological Propositions," 469.
[451] Ibid. Stålsett refers to Jeanrond, *A Theology of Love.*
[452] Stålsett, "Towards a Political Theology of Vulnerability: Anthropological and Theological Propositions," 470.

The risky business of love appears in the vulnerability that being loved creates in the person who is the object of love as well: Stålsett holds that "love creates a certain sense of vulnerability in the person being loved" because it "seems impossible to turn away from, or even turn down, the love of another person without in some way, at some level, being affected by one's own act of rejection."[453]

Stålsett makes some further observations that are profoundly relevant from the point of view of Christian theology. He claims that "only the one who recognizes him or herself to be vulnerable can truly be an agent of love."[454] This claim is important because it qualifies the conditions under which our desire can appear as something else than seeking itself: it is in being open to the other in vulnerability that love can be practiced. If vulnerability is not part of what shapes desire, the other cannot be loved, and desire becomes a mere tool for self-gratification. The triad love-desire-vulnerability thus appears as significant for shaping what matters in human life in the best way possible. I suggest that this triad is the best point of departure for understanding what it means to live as an image of God.

Moreover, Stålsett makes an important observation to consider from the theological point of view: that humans are not justified by their works and merits, but by their relationship with Jesus Christ through faith. He claims that "only the vulnerable person can be truly loved."[455] His argument for this claim is that someone considered by others to be invulnerable can be an object of admiration, respect, or reverence, but not of love. Moreover, the invulnerable may instead instigate fear as a likely response.[456] Hence, it is not *what* a person can show for herself that makes her loveable, but *how* she shows herself as truly human – as vulnerable. From the point of view of the doctrine of justification, this analysis implies that one can consider the attempt to establish justification by works as an attempt to make oneself resilient to the fundamental condition of vulnerability. Such struggle implies a misguided desire because it is basically a desire for oneself.

Against the backdrop of the above, it makes sense to say, with Springhart, that "Love has an anthropological and a theological dimension and as such, it

---

[453] Ibid.
[454] Ibid., 469.
[455] Ibid., 469f.
[456] Ibid., 470.

is a paradigmatic focal point for valuing vulnerability."[457] She sees divine vulnerability becoming visible in the incarnation of Jesus Christ and in particular at the cross. This vulnerability and divine love are connected to each other. Springhart here deepens Stålsett's reflections as referred to above, by stating that "the transformative power of God's vulnerability characterizes the incarnation." In the incarnation, "love increases vulnerability and requires vulnerability." Therefore,

the incarnation as expression of God's love increases Divine vulnerability. Also divine love requires vulnerability in order to really adopt humanity and to be affectable and susceptible to human life in general and the encounters with specific human beings in particular situations of healing, for example. The Cross then reveals the connection of shame with vulnerable love, as part of the passion of Christ is the humiliation that comes with it. The risk of love is the possibility of shame and of being shamed, while shame at the same time protects vulnerability and increases it.[458]

It makes no sense to speak of vulnerability without speaking about community. If we understand the church as a model for how love can express itself in vulnerability and the desire for justice, we can develop this as a model that is of significance for others than those who take part in the community of believers. Springhart points to how the church is "the community of vulnerable limbs of the vulnerable body of Christ. Love's vulnerability in the social, communal and ecclesiological sense is related to the aspects of care and vision."[459] In this respect, the church is not a self-enclosed entity, but a model for human life in general. The practices of the church in love and its concomitant shaping of human features like desire and vulnerability are relevant beyond its walls.

Love as a process, love as a mode of growth (unfinished business)

To describe the human being from the point of view of desire and vulnerability provides us with a specific perspective on its relational being: it implies that growth, development, maturation, and formation also have to do with these features. However, this approach makes it possible to see humans not only from the point of view of what and how they are, but also allows us to address the *de-centered* character of the constitution of human life and experience, because

---

[457] Springhart, "Exploring Life's Vulnerability: Vulnerability in Vitality," 32.
[458] Ibid.
[459] Cf. Ibid., 33.

both desire and vulnerability points to how we exist in connection with something or someone else. Accordingly, we need an account of the human that transcends individual and merely empirical perspectives. We have seen how this is exemplified in the description of love as a transcendental condition for life. Being and becoming, desire for love and love in desire are all elements that point towards a field in which the "self" exists as conditioned by otherness and by something beyond its own control and power. The theological symbol of *imago Dei* articulates these elements further because it goes directly to the heart of understanding the human being as decentered.

Whereas a center stabilizes and creates the impression that there is a given stance on which we can build and make sure that we grasp the identity of the human being, an analysis of the human condition that draws on the resources that this book employs from the Christian tradition precludes a centered understanding of human beings that sees them only from the perspective of their own (empirical) and determined presence in one specific situation. Human existence is not determined from one punctual stance but must be seen as a historical being that is partaking in a lifelong process where its relationships to others and to God are the main, determining elements. This point is intimately linked to an understanding of God as love and as the ultimate source of self. Most people may think that this is a likely approach because the human being cannot be understood from itself, but only from its relation to God. That is correct, but there is more to say about it. It is true that the very notion of the human being as created by God decenters the human and makes her or him what they are only in the relation to God. But what exactly *are* we, then? To this, as well, there is no final answer. There are several answers, a *plurality* of answers, all contained in the historically established bulk of Christian doctrine, and they all contribute to underlining the provisional character of human self and identity, and thus every attempt to have a final understanding of what it means to be human. Let me spell this our more concretely:

According to the doctrine of creation, God creates the human being in God's own image. This gives the human being a distinct qualification. Humans are willed by God, recognized by God, loved by God. We emerge out of the love of God. This very relation to God gives us our human dignity. It also makes humans *persons*, in the sense that God calls forth a distinctive awareness of our selves as being something more and other than what we actually are and do. We are more than the present. To be a person is to transcend the perceptible positivity of our actions and capabilities – it is to have a distinct identity that is grounded in something not positively given, but yet present – in hope and de-sire, which relates us to a future yet unfulfilled. Accordingly, being a person is the opposite of being a *thing*. A thing cannot relate to its own future as the determining factor for its presence. However, human beings can experience themselves and others to be more than things, and also realize that if we con-ceive of ourselves or others as things, we are degraded as humans – and that there is something lacking in such an approach to humans.

Because being created as a person by God implies that we are called to goodness, and to witness and to realize the good of the loving God who created us, goodness is internal to human life. God made us capable of doing good, leading good lives – and of desiring goodness. Created life is good and God-willed, and our destiny as humans is, from the point of view of the doctrine of creation, that we live according to the desire for the goodness that emerges out of the fact that we are created in the image of God. That is to say that we live in such a way that God's goodness and love are made manifest in the world, thus expressing his glory.[460] Hence, *our love and our hope and desire for good-ness are related intrinsically to being created in the image of God.*

In this way, the Christian doctrine of human beings as created in the image of God relates God and humans to each other and allows us to develop practices in which the goodness of God and the desire for love and for goodness in human life are closely related. Simultaneously, the destiny of the human being as cre-ated in the image of God not only lends the human his or her dignity, but it also offers us the task set for our lives: to be mirrors of the God who created us.

Can this then be a center, a way of creating and even stabilizing human identity in spite of the fragility and vulnerability that we are exposed to when being thrust into the desire for others' love? Does the logic inherent in this ap-proach to human existence create a pattern in which everything that is possible to say about us and human experience fits in and is made meaningful? This is exactly *not* the case, and Christian theology has always made it clear that this perspective of the human being as created is insufficient – even false – when taken to be the sole and only description of what it means to be human. The reason why is identified in the notion we already have met several times in this chapter: sin. Consequently, to say that the human being is created in the image of God is not the last or only word theology has to say about being human. But sin is not identical with moral failure. *Sin is a lack in the future of God*, it is the

---

[460] Cf. Christof Gestrich, *The return of splendor in the world: the Christian doctrine of sin and forgiveness* (Grand Rapids, Mich.: W.B. Eerdmans Pub. Co, 1997), passim.

absolutizing of the present and the past conditions of life for the sake of one's own self-centered desire for security against all the treats of vulnerability. It is holding on to the finite and thereby absolutizing it. As such, sin may also express itself in the way human beings think of and interpret themselves only as products of the past – including the past of a blind evolutionary process. Such an understanding excludes the practices that are open to the transformative future of love and the relationship with God as the power of the future.

Whereas the description of reality as God's creation spells out humanity's relationship with God and how the human desire for love and loving desire are what orient us and may shape our being in the world, the doctrine of sin spells out how the human being separates itself from God in ways that alter this fundamental situation. God addresses this specific situation concretely in the *incarnation*, by inviting concrete human beings into a concrete and caring community with his representative, Jesus Christ. If Christians do not continue this practice of inviting into such a community after Jesus' model, they are not fulfilling their calling to live as images of God and as God's representatives.

Furthermore, while the doctrine of creation affirms the goodness of the human being and its origin in the love of God, the doctrine of sin articulates how the will of the human being is not shaped by love and by the desire for the other as one who may open up my world. Instead, sin implies, as already suggested, that human desire is lacking in true *eros*, and exchanged for a desire for what is already present in me and my perception of how the world should be, a perception not shaped by interaction with or openness toward others, which would imply vulnerability. This closing off to others, or absolutizing of our own finitude, is the reason why Augustine and other theologians locate sin in the will – as the faculty that is shaped and oriented by desire, be it for good or for bad.

Accordingly, whereas understanding of the human being as created in God's image articulates the human being as dependent upon God's loving and creative powers and as called to witness to this designation in life and deed, the doctrine of sin opens up an understanding of humanity that describes our attempts to be self-sufficient and independent of God, as well as our attempts to construct our own reality without openness towards God and without being shaped by vulnerable love. Thereby, we not only attempt to construct our reality and our self in ways that neglect the given qualities of God's creation, but we are also ourselves – tacitly at least – trying to establish ourselves as God, i.e., as the center of reality and with the power to uphold and control it – by shielding ourselves from the consequences of life's inherent ontological vulnerability.

Hence, as sinners, we not only oppose God – we negate God by our very lives by excluding love from what constitutes our selves. True *eros*, on the other hand, is characterized by the quest for self-transcendence with the aim of achieving liberation from those elements in the past which manifest inadequacy and failure. It is against this backdrop that we can interpret the human quest for beauty and goodness:

> This orientation to the future of the good finds its purest and most comprehensive expression in trust and hope. These are attitudes which from the very beginnings of human life accompany the process whereby the person is formed; they give this process space to breathe in, so to speak. Trust, no less than hope, is characterized by a reference to the future, because those who trust believe that the future of their own being is made secure by the one in whose hands they place themselves.[461]

It makes no sense to say that the description of what makes humanity human is something to which we *add* an understanding of the human as a sinner to complement the understanding of the human as created. The understanding of the human as sinner opposes the very description of the human being as created from the loving desire for otherness in God, while at the same time it presupposes it. There is a contradiction here that cannot be sublated (in the Hegelian sense), but which also does not lead to the denial of the validity of either of the alternative perspectives. Neither perspective on the human can be taken for granted, but each is put to the question by the other. Moreover, both the creaturely and the sinful character of human life shape and form desire and vulnerability, and determine the effect these features have on realizing oneself as the image of God. The existence of sin in human life nevertheless does not repeal the determination to be and become this image. As different approaches, these theological descriptions offer alternative types of logic of the constitution of the self (with or without love as the content of desire) that can be read off in the concrete experiences of love and vulnerability, so that what is implied in one type of description, allows a coherent explication of the basis given for it – but without any chance of being reconciled with other approaches.

The third possible perspective on humanity that is offered by theological anthropology is that of the human being as being offered grace and salvation by God.[462] This understanding presupposes insights gained by the two previous

---

[461] Pannenberg, *Anthropology in Theological Perspective*, 526.

[462] Miroslav Volf, *Exclusion and embrace: a theological exploration of identity, otherness, and reconciliation* (Nashville: Abingdon Press, 1996) states that the new identity of the self in Christ implies both a de-centering and a re-centering of the self. However, the following description

ones, but there is no transformation into a third and higher, more all-encom-
passing perspective here: God's recapitulation of humanity is more than the
restoration of creation – an insight that theology has affirmed since Irenaeus.[463]
Just as speech about the human being as a sinner is related to speaking about us
as created, so too is speech about the human being as being saved by the grace
of God related to, but not reduced to, what is said by or within the two perspectives expressed in the doctrines of creation and sin.

From this, we can draw the conclusion that the desire that comes from
goodness, and which expresses itself in every part of human activity and desire,
emerges from our relationship with God. It is an expression of how we, from
the outset, are determined by God's love in the innermost core of our being. It
is when we attempt to separate ourselves from the love of God and stop loving
God that our desire goes astray, and we no longer express to a full extent our
calling to be the Image of God and bear witness to God's love and God's desire
for goodness and justice. But when we do, our *eros* may be seen as the presence
and manifestation of divine creativity, and as something that opens both us and
others up to engaging the world as God's creation again.

To be part of a history in which one is called to realize one's destiny as the
image of God through practices of faith, hope, and love implies the following
three elements:

- The recognition that we are ourselves not God (God is the Other), but
that we are nevertheless related to God in love and in our hope and desire for
goodness. Faith opens up to this relation and expresses the trust in the fact that
life is lived best in this way.

---

offered by Volf does not rule out the necessity of maintaining and expressing the human being
in terms of the perspectives I have elaborated here. Writes Volf: "By being 'crucified with Christ'
the self has received a new center, – the Christ who lives in it and with whom it lives. Notice
that the new center of the self is not a timeless 'essence,' hidden deep within a human being,
underneath the sediments of culture and history and untouched by 'time and change,' an essence
that waits only to be discovered, unearthed, set free. Neither is the center an inner narrative that
the reverberating echo of the community's 'final vocabulary' and 'master story' has scripted in
the book of the self and whose integrity must be guarded from editorial intrusions by rival 'vo-
cabularies' and competing 'stories.' The center of the self – a center that is both inside and outside – is the story of Jesus Christ, which has become the story of the self. More precisely, the
center is Jesus Christ crucified and resurrected who has become part and parcel of the very structure of the self" (70). This story and this center is open, it cannot be seen as a closure of the quest
for the human being's identity.

[463] Cf. e.g., Irenaeus and James R. Payton, *Irenaeus on the Christian faith: a condensation of
Against heresies* (Eugene, Or.: Pickwick Publications, 2011), III,18,7.

- Thus, understanding oneself as an image of God means that human identity is perceived as not yet fulfilled and that it contains an element of futurity that humans are directed towards in faith, hope, and love. Hence, human identity is not yet realized but is present in the human desire to become a self by means of participating in the world in practices shaped by faith, hope, and love. To become a mature human being is accordingly also to be able to recognize oneself as an unfinished project, and as someone who is related to others and to God in order to be able to grow further toward this destiny.

- In relation to other humans and to the world, human beings are called to represent and manifest God's care, goodness, and love, while at the same time recognize them be carriers of God's gifts to me. Thus, to recognize the image of God in oneself and in others is a way of realizing our common destiny as human beings, which is to *represent* God in the world.

When we relate to our future and see ourselves in a not yet fulfilled destiny, and realize that it cannot be wholly appropriated or fulfilled at present, this attitude safeguards the possibility of living here and now in a way that recognizes the vulnerability of both others and oneself. Humans are not perfect, and to realize this is to be confronted with the vulnerability that is given with the fact that we are dependent upon others, live exposed to the power of others, and have a responsibility for them as well. This is one of the reasons why love and the safeguarding function that love has are so important in human life.

Love is not blind. Love provides us with the opportunity to see ourselves as human beings in our distinct otherness – from different centers and perspectives – and in a way that still recognizes how we are related to other living beings, are dependent on them, and partake in evolutionary history with them. It is only against this background that we can interpret our experience of what it means to be human, harboring love, desire, and the struggle to become a self and find our own identity by means of faith, hope, and love. Who we are is not based on what we already have in our possession, but on what we still are to become and what we relate to in our desire. Desire and the vulnerability that is open to transformation are the very embodied manifestations of God's future in us.

When Paul Tillich in *Love, power, and justice*[464] places together three elements that are not usually considered in the same category, he makes visible

---

[464] Paul Tillich, *Love, Power, and Justice; Ontological Analyses and Ethical Applications* (New York,: Oxford University Press, 1954).

that they all are *relational categories* that presuppose that individuals exist in relation to each other. None of these phenomena can be realized without relation. Moreover, neither of them exists without being practiced. All three are dependent on more than the individual in order to become manifest: they all point the individual beyond himself or herself and toward some types of practices. Love enables humans to participate in the world in a manner that is shaped by something other than just a detached or distanced attitude. It involves our *being as relational,* which means that life can flourish, and new opportunities *can be revealed,* which the self does not possess in himself or herself. This is why the first-person perspective is so crucial for understanding and articulating a religious mode of being in the world. Tillich points to the profound theological implication of this point when he connects love and life: "Life is being in actuality, and love is the moving power of life. In these two sentences, the ontological nature of love is expressed. They say that being is not actual without the love which drives everything that is towards everything else that is. In man's experience of love, the nature of life becomes manifest. Love is the drive towards the unity of the separated."[465] A better way to state how religion aims at uniting God and the human being is hard to find.

Tillich's analysis of the role of love in human life thus points toward the participatory character of love, in which, by love, one relates to and involves the loved one in a relationship with oneself that makes oneself become more and other than what we are as individuals. If we link this feature to the understanding of God as love, we might say that, in instances of love, the human participates in the reality of God and that something about God is thus revealed when love takes place. To become human – and to be an image of God; that is, display who God is and be a witness about God – is something that is realized in human reality when love is present. Tillich points to the relationship between love and true self-realization when he writes that the ultimate form of self-fulfillment is found in the reunion of the personal self with the God who is the "principle of participation as well as the principle of individualization."[466]

Furthermore, Tillich's understanding of the dynamics of life as striving for both unity and individualization identifies the conditions for being able to talk about *participation* at all. This dynamic is not driving toward a narcissistic replication of one's world, but toward an *extension* of one's world by participating

---

[465] Ibid., 25.
[466] Tillich, *Systematic Theology* (London: SCM, 1978), Vol 1, 245.

in and uniting with something beyond oneself. Hence, it marks an *open mode of desire.*

Emergence as the condition for agency manifesting faith, hope, and love

Because faith, hope, and love are the basic elements in human life that embody the human relation to God in specific practices, these elements must be offered chances to develop. Then, they also provide new conditions for agency: they open up to visions of and attitudes towards the world and of the relations that are not bound to the present and what is immediately in front of us. They motivate and orient agency in new ways and, thereby, enable transformations of the present.

As already indicated, faith, hope, and love are characterized by how they point the individual beyond himself or herself, and by how they reveal elements in the world of the individual that are not solely under his or her control. They involve risk, vulnerability, and chances of failure. But they also mean that something new and unprecedented can take place, given that love or hope is realized.

Human agency based on faith, hope, and love is not the result of human capacities only, but of specific human *responses* to experiences of and engagements with the world. It is the result of specific forms of participation with the world that go beyond what the individual can produce by himself or herself.[467] Such response is due to how love spontaneously shapes a mode of being in the world in which faith and hope can emerge. This mode does not emerge out of human decision alone, or as a result of mere will. It is conditioned by how the world as the object of love presents itself. Theologically speaking, when God is love, God is the basic condition of the human experiences of love. In such instances, God is not only revealed in this way, but also reveals the world's possibilities through faith, hope, and love.

We can understand the revealing character of faith, hope, and love more fully from the point of view of emergence theory. One version of this theory implies that what emerges, in reality, cannot be reduced fully to earlier components and causes and must instead be seen in the light of higher elements and the wholeness of a wider development/context. From a theological perspective, this approach has the following implications:

---

[467] Cf. Paul S. Fiddes, *Participating in God : A Pastoral Doctrine of the Trinity* (London: Darton Longman & Todd, 2000).

When God reveals Godself to humans in and by their participation in love, power, and justice, God does so in a way that affects the whole human person. This includes and is conditional upon human agency. Such agency is related to all dimensions of human life: the psychological, emotional, cognitive, embodied, and reflective. When Paul Fiddes considers mind-body dualism to be one of the problems regarding how we conceive of God's agency, he addresses positions that "are content to speak about God's loving persuasion in the human consciousness,"[468] and in the subjective expertise of wisdom, but which can nevertheless only conceive of God's action within physical matter as purely unilateral. However, such dualism ignores how human beings are psychosomatic unities involved in their environment; or, in other words, are conditioned by the reality in which they participate. Accordingly, it makes no sense to make a strong distinction between mind and body: "If the mind is not separable from the physical substratum of the brain [...] and the physical brain is embedded in the materiality of the world, then we cannot have any duality in the activity of God."[469] Thereby, Fiddes points to how part and whole are related in human reality in a manner that also opens up to a wider theological interpretation of God's agency:

If we are to conceive God's action in and through human wisdom as persuasive, then we must also perceive God as working in this way within the whole of nature, guiding it patiently, offering innovation through the influence of the Holy Spirit and calling out response from it. In the world as an organic community, all its members work together, affecting each other. If the human mind can respond to God, then it is not unreasonable to think that there must be something at least akin to response to God at all levels of creation, some 'family-likeness' within the cosmos.[470]

Fiddes connects this way of thinking to both process theology and to ideas about "top-down" influence of holistic causation on complex systems; for example, when larger social systems help to shape altruism in a species.[471] It is possible to link this idea to a way of thinking that allows for an approach to nature, where one still can think of God as active. The model for this is found in the emergence theory developed by Philip Clayton.

Emergence implies that we can distinguish between different levels of reality, where a level 1 (L1) phenomenon is prior in natural history to what takes place at level 2 (L2), and one cannot understand what takes place on L2 unless

---

[468] Fiddes, *Seeing the World and Knowing God : Hebrew Wisdom and Christian Doctrine in a Late-Modern Context*, 163.
[469] Ibid.
[470] Ibid.
[471] Ibid., 164.

something prior happens at L1. L2 can be seen as the result of the development of complexity in L1. However, what happens at L1 is not in itself enough to predict in detail what qualities L2 will have, be it "(i) the precise nature of these qualities, (ii) the rules that govern their interaction (or their phenomenological patterns), or (iii) the sorts of emergent levels to which they may give rise in due course." Furthermore, L2 is not reducible to L1 in any of the standard senses of 'reduction.' The most important element in Clayton's proposal about emergence is his claim that what happens at L2 may also have some effect on what happens at level 1.[472] Therefore, Clayton is able to propose what I have referred to above as downward causation. He writes:

In some cases, phenomena at L2 exercise a causal effect on L1 which is not reducible to an L1 causal history. This causal non-reducibility is not just epistemic, in the sense that we can't tell the L1 causal story but (say) God could. It is ontological: the world is such that it produces systems whose emergent properties exercise their own distinct causal influences on each other and on (at least) the next lower level in the hierarchy. If we accept the intuitive principle that ontology should follow agency, then cases of emergent causal agency justify us in speaking of emergent objects (organisms, agents) in natural history. Emergent properties are new features of existing objects (e.g., conductivity is a property of electrons assembled under certain conditions); emergent objects become centers of agency on their own behalf (cells and organisms may be composed of smaller particles, but they are also the objects of scientific explanation in their own right).[473]

Although it may seem strange at first, the theory about emergence is not only a way of explaining why we can speak about two aspects of (natural) reality without having to end up in a mind-body dualist position. The theory also enables us to see the development of the human community and the shared visions of what this community can accomplish through shared practices, as something that is the result of human natural history, without having to see that all such practices are the result of evolutionary principles (at L1). Instead, we can see such practices as results of emergence processes that surely build on such processes, but not as fully determined by them.

If we now look at practices of faith, hope, and love from this perspective, it is evident that such practices cannot be seen as the result of individual components at L1 in evolution. Instead, they must be seen as the result of how humans have been able to evolve and develop ways of being in the world that display emergent properties compared to those determined by evolution. This,

---

[472] Philip Clayton, *Mind and Emergence : From Quantum to Consciousness* (Oxford England ; New York: Oxford University Press, 2004), 61.
[473] Ibid., 61–62.

in turn, may also explain why such elements as faith, hope, and love can appear meaningful even when they do not serve, or even when they contradict, evolutionary purposes such as fitness. The unfinished character of human evolution thus manifests itself at all levels, as does the potential realizations of God's love. They cannot be reduced to conditions at the initial stages of evolution.

Emergence also suggests that wholeness is more than what can be determined and delineated by individual parts, and as caused by them; this may also shed light on how we have to see the feature of love as more than single factors. At the stage in human history where love enters into human practices, human agency finds a new mode of being, not only in motivational terms, but also in terms of how one orients the development of knowledge, relates to and interprets history, and develops visions about transformation and perceives one's potential for future agency in general.

The emergence of this appearance (or revelation) of love in human history makes it possible to see instances of love as displaying a type of power other than that which is present in the mechanisms of evolutionary history. Humans may experience that, through glimpses of love, they participate more intensively in the fullness of God, who is love. By revealing God, these glimpses may also shape new and different conditions for human agency, just as social practices cannot be reduced to one single component. However, given that this capacity for practicing, experiencing, and making love is emergent, it cannot be reduced to either a physical or a mental state only. Hence, the way God influences human agency when it comes to practicing faith, hope, and love is not either mental or physical. Given that the reality in which God works is one, we can also see God's work to promote such agency as something that displays the unity of God's own agency in reality: where humans practice faith, hope, and love, God is at work and performs God's own agency in the world. Thus, through faith, hope, and love, God participates in the human reality and reveals Godself just as much as humans participate in the reality of God and experience (albeit in a finite manner) what God is. As Arthur Peacocke writes, "God is best conceived as the circumambient Reality enclosing all existing entities, structures, and processes; and as operating in and through all while being more than all. Hence, all that is not God has its existence within God's operation and being. The infinity of God includes all other finite entities, structures, and processes – God's infinity comprehends and incorporates *all*."[474]

---

[474] A. Peacocke, "Sciences of Complexity: New Theological Resource?" in P. C. W. Davies and Niels Henrik Gregersen, *Information and the Nature of Reality : From Physics to Metaphysics* (Cambridge, UK ; New York: Cambridge University Press, 2010), 262.

Hence, we return here to the panentheist approach to God's agency that was described in the previous chapter. This approach implies that there is no place "outside" God where something exists. One of the main advantages of this way of understanding God's agency is that it does not imply that God intervenes from the "outside" or "sets aside" natural laws or processes. Instead, it allows us to see that God is working in, with, and under the reality that God has created. God creates dynamically and continuously in response to the development and the response of God's creation. This claim entails that there is risk and vulnerability involved in God's creative work. God is the *immanent* creator who works in and through the processes of the natural order. However, Peacocke is clear that this does not mean that the processes are themselves God. They are the *action of* God-as-creator.[475] Therefore, we do not need to take on the conception of an interventionist God.

Human intentions and purposes seem to transcend our bodies, despite the fact that they are intrinsically related to our brains and can only be performed through our bodies. This gives a holistic understanding of human agency where the embodied character of such agency cannot be ignored. Accordingly, agency has an immanent and a transcending element, both of which are deeply connected to the embodied character of human life. Peacocke holds that this understanding of agency has implications for how one understands God's relation to the world. As *internally* present to all of its entities, structures, and processes, God is related to the world in a way analogous to how humans are related to their bodies.[476] However, as is evident from the above, I argue that there is more than just a mere analogy here when it comes to an understanding of how God acts in order to reveal Godself: it is in a way that conditions human agency in specific practices that God acts in this world, in ways that reveal Godself. This is perhaps most evident in how God was revealed in the life of Jesus Christ.

Divine agency as human practice: Relation and participation

Through practices of faith, such as reading the Bible, listening to sermons, and caring for the poor, humans may be partaking in the reality of God and become inspired by God's spirit. These practices do not need to be considered as a kind of supernatural *extra* but should rather be seen as opportunities in which God enhances the capabilities that belong to the created world. These capabilities are now seen in a new light, due to the possibilities for agency that present

---

[475] Ibid., 259–260.
[476] Ibid., 263.

themselves through such practices; possibilities that could not be produced by the conditions for human agency determined by either evolutionary mechanisms or by conditions restricted by human sin. These capabilities are opened up by faith.[477]

Faith means participation because faith allows humans to relate to and take part in God's intentions for the world. Participation is a key element in our relation to the world, from a religious point of view. This notion enables us to see our relationship from perspectives other than those that see our relation to the world only in *instrumental terms,* as something we relate to only in order to, by our actions, achieve external goals. Faith enables and enhances participatory practices. A suitable definition of practices that can deepen our understanding of these has been presented by Alasdair MacIntyre:

By a 'practice' I [...] mean any coherent and complex form of socially established cooperative human activity through which goods internal to that form of activity are realized in the course of trying to achieve those standards of excellence which are appropriate to, and partially definitive of, that form of activity, with the result that human powers to achieve excellence, and human conceptions of the ends and goods involved, are systematically extended.[478]

The *internal* goods of religious practices are faith, hope, and love, exactly because they enable participation. It is in these practices that God reveals Godself – and his purpose for the world. We do not love in order to achieve something external to the loving relationship. Accordingly, theology has always criticized instrumental approaches to faith, hope, and love, as such approaches destroy their character as religious virtues. This approach also implies that to engage in faith, hope, and love in order to overcome the challenging dimensions of vulnerability is mistaken. One does not believe in order to get saved, but because one is saved by the grace of God. My faith rests on what God does, not in what my faith can achieve for me of external goods. Likewise, I hope not in order to get something for myself, but in order to participate in a community where justice rules and where goodness flourishes among all creatures. And I do not love

---

[477] Cf. Schwöbel, "Divine Agency and Providence," 239. He also wrote aptly about such inspiration: "If God is the one who inspires the believer, the freedom of the believer is in no way denied or destroyed. God does not coerce human beings to obey his commands; nor does he use us as impersonal instruments for achieving his hidden purposes. Rather, he opens up new possibilities for us which we can realize by using our own personal finite freedom." Ibid., 239.

[478] Alasdair C. MacIntyre, *After Virtue : A Study in Moral Theory*, 2nd ed. (Notre Dame, Ind.: University of Notre Dame Press, 1984), 187. Some of the paragraphs in the following are reworkings of a more comprehensive analysis in my *Christianity as Distinct Practices* (London: T&T Clark, 2019).

in order to get something in return, but in order to participate in a loving relationship, which may also fulfill my internal goal of being the human being I am called to be.

We can deepen and expand this idea of the internal goods of practices through which God can reveal Godself through our agency if we add to MacIntyre's understanding of practices some perspectives from social practice theory. This approach makes it possible to see further relevance of the emergentist perspective presented above. A practice is socially and culturally conditioned, and accordingly, it cannot be seen as merely the result of evolutionary mechanisms. Thus, from a theological point of view, evolution had to take a specific turn and allow for the emergence of social and cultural capacities that are not reducible to such mechanisms. The next step is to see how such cultural and social conditions may enable practices in which God can reveal Godself. It is exactly these social practices that can be most clearly identified as contributing to such revelation.

Andreas Reckwitz' analysis of social practices allows for a profound understanding of what I have called participation from a theological perspective. For him, the social dimension in human life is constituted by practices. Thus, he avoids approaches that identify the condition for the social in mental qualities, in discourse or in interaction. Instead, he sees "social practices" as the smallest unit for understanding the social. Hence, it is crucially important to develop a definition of 'practice' that can open the notion of human participation in the world and in God. His understanding of social practice meets this requirement, I argue: "A 'practice' (*Praktik*) is a routinized type of behavior which consists of several elements, interconnected to one another: forms of bodily activities, forms of mental activities, 'things' and their use, a background knowledge in the form of understanding, know-how, states of emotion and motivational knowledge."[479] Reckwitz' understanding of practice implies three things that are important for the present treatise. The first is that every practice is a "block" consisting of different elements. No practice can be reduced to a single one of these elements.[480] Thus, practices are irreducible to specific, evolved elements that can be identified as their causes. Second, Reckwitz sees a practice as a pattern that can be filled with a multitude of single and often unique actions that do not always need to be coordinated with each other. As Reckwitz writes, "Thus, she or he is not only a carrier of patterns of bodily

---

[479] See Andreas Reckwitz, "Toward a Theory of Social Practices: A Development in Culturalist Theorizing," *European Journal of Social Theory* 5, no. 2 (2002), 249.
[480] Ibid., 250.

behavior, but also of routinized ways of understanding, knowing how, and desiring."[481] He sees these routinized, mental activities as being "necessary elements and qualities of a practice *in which the individual participates*, not qualities *of* the individual."[482] Hence these elements manifest themselves in the individual when he or she participates in the actual practice. They are not solely the result of the individual agency but point beyond it.

The theological implications of this understanding of practice become obvious when we consider the ways in which people act on the basis of faith, hope, and love. My argument rests on the fact that faith, hope, and love are only accessible as related to practices or as internal to *modes of practice*, and that it makes little or no sense to speak of them as manifesting themselves apart from specific practices.

As for the *composite* character of practices that blocks their reduction to one or a few components, it is clear that faith, hope, and love cannot be reduced to a single component: they all have motivational, orientational, and practical implications. We act on faith and hope, as well as on love. All three elements imply some type of bodily activity and an emotional component: there is no love that is not related to some kind of bodily activity (even if it is only a gaze or a small gesture), just as there is no hope or no faith that does not direct us towards something outside ourselves. However, the irreducible character of such practices to one single component is evidence for the relevance for a practice-oriented interpretation of these. By participating in such practices, humans participate in something that transcends their individual competencies and abilities – as the desires, knowledge, and other elements required for a practice are something they must acquire by learning from others. A practice opens up to different dimensions of human experience, and to processes of learning that can expand the range and potential of human agency. As contexts for learning, religions can thereby also be seen as places where practices not only take place, but also where one may learn more about *how to practice* faith, hope, and love. Furthermore, it almost goes without saying that practices of faith, hope, and love can be carried out in a multitude of different ways. It is not predetermined how and who one loves, what one hopes for, or how one lives one's faith. There-

---

[481] Ibid.
[482] Ibid. My italics.

fore, what was previously said about religions as providing resources for orientation and transformation may here be specified further, as they provide and expand the repertoires of learning practices.[483]

A human being can be a carrier of different practices, which are often not coordinated with each other. This is also apparent in how believers may not always be consistent when it comes to the relation between their faith and other things they practice. Reckwitz points to a reason for why this may be the case: Humans are involved in different projects – some are selfish, some are not; some are oriented by faith and love, whereas some are short-sighted and instrumental. The theological implication of this point is that even though one might say that the reality of God is revealed in practices of faith, hope, and love, human practices may still, in total, display ambiguity and inconsistency, which makes such revelation far from obvious.

Preliminary conclusion

Humans realize God's intentions by freely appropriating, and thereby also participating in, the reality of God as they engage in practices of faith hope and love that shape their desire and vulnerability. Thus, they realize what it means to be created in the divine image. A full realization of this participation requires that humans recognize God as the condition for their own agency. Nevertheless, in cases where such recognition is lacking, people may still realize some of God's aims when they perform actions of love and care, provide comfort, and offer reasons for hope. Then, they are still conditioned by God's creative work for creation, even though they do not recognize it. However, because faith opens up the full relationship between God and humans, we can say that it is in faith, hope, and love that God's agency for humankind is most fully realized, and so in ways that also allows human beings to fulfill their calling and destiny to be and become an image of God.

The conditions for human agency, and therefore also for God revealing Godself in human reality, in experience, and participatory practices, are the result of processes that enable humans to become embodied agents. Humans are the result of an interplay of different elements that can only be interpreted as the result of unfinished historical processes. History is the realm in which God realizes Godself through human agency. This approach allows us to see God as the creator who allows the emergence of forms of life that reveal God in ways

---

[483] Cf. Geir Afdal, *Religion som bevegelse: Læring, kunnskap og mediering* (Oslo: Universitetsforlaget, 2013).

that are less ambiguous and more clearly shaped by love and care than what would be the case at earlier stages of evolution. Thus, all God's actions in order to manifest Godself as love is the result of the many and diverse actions and practices that God has allowed to emerge, both in the totality of creation and through human agency.

Practicing the divine image: Forgiveness as transformation

Human life is vulnerable and often in need of healing. Healing can happen through forgiveness. However, sometimes, it may not. Therefore, we need to consider to what extent forgiveness is a transformative practice that relates to the consequences of hurtful human agency in a positive way, and in what way it may contribute to simply perpetuating the hurt. For many, forgiveness is among the central virtues in religion, and therefore also the model transformative practice of religion. This is also the case in Christianity. However, forgiveness is a complicated topic – and the Christian tradition contributes to the never-ending task of keeping it open for discussion by addressing the diversity of the challenges it raises. It is a topic that calls for nuances, clarifications, and careful considerations. Moreover, it is not at all clear what forgiveness implies, and what conditions are the best for its practice.

Against the backdrop of the previous sections of this chapter, one can argue that the approach to forgiveness as a transformative practice can take its point of departure in the following considerations: Prior to us becoming human beings with transparent conditions for agency, we take part in a reality not determined by ourselves. The most obvious example of this is how we are born into a community and into relationships with others. It is the others who determine our further development and shape the conditions on which we will subsequently lead our lives. The presence or absence of love, power, justice, affirmation, recognition, and safeguarding point to elements in a community that will affect and determine the shape of our desires and our experience of vulnerability. Against the backdrop of the existence of this realm that goes beyond the individual, it makes sense to talk about forgiveness. The reason is simple: forgiveness is about the restitution of relationships and life-conditions, in some form or other. Although only individuals can practice forgiveness, it is about living with others in a community where the vulnerable character of life is recognized. One of the initial conditions for forgiveness is that it entails the recognition of vulnerability in oneself *and* others.

To speak of forgiveness as a practice along the lines suggested by Reckwitz above means that we can see forgiveness as possible to practice in a multitude of ways. How and when it is done cannot be prescribed beforehand and in detail but is conditioned by various situational factors. This makes it an elusive phenomenon, as most writers attest to. Moreover, from a Christian point of view, this practice emerges out of faith and hope that practicing forgiveness will cause something good (although this outcome is never guaranteed), as well as sometimes love (for oneself, and/or for the one who is forgiven). It is probably not recommendable to practice forgiveness if it cannot be linked to any hope for the good. Forgiveness need not be dependent on love for another, but as we shall see, it may entail, at least occasionally, that one can face the other with some degree of empathy.

Despite its central place in many religious traditions, forgiveness is nevertheless not a religious virtue or a specifically religious phenomenon. However, when practiced, it can engage our relationship with the ultimate conditions for our lives: it can help overcome some of the destructive features of life and connect us to the fundamental conditions for future flourishing. Anthony Bash formulates it well, in saying that, "On pragmatic grounds, one can infer that those who experience forgiveness will often be better able to forgive others; one can also say that forgiveness multiplies forgiveness. When forgiveness is not a moral ideal of human behaviour, revenge, retaliation, anger and bitterness are the principal alternatives, together with the destructive personal and social consequences that they bring."[484] To speak about forgiveness as a moral aim, as Bash does here, suggests that this aim is not possible to relate to all situations and circumstances, but must be considered under specific conditions. It is therefore important to distinguish forgiveness as a moral aim from seeing it as a moral duty.[485] Relating to what was just said about the practice of forgiveness as conditioned by the hope for the good, we can say that *forgiveness aims to open the future which has been denied in previous practices and has become impeded by destructive human activities.* With this aim in mind, we can assess some of the elements present in the comprehensive contemporary discourse on forgiveness, and address its more ambiguous features, as well. The aim is not

---

[484] Anthony Bash, *Forgiveness and Christian Ethics*, New Studies in Christian Ethics (Cambridge, UK ; New York: Cambridge University Press, 2007), 100.
[485] "Forgiveness is not a duty but goes beyond duty, as a free gift to the off ender. It is to be distinguished from forgetting, denying, condoning, and excusing." Eve Garrard and David McNaughton, *Forgiveness* (Durham: Acumen, 2010), 70.

to comment on all of this discussion, but to disclose how forgiveness as a transformative practice can be related to living as the divine image.[486]

Forgiveness: Fundamental considerations for theological discourse

Biblical material displays God as forgiving, and the ideal of forgiveness as the
alternative to a culture in which retaliation was legitimized theologically.[487]
This fact immediately sparks the question: Should human beings who want to
live and practice the calling to be the image of God emulate God in this regard?
Not without reserve, it seems. There are important differences between God and
humans. If we, as suggested in the previous chapter, understand the "essence"
of God as love, it means that God continuously struggles to shape the world
according to God's love. This cannot be done unless God relates to humans in
love. For God, forgiveness is a way to offer human beings new chances to live
in love and to practice the divine image. However, as we will see shortly, on
the side of humans, forgiveness is related to conditions in their identity and life
story that complicate practicing forgiveness unconditionally. Moreover, "to experience God's forgiveness, human beings must seek forgiveness and respond
to God's grace. In other words, they must seek the gift in the way that God will
give it."[488] To seek God's forgiveness presupposes faith in God and God's
grace. It also implies that one is already related to God as the ultimate source
for life, and as love. This relationship with God contributes to the transformation of the self that seeks forgiveness. Thus, the subject who forgives here
(God) appears as fundamentally different from the human who is asked to forgive, and for whom the relationship is shaped very differently. Hence, "the reasons God might have to forgive sinners aren't the same as the reasons we humans might have to forgive wrongdoers."[489]

Furthermore, some important traits in connection to God and forgiveness
are important to note from the outset:

---

[486] To qualify all conditions for when forgiveness and mercy can be practiced in a way that has
a positive outcome for all involved parties, is a larger task than what I aim for in this section. My
main aim here is to relate the practice of forgiveness to some of the features discussed in previous
sections, and not to deal with all of the psychological and other conditions that one has to bear
in mind. For the complexities of the emotional and juridical elements involved, see Jeffrie G.
Murphy and Jean Hampton, *Forgiveness and Mercy*, Cambridge Studies in Philosophy and Law
(Cambridge ; New York: Cambridge University Press, 1988); Bash, *Forgiveness and Christian
Ethics.*
[487] For a detailed account of the New Testament material on forgiveness, see Bash, *Forgiveness
and Christian Ethics*, Chapter 5.
[488] Ibid., 106.
[489] Garrard, *Forgiveness*, viii.

a) That God forgives does not mean that God ignores the question of justice. This is mirrored in how one must recognize the limited character of human
forgiveness. The latter "does not – and cannot – undo the past or free people
both from the consequences of what they have done and from what [Hannah]
Arendt calls "the predicament of irreversibility." Human forgiveness and the
process of which it is part do not exculpate the wrongdoer.[490] Accordingly, forgiveness is not the opposite of justice, or in contradiction to it. Instead, it is,
under given circumstances, an alternative to the perpetuation of conflict, as it
implies that retaliation and vengeance are not the only ways to deal with injustice, harm, and hurt.

b) God's forgiving always means that the forgiven is given a new chance
to live according to the ultimate conditions of love and justice.

c) Even though the biblical material suggests that humans should not set
any numerical limits to how often one should forgive someone, nothing in it
suggests that everything can be forgiven or should be unconditionally forgiven.
E.g., the spilling of the blood of innocents is something that God is depicted as
not willing to forgive (cf. 2. Kings, 24:4). The Bible presents no demand to
forgive those who kill children or push them into the gas chambers. Forgiveness
seems to be primarily a moral ideal for how to go about with those whom we
will have to live with as our equals in the future. "The New Testament docu-
ments do not insist that there is a Christian moral duty to forgive."[491]

d) In the New Testament, forgiveness is addressed in a context where it is
acknowledged that all human beings have trespassed against each other. The
realization that oneself is subject to the need for forgiveness, and God as willing
to forgive, motivates the exhortation to forgive. When Jesus explains the Lord's
prayer and says that God will forgive if we forgive (Matt 6:14–15), this seems
to place forgiveness in a context of relative symmetry among humans. It must
be assessed against the goal it is meant to achieve: the restoration of human
relationships without resentment or grudge, which can only happen in the context of relative symmetry.

e) Hence, the Lord's prayer, as well as Jesus' words that we should forgive
those who trespass against us, presents human beings with the constant challenge to consider the transformative practice of forgiveness as a possibility that
can reshape human relationships.

---

[490] Bash, *Forgiveness and Christian Ethics*, 168.
[491] Ibid., 104.

f) Forgiveness must be considered being a moral virtue or a moral aim, but not a moral duty. Consequently, the wrongdoer has no right to be forgiven. Forgiveness cannot be earned.[492] But as with all virtues, it requires contextual considerations in order to determine its adequacy.

g) Forgiveness cannot be the result of a demand or simply be an instrument for other purposes. "The biblical story does not recommend or display forgiveness as being of primarily therapeutic value for the victim who forgives, but rather as being the generous and loving response to the recovery of a person and a relationship that had been thought to be dead."[493] This point echoes my comments above about the possible restoration of relationships as an aim.

A careful reading of biblical material that takes the points here listed into account, must realize that symmetrical relationships are not always the case, that forgiveness does not imply acceptance or condoning of injustice, and that there is no suggestion that everything can or should be forgiven unconditionally. Forgiveness must therefore primarily be considered as a composite practice, in which one, a) relates to oneself as a person in relationship with others and under self-examination in order to avoid being or becoming sanctimonious, and b) to be open to the other person who asks for forgiveness, in order to establish new and better conditions for future relationships in community with him/her. Furthermore, c) to ask forgiveness from God presupposes entering into a transformative relationship in which God's love is considered as the ultimate condition for one's love, and this may motivate and shape the desire to be forgiving towards others.

Forgiveness means taking personal responsibility for the future of a community that shares life. Forgiveness cannot be practiced by anyone else than persons, individuals. An institution cannot forgive, and only a person can be forgiven. This is due to forgiveness as a moral response to wrongdoing. Moreover, this fact does not mean that forgiveness is easily delineated, or only takes place in an event or through a speech-act that says, "I forgive you." It is not necessarily the endpoint of a process.[494]

---

[492] Cf. Ibid., 103.

[493] Garrard, *Forgiveness*, 16. In the following, I ignore the topic of therapeutic consequences of forgiveness, because they are ambiguous, and it follows from this that the recommendation to forgive with this aim in mind may at best achieve its goal, but it may also lead to more pain and more difficult relationships. Cf. Ibid., 29–32, and Christiane Sanderson, "The Role of Forgiveness after Interpersonal Abuse – Danger or Road to Recovery and Healing?," in *Forgiveness in Practice*, ed. Stephen Hance (London ; Philadelphia: Jessica Kingsley Publishers, 2019).

[494] Cf. Bash, *Forgiveness and Christian Ethics*, 166.

At the concrete level, practicing forgiveness is thus about establishing a more symmetrical relationship outside the parameters of power. According to A. Bash, this is exemplified when Jesus forgives those who offend him. This practice is non-retaliatory and not vindictive and marks a contrast to those who are unforgiving and seek revenge. Bash claims that this contrast or difference has to do with power. To be *unforgiving* expresses a wish to exercise power over the offender. It seeks retribution and emerges out of the desire to redress "the sense of powerlessness that the wronged person may feel. It is also a way to restore the imbalance in the power relation between wrongdoer and victim: the wrongdoer abused the victim, and so the victim, to 'get even,' exacts revenge or retribution."[495] Forgiveness breaks this circle of wrong and retribution and establishes another set of conditions – conditions that may seem impossible only from the perspective of the situation thus far.[496] It is against this backdrop that forgiveness in Jesus' parables can appear as "a gift to the undeserving, often of unimaginable generosity."[497]

The goal of achieving symmetry and still maintain some type of undeserved gift-character for forgiveness can nevertheless be problematized. Derrida, who will be treated more extensively below, emphasizes the tension between unconditional and conditional forgiveness to the extent that he makes the first almost impossible to practice. He does this by a discussion of Vladimir Jankelevitch's complaint that the Germans responsible for the Holocaust failed to ask for forgiveness because they did not admit their crimes. Derrida's response is that had they done so, the forgiveness offered would not have been "pure," i.e., unconditioned. His valid point here is that if forgiveness is a matter of exchange of attitudes, then withholding forgiveness is, in this case, an adequate response.[498] As Paul Fiddes points to, "even if forgiveness had been asked for, no request could restore symmetry or equilibrium after horrendous evil."[499] Some cases exclude the possibility of (re-)establishing symmetry. However, Derrida sees forgiveness primarily from the perspective of a *gift* (which must be unconditional in order to be a gift), and it causes him to interpret it from another context than the one of exchange or reciprocation. There is an absolute contrast between

---

[495] Ibid., 93.

[496] For more on forgiveness and the impossible, see the next sub-section, on Derrida.

[497] Bash, *Forgiveness and Christian Ethics*, 94.

[498] Jacques Derrida, *On Cosmopolitanism and Forgiveness*, Thinking in Action (London ; New York: Routledge, 2001), 34–37.

[499] Paul S. Fiddes, "Memory, Forgetting and the Problem of Forgiveness. Reflecting on Volf, Derrida and Ricoeur," in *Forgiving and Forgetting : Theology and the Margins of Soteriology*, ed. Hartmut von Sass, Zachhuber, Johannes (Tübingen: Mohr Siebeck, 2015), 123.

the "demand for the *unconditional*, gracious, infinite, aneconomic forgiveness granted to the guilty as guilty, without counterpart, even to those who do not repent or ask forgiveness, and on the other side [...] a conditional forgiveness proportionate to the recognition of the fault, to repentance, to the transformation of the sinner who then explicitly asks for forgiveness."[500] In setting up this contrast, Derrida exemplifies a tension that runs through much of the discussion about forgiveness, between understanding it from the point of view of an absolute or ultimate demand on the one hand, and from the point of view of conditional circumstances on the other hand. However, there is no reason why a gift needs to be totally unconditional. It is possible to offer a gift without it being conditioned by a request from some other.

Forgiveness, symmetry, and justice

To some, the practice of forgiveness may seem morally offensive. This reaction makes it important to underscore that practicing forgiveness in many cases is most wisely done in a context shaped by relative symmetry and justice. It is only in such a context that forgiveness appears as a truly transformative practice. The main reasons for this point are as follows:

Forgiveness needs to be coupled with justice in order to acknowledge the truth of what happened to the victim; and hence, to recognize the hurt inflicted on her. This prevents the practice of forgiveness to do no further harm to victims. Furthermore, it prevents pressure for victims to respond in ways they find unacceptable. The context of justice also makes possible the instigation of a new status for the one who was a victim – and establishes for them a new identity in which victimhood is taken off their shoulders. This is important in order to allow them to move on from the offense without permanent psychological damage; although "it should also recognize that 'moving on' is sometimes morally inappropriate, and that resistance to this needn't be either psychologically or morally pathological."[501] When practiced in this way, forgiveness can re-establish the victim's self-respect. Justice manifests the equality and "the recognition that all of us are worthy of respect for the individual persons that we are. Just as we should show respect to others, so they should show respect to us. Where offenders fail to do so, the fault is in them, not in their victims."[502]

---

[500] Derrida, *On Cosmopolitanism and Forgiveness*, 34.
[501] Garrard, *Forgiveness*, 46.
[502] Ibid., 101.

Hence, justice manifests a fundamental symmetry, even when this is not recognized by perpetrators. In a legal system, perpetrators are offered the chance to express this recognition, which was denied by them in the carrying out of the offense. Such recognition may establish new chances for forgiveness.

Forgiveness does not necessarily entail reconciliation. This point seems to have been overlooked in the practice of the *Truth and Reconciliation Commission* that we look further into below. The most obvious example of this is how people who have been subjected to abuse can forgive their perpetrators but refuse to continue any type of relationship with them. Forgiveness, furthermore, and concomitantly, needs not to imply forgetting, and therefore, the presence of the perpetrator may cause pain, still. "Even where there are no reasons of prudence to block reconciliation, it may still be intrinsically inappropriate in the wake of certain crimes, even where forgiveness has taken place."[503]

Accordingly, "forgiveness won't involve either ignoring, or forgetting, what was done to the victim. When you forgive someone, you forgive them for something wrongful that they've done."[504] Forgiveness implies the awareness of the wrong done. If the wrong was not large, it might be forgotten in time, but this is not always, and cannot always be the case,[505] as we shall see in the example of Améry below. However, forgetting may be a dimension of the transformative power of forgiveness to "let go." But for large offenses, the transformative elements presuppose an awareness of it that neither ignores nor forgets because it will have such an impact on future life, even when forgiven.

This point is important to raise against Derrida's claim that forgiveness must be unconditional – and hence also not caused by any type of remembrance of what has happened. For him, forgiveness implies forgetting. Fiddes comments that "the absolute unconditionality not only of forgiveness but forgetting surely opens up danger for justice. In forgetting the act of forgiving, it seems that the object of forgiveness will be also forgotten." He goes on, writing that

Forgiveness is appropriate for radical evil, but it seems that memory of the atrocious crimes that have prompted this 'impossible forgiveness' is lost. If there were a response of repentance from the recipient, then the horrific acts committed would not be lost to memory; they would be present in the repentance and recalled in the reconciliation, even if the forgiver did not draw attention to them. In Derrida's view of absolute unconditionality, there seems to be an encouragement

---

[503] Ibid., 59.
[504] Ibid., 89.
[505] Ibid.

to forget the very historic events that should remain in the community's memory as a terrible warning.[506]

Because 'forgiveness' is an equivocal term, it is important to distinguish it from excusing someone for what they have done. Excusing reduces, "sometimes to nothing, the scope for forgiveness. If there's a full excuse for what the wrongdoer did, then he's not to blame for it. And if he isn't to blame, then there's nothing to forgive."[507] The excuse takes the wrong done out of the context of both forgiveness and justice. It has no transformative power similar to forgiveness as here delineated. It is, therefore, crucial to distinguish clearly forgiveness from condoning or excusing or wiping the slate clean.[508]

Garrard and McNaughton, on whom most of the reflections in this subsection are based, summarizes their approach to forgiveness in the following quote, which also underscores my initial point about the transformative power of forgiveness with respect to the future:

Forgiveness is hard. It has forms that are morally negligible or worse. But at its highest, it shows solidarity with our fellow humans; not when they're at their magnificent best, but when they're at their worst, tainted with evil and low in the dust. It's a strike in favour of love, for the worst of us as well as for the best: that is, for what any one of us might, or might have, become. The needs of victims, and solidarity with them, are always more important than solidarity with perpetrators. Nevertheless, we still have to decide what attitude to take to wrongdoers. Choosing to forgive them acknowledges the nature of what they've done, terrible as it sometimes is, but also remains open to hope for something better in the future: a hope that is often utterly disappointed, but which nonetheless returns again and again.[509]

Thus, forgiveness does not appear as easy to practice. Nevertheless, the reason why it is maintained as a moral ideal in many traditions is that it has demonstrated its transformative power. However, there are deep problems with approaching forgiveness as an unconditional phenomenon. This is perhaps most obvious in the current debate about Derrida's writing, which can be analyzed as pointing to elements that also recur repeatedly in some strands of religious

---

[506] Fiddes, "Memory, Forgetting and the Problem of Forgiveness. Reflecting on Volf, Derrida and Ricoeur," 126.

[507] Garrard, *Forgiveness*, 87–88.

[508] Cf. Ibid., 105. Derrida, on his part, also points to the need for there to be a shared language practice of forgiveness that entails "an agreement on the meanings of words, their connotations, rhetoric, the aim of a reference, etc." His argument for this is that "when the victim and the guilty share no language, when nothing common and universal permits them to understand one another, forgiveness seems deprived of meaning." He admits that this makes forgiveness hard, sometimes even impossible. (Derrida, *On Cosmopolitanism and Forgiveness*, 48).

[509] Ibid., 125.

discourse that advances forgiveness as an unconditional demand and as a gift. Derrida's analysis can thus offer further reasons for why it is so important to distinguish between divine and human forgiveness.

A difficult practice

When humans are on relatively equal terms, the chances for practicing forgiveness may not appear as absent, and the process towards it does not present us with insurmountable challenges – despite the fact that even in such circumstances, it can be difficult enough to forgive. However, the main discussion of forgiveness in the contemporary debate is about the times atrocities have been committed, or where people have had their lives destroyed by abuse, violence, or psychological terror to such an extent that any chance for repair or restoration of relationships seems impossible. These instances complicate the demand for the transformative practice of forgiveness considerably. In these instances, the relevance of vulnerability for this practice comes to the fore in a serious way.

We can elaborate the discussion of the complicated conditions for the transformative practice of forgiveness by addressing two positions advanced by contemporary philosophers: French-Algerian philosopher Jacques Derrida and Danish philosopher Thomas Brudholm.

Derrida can be criticized for making forgiveness impossible, and there are good reasons for this critique, as we shall see. The main point in introducing him here, however, is that he, more than most authors, points to how there must be an ultimate reference point for forgiveness, even when we discuss the conditions under which it can be practiced. Hence, Derrida contributes to deepening the discussion, and tacitly shows how it must be seen as related to the notion of ultimacy that makes religious approaches to it so powerful.

From what I have developed so far, forgiveness is understood properly as a gift, albeit an elusive gift. Bash can side with Derrida in claiming that "A naive and simplistic approach to forgiveness robs the concept of its moral richness and its transformative power. To engage with the complexity of forgiveness is to engage with an ideal that affects people – wrongdoers, victims and even onlookers – relationally, psychologically, morally and spiritually."[510] Derrida therefore also addresses elements of forgiveness as it is dealt with in the Judeo-Christian tradition.[511] A crucial element in his approach is that he

---

[510] Bash, *Forgiveness and Christian Ethics*, 186.
[511] Derrida, *On Cosmopolitanism and Forgiveness*.

introduces the already mentioned distinction between conditional and unconditional forgiveness,[512] and starts out his essay with the latter, of which he writes: "In principle, there is no limit to forgiveness, no *measure,* no moderation, no 'to what point?'"[513] Moreover, he points to how forgiveness appears in the public arena in a diversity of ways, making it an equivocal concept. Accordingly, it is "often confounded, often in a calculated fashion, with related themes: excuse, regret, amnesty, prescription, etc.; so many significations of which certain come under law, a penal law from which forgiveness must in principle remain heterogeneous and irreducible."[514] Derrida articulates a provocative proposition against this backdrop when he writes that if there is something to forgive, it should be the unforgivable. He formulates this aporia thus: "Forgiveness forgives only the unforgivable. One cannot, and should not forgive; there is only forgiveness, if there is any, where there is the unforgivable. That is to say that forgiveness must announce itself as impossibility itself. It can only be possible in doing the impossible."[515] How can we interpret this claim?

The point of view from where Derrida's radical claim must be interpreted is his insistence on the gift-character of forgiveness, which implies that there can be no conditions that make it possible to expect or assume that forgiveness can take place. It must be considered as impossible. Moreover, in insisting on forgiveness as only possible in the face of that which appears as unforgivable, Derrida seems to address the need to avoid understanding forgiveness as an excuse, as condoning, or similar attitudes. In his perceptive discussion of Derrida which I have already referred to above, Paul Fiddes comments that not only is "Derrida's view of unconditionality [...] undeniably extreme. For him, unconditionality does not just mean that forgiveness does not require evidence of repentance and transformation from the offender before offering forgiveness."[516] Hence, forgiveness cannot be determined or preceded by any response from the offender. "In Derrida's view, forgiveness in its purity must be offered without any hope, expectation or intention that the offender will in due

---

[512] Ibid., 34–35.

[513] Ibid., 27.

[514] Ibid., 27. Derrida's comment here can also be related to Bash, who writes that "In the New Testament, as in the popular mind, there is undoubtedly a degree of confusion about forgiveness." See Bash, *Forgiveness and Christian Ethics*, 99.

[515] Derrida, *On Cosmopolitanism and Forgiveness*, 32–33.

[516] Fiddes, "Memory, Forgetting and the Problem of Forgiveness. Reflecting on Volf, Derrida and Ricoeur," 124.

time face up to his or her crime, be repentant, seek reconciliation, offer repara-
tion and be transformed. Even holding hope for the offender is, in Derrida's
view, entering an economy of exchange."[517]

We observe that Derrida's position here is contrary to the one I have delineated above when suggesting that practicing forgiveness should be done with
faith and hope that it may bring something good about. If forgiveness is made
unconditionally to the extent he describes, one can ask with some legitimacy
what the point is of forgiving at all? It would be adequate to ask this if Derrida
had not added another dimension to his discussion. His point is that all conditional talk about forgiveness can only be assessed against the backdrop of some
notion of its unconditional or ultimate character. This complicated situation is
also the reason why the tradition is so equivoque regarding the understanding
of forgiveness. Derrida writes:

Sometimes, forgiveness (given by God, or inspired by divine prescription) must be a gracious
gift, without exchange and without condition; sometimes it requires, as its minimal condition,
the repentance and transformation of the sinner. What consequence results from this tension? At
least this, which does not simplify things: if our idea of forgiveness falls into ruin as soon as it
is deprived of its pole of absolute reference, namely its unconditional purity, it remains nonetheless inseparable from what is heterogeneous to it, namely the order of conditions, repentance,
transformation, as many things as allow it to inscribe itself in history, law, politics, existence
itself.[518]

This quote makes apparent how important it is to separate human and divine
forgiveness. Only the latter is unconditional. In Derrida's view, "they are absolutely heterogeneous and must remain irreducible to one another. They are
nonetheless indissociable."[519] It is in the tension between these two poles that
human decisions about forgiveness must be taken – a point that makes much
sense, because if we were only referred to the pole of conditions, forgiveness
would be a mere result of a calculation and clearly defined aims. This is the
reason it is, in addition, necessary to maintain an "idea of pure and unconditional forgiveness, without which this discourse would not have the least meaning."[520] Furthermore, it is the latter pole that also opens up to speaking about
grace in the context of forgiveness. Thereby, he introduces the central notion
for describing the unconditional element in forgiveness, and one that has profoundly theological connotations. Thus, he also identifies the element that

---

[517] Ibid.
[518] Derrida, *On Cosmopolitanism and Forgiveness*, 44.
[519] Ibid.
[520] Ibid., 44–45.

seems absent in much of contemporary discussion of forgiveness, including the one to which we now turn.

Thomas Brudholm argues that to forgive others for atrocities and crimes might have severe consequences and that it might even be in the interest of morality to refuse forgiveness.[521] Thus, his book can be read as one in which the *limits of forgiveness* are identified. Brudholm argues along lines that explicitly critique some of the more hasty and rapid processes of forgiveness that have followed the overturning of political regimes with major and systematic violations of the human rights of large groups of people: the victims of the Holocaust and the victims of apartheid South Africa. In this regard, he seems to address contexts which are more similar to what God seems unwilling to forgive in 2. Kings 24, than the forgiveness one is exhorted to practice in relation to petty transgressions among humans in a context of more or less symmetrical level.

Brudholm is not against forgiveness and reconciliation in principle, but he points out how difficult it is to establish processes that can lead to a better future unless one is also taking sufficiently into account the justified anger or resentment of the victims of violations. His critique of concrete practices of reconciliation and forgiveness is especially relevant with regard to religious ideals that promote such practices. To consider his contribution is therefore important in order to develop an understanding of how forgiveness can appear as a positive transformative practice that benefits all involved parties (if they still exist, that is).

The main voice in any discussion of crimes and atrocities has to be the victims'. This point must be repeated here, as it is an important premise in Brudholm's work. If the leading voice is that of the one craving forgiveness or that of those who want to harmonize circumstances and get on with it (whatever it is), it is always the power and desire of the perpetrator and his/her deeds that still rules the world. To take the victim seriously is to acknowledge her vulnerability, This can only happen if her voice is heard, and is heard as a morally relevant voice, not as a voice that "we have to hear" in order to go on, or in order for her to be healed or reconciled with the crimes done to her. In other words: this vulnerable voice is the precondition for the experience that her world is recognized as the world destroyed, the place where transgression took

---

[521] Thomas Brudholm, *Resentment's Virtue : Jean Améry and the Refusal to Forgive*, Politics, History, and Social Change (Philadelphia: Temple University Press, 2008). See also Thomas Brudholm and Thomas Cushman, *The Religious in Responses to Mass Atrocity: Interdisciplinary Perspectives* (Cambridge ; New York: Cambridge University Press, 2009).

place and in which the parties still have to face each other in recognition of the atrocities.

To practice forgiveness in the context of vulnerability also implies opening to strong emotional elements. Religious conceptions of forgiveness need to open up to such emotions and not suppress them by ideals of tranquility and calmness. Anger, rage, and resentment are spontaneous and justified responses to injuries, insults, or atrocities, and it is part of taking care of the vulnerable other to allow these emotions to be expressed. Among the shortcomings of much Christian theology is that it has not been able to deal with these strong emotional states, because they appear as disruptive, uncontrollable, and potential disturbers of harmony and tranquility.[522] Thereby, traditional religious piety has contributed to silencing the wisdom of such emotional states and has not been helpful in interpreting them as important to any other than the individual who holds them. Among those who have expressed this most profoundly is feminist theologian Rita Nakashima Brock:

Anger is a key to both love and nonviolence, and it is pivotal to self-affirmation and liberation. It is the healthy response of a self to violation and a crucial avenue to self-acceptance and acceptance of others. But this anger must be deeply personal, tied intimately to its roots in experience. This anger, when we take responsibility for it as part of our own damage, leads to mourning the loss of self and to the first steps to reclaiming self and intimacy.[523]

The immediate consequence of this for the human being's relationship with God is that this relationship must be perceived and expressed in a way that makes it possible, and even encourages, voicing such emotions. Much biblical material supports imagery for such emotions. It also has important effects on healing, a point that advocates of forgiveness sometimes forget when they "argue that forgiveness will release survivors from negative emotions such as anger, rage, resentment and the desire for revenge." Accordingly, Christiane Sanderson questions the idea that forgiveness will open up to more satisfactory lives and improved relationships if it overlooks "that feelings of anger, rage and the sense of betrayal need to be legitimized, validated, felt and processed for healing to occur. This challenges the notion that to forgive facilitates healing, and argues that healing must come first before forgiveness can take place."[524]

---

[522] I develop more in detail how devastating such suppression is in Henriksen, *Relating God and the Self : Dynamic Interplay*.

[523] Rita Nakashima Brock, *Journeys by Heart : A Christology of Erotic Power* (New York: Crossroad, 1988), 19.

[524] Sanderson, "The Role of Forgiveness after Interpersonal Abuse – Danger or Road to Recovery and Healing?," 138.

Brock's insistence above that the anger must be deeply personal and tied intimately to its roots in experience is met in the case of Holocaust survivor Jean Améry, who is among the main sources of Brudholm's reflection. Améry never lets go of his own subjectivity, his own point of view, and demands its recognition and affirmation. Hence, he allows himself to be vulnerable. It is only by being recognized for what life is for him, after Auschwitz, that the possibility of a shared world with others is present. However, this world has been denied him because no-one seems interested in sharing with him the atrocities and murders that he experienced.

Acknowledgment of vulnerability, and of hurt inflicted on others, is a basic demand in Améry's approach to issues about forgiveness. It is the lack of recognition, this absence of will to truly recognize the content of his moral judgment of the atrocities, that blocks the way to forgiveness and reconciliation for him. If my reading is correct, it implies that it is not Améry on his own, so to say, who rejects the possibilities of forgiveness, but the others' lack of recognition of the importance of *not* reconciling with the past. Holocaust is an event in history with which there can be no reconciliation. Here, Brudholm makes an important distinction between reconciling with others and reconciling with the past. Améry's resentment, his anger, is directed not only against the past and what happened, but also against those who are not able to share, or willing to share, his relation to the past with him. They simply do not seem to take his moral concerns seriously enough for him to be able to reconcile with them. Améry's anger continues, rightly, to feed on this situation. Any expectancy of, or demand for, reconciliation before this situation changes would be inappropriate.

Accordingly, Améry's conception of justified resentment is just as strongly directed towards an indifferent present as it is a relation to an atrocious past. Moreover, he refuses to be seen simply as traumatized or as a psychological case – and insists that his case is profoundly *moral*. This is why he refuses to reconcile with the irreversible. To keep the past open and unfinished, something that is not to be left, bygone, surpassed, represents an attitude that will ascribe an impact to what happened in the Holocaust that is impossible to ignore for all future. It is for everyone to remember. The impact is so vast that it can never be undone. However, it seems impossible to sustain this insight once one introduces speech of reconciliation or forgiveness.

Brudholm discusses Améry's position against the backdrop of the proceedings of the *Truth and Reconciliation Commission* (TRC) in South Africa, which was chaired by Archbishop Desmond Tutu in the aftermath of the dissolution of the apartheid regime in order to deal with its atrocities. Analysis of the material related to the TRC shows how the victims' anger was actually dealt with in the hearings of the commission, and also how it was considered by some of its members. Siding with the critics of the hearings, Brudholm addresses the strong bias in favor of recognizing those victims who were ready to forgive and to rapidly pass over instances in which this readiness was not present or did not express itself. In some instances, this pressure appears to have led to more resentment among those who were not "ready to forgive." The counter-posing of forgiveness vs. vengeance-hatred-bitterness among representatives of the commission seemed to overlook important alternative ways to approach the situation, among which one prominent is that there can be no real reconciliation without justice. It also seems, at least sometimes, to have favored the desire for going on at the expense of recognizing how deeply hurt and vulnerable the victims were.

The systematic problem inherent in the background of the proceedings seems to be that justice was bracketed in order to be able to move on. But the demand for justice cannot be established unless vulnerability and transgression are recognized. The theological insight expressed in the dictum "no reconciliation or peace without justice" seems to have been ignored. Looking at it from the history of theology, this is a position that we, with Anselm of Canterbury, can say that privileges the culprit instead of the victim, by placing him above the law.[525] One could also ask if forgiveness was – if not in principle so at least in practice – here expected in ways that put pressure on the victim and disregarded its need for being given unconditionality.

From a critical perspective, one could say that the TRC instrumentalized the demand for forgiveness in order to promote national unity and reconciliation. The framework into which testimonies were integrated and seen as instruments established a conception of forgiveness and personal confession that in practice to a large extent seems to have uncoupled the insights into the conditions of justice and its importance for reconciliation. The instrumental character became even more enhanced when it was coupled with therapeutic language. On a more positive side, Tutu's employment of the conception of Ubuntu as the

---

[525] Anselm's discussion of why God cannot simply forgive out of mercy alone is based on the point that some kind of punishment of and satisfaction for sin implies a recognition of the fact that humans live under the law. If someone is forgiven out of mercy alone, that would imply that they are no longer under the law, and that they accordingly find themselves in a position that makes them privileged. This interpretation basically implies that the just and the unjust are treated as equals, which in turn implies that injustice is more privileged than justice. Cf. Anselm, *Cur Deus Homo* I, 12.

major ideological resource for the work of the TRC can correct an individualistic European tendency to overlook the importance of the community for the
individual identity. However, one can nevertheless ask if Ubuntu can be expected to deal with social conditions like those under apartheid – or, to take
another example, the genocide in Rwanda. If one takes a concept based on people of relatively equal terms and assesses conditions where the basic conditions
for this concept and its practice are violated, one might easily end up with more
violation of those who are the victims of the first condition.

Brudholm's critical discussions show how resentment precludes from engaging forgiveness as a moral ideal and fastens the victim in a situation in which
it is impossible to relate to forgiveness on unconditional terms. Therefore, resentment also excludes the possibility for grace. The reason for this must, however, not be identified in the victim's lack of willingness to forgive, or his ar-
rested psychological development, but must be seen as caused by the extent of
the atrocities that he has suffered, and the lack of recognition of their extensive
impact on the continuing social order. Sometimes the destructive deeds also
destroy the future conditions for forgiveness, for empathy with the perpetrator,
and the ability to relate to it within a horizon of ultimacy.

However, Brudholm's analysis should not be seen as an argument against
forgiveness as such, but only against practicing forgiveness unconditionally in
any given context. Forgiveness calls for prudence. "A world without forgiveness will be an impoverished world; a world with an impoverished notion
of forgiveness will also be an impoverished world."[526] Therefore, to discuss
how we should understand forgiveness and its conditions is not an academic
enterprise, but is meaningful only to the extent that has concrete implications
for how humans can practice the divine image in order to restore a broken world
and transform the conditions for flourishing to the benefit of all involved. How
to find good ways to practice forgiveness is among the unending tasks of religion. To approach it simply from the abstract points of view of either unconditional or conditional forgiveness will not help us sufficiently, as the above discussions aim at making apparent.

Using Sacred Scriptures as a practice of orientation (mainly descriptive)

Humans are guided and oriented by something other than themselves. This fact
belongs to the human condition and is among the reasons why life is a process

---

[526] Bash, *Forgiveness and Christian Ethics*, 186.

of constant learning. The relational character of existence expresses itself in this fact. In a recent book that addresses the uses of scriptures for guidance and orientation, Steven G. Smith can therefore claim that

it undeniably belongs to our animal condition that we depend on cues from other beings and consistencies in our interactions with them to live successfully. The human experience of "relationship" and practical "knowledge" is based on this relatedness. One could not carry on a human conversation if one did not possess beelike perceptual and motor responsiveness and if one's interlocutor did not provide a flowerlike structuring of the situation. One had best be aware that one's prospects for successful life can be affected favorably or unfavorably by changes in these dimensions of the interactive situation.[527]

Some sources for guidance stand out as more significant than others when it comes to finding guidance and orientation. Religious texts are perhaps the most obvious example. They are the result of the human communities' desire to pass on and share what some of their members have seen as wisdom.[528] When we look for religious representations, perhaps there is no material thing more powerful than a text. Words are less equivocal than symbols – and often more instructive. The presence of text opens immediately to a variety of different practices: reading, interpretation, sermons based on text, discussion, contemplation, recitation, prayer, singing, etc. A text can thus be used with a multitude of purposes, all of which involve specific practices. Because a text has cognitive content that is immediately accessible (for some, at least to some extent), it provides opportunities for a larger repertoire of *reflection* than other religious representations do. Its material and fixed character also implies that it can appear as a stable entity and a reference-point one can return to. If one is insecure about the meaning the text conveys, or what kind of guidance it offers, it can be re-read, read with other, or provide a reason for consulting others on what it means.

This subchapter is not primarily discussing the *doctrinal* approach to holy scriptures, which identifies these scriptures, in some way or another, with revelation. Such doctrinal convictions about the text have their origin already in specific practices and uses of the text. Instead, I want to address some of the basic features that constitute *practices related to text*. Of course, this cannot be

---

[527] Steven G. Smith, *Scriptures and the Guidance of Language : Evaluating a Religious Authority in Communicative Action* (Cambridge; New York: Cambridge University Press, 2018), 11.
[528] I phrase it thus, since the last decades of scholarship (especially feminist) have disclosed how the content of many of these texts have been far more influenced by the perspective of those in power or representatives of patriarchy, than being representative for all members of the society from which they emerged.

done without some reference to the convictions that people may hold with re-gard to the texts, but these are not my main object of analysis. Rather, such convictions are expressions of the experience of interacting with and using text for specific purposes. The main element in making a religious text relevant for use is the conviction that it identifies points of ultimacy and by doing so, offers important elements for orientation. It cannot do this unless the text is also con-sidered *a representation of ultimacy*. However, already here it gets complicated because a text is always – by means of saying something about something – a representation of a representation of ultimacy. The New Testament text repre-sents the story about Jesus, which in turn is considered by Christians to repre-sent (and therefore to reveal) God.[529]

That the text opens to engagement with ultimacy means that it cannot pri-marily be considered merely as mediating information (which would be the usual way to think of the text as revelation). Nicholas Wolterstorff has argued that prior to understanding the text as a revelation, one needs to consider that a text *does* something – and that the illocutionary actions of a text establish the conviction that God speaks through them by speaking through humans. Thus, he sees the constitution of the text as divine speech as conditioned by a specific experience: the experience that the text *addresses me, promises me, exhorts me, asks or commands me, even when this is done by someone else on God's be-half.*[530] Without this experience of being addressed, the text(s) would not have the status it/they now have.

The main point in employing a text is, therefore, to identify and establish points of orientation and validate those. Points of orientation can be what the texts seem to promise to the believer, what it identifies as valuable, what it says about what someone did for me, and so on. Therefore, the text does more than simply convey information. A religious text always establishes a practice, an attitude, or orients you in some direction, or intends to do so. Its meaning cannot be separated from its use and from the consequences of this use. The text must, therefore, be seen in relation to how it legitimizes, or de-legitimizes, specific practices – some of which can be identified as religious, some as moral or im-moral, and some simply as human in some way or another. Hence, texts provide

---

[529] Similarly, the Qur'an as text represents what Allah revealed to Mohammad – and even when it is seen as a direct revelation of this, the text is nevertheless a representation of Allah's words.
[530] Cf. Nicholas Wolterstorff, *Divine Discourse : Philosophical Reflections on the Claim That God Speaks* (Cambridge England ; New York, NY, USA: Cambridge University Press, 1995), 7, 13.

justification of positions, explanation of them, warrants for claims and practices, and offer resources that make them plausible.[531]

A religious text, such as the Bible, therefore, achieves its status due to two,
interrelated features: first, it is seen as a representation of the divine, and
thereby, a mediator that makes it possible, to engage with ultimacy in some way
or another. Second, it cannot appear as such representation unless it is engaged
in practices that also aim at orientation, reflection, and sometimes even transformation. All uses of the Bible, all practices that it gives rise to, are shaped
with one or more of these aims. Hence, it is not the meaning of the text in itself
that constitutes its sacred status, but the fact that it can be involved in such
practices. Thereby we get an important glimpse into how religious practices, by
means of engaging representations, can mediate between the human and the
divine.

The fact that a text's meaning is dependent on how it is used, and for what
purpose, implies that there is no immediate access to it.[532] The text is always
mediated not only by specific practices, but also the concrete communities in
which it is employed. In another context, I have argued more extensively for
the position that practices related to orientation and reflection on the basis of
texts involve three different but interrelated elements[533]: a) the individual,
which relies on b) the community to which the individual belongs, which would
not exist apart from c) the religious tradition that constitutes the community and
provides practices through which it lives and articulates itself.

Every religious tradition that relates to texts is based on a cluster of practices that are mediated in and through the interplay between these instances.
The individual would not be a religious practitioner without relating to the tradition by taking part in the community (although not necessarily in an uncritical
way).[534] The community exists because it is constituted by the chain of memory

---

[531] I have developed these points more extensively in Henriksen, *Religion as Orientation and
Transformation : A Maximalist Theory* (Tübingen: Mohr Siebeck 2017).

[532] This point is perhaps most strongly reflected in Gadamer's hermeneutics, which not only
underscores that all reading is dependent on the prejudices mediated by the text's *Wirkungsges-
chichte,* but also that the immediate reading of a text as meaningful in the context of the reader's
world constitutes it in another way than the mediate reading where one has to thematize what the
author meant, because there is no immediate way to understand and apply it. The hermeneutical
points I develop in the following owe much to Gadamer's analysis of the hermeneutical process.
See Hans-Georg Gadamer, *Truth and Method,* (London ; New York: Continuum, 2004).

[533] See Henriksen, *Christianity as Distinct Practices: A Complicated Relationship,* 91–107 *et
passim.*

[534] This relation between the individual and the community as a point of departure for theological
reflection is recently articulated comprehensively in Eilert Herms, *Systematische Theologie: Das*

that also constitutes the tradition that individuals relate to as a community.[535] Furthermore, the tradition would not exist apart from the community that mediates specific memories, skills, and points of orientation in and through a diversity of practices. Nevertheless, these practices must always be appropriated by the individuals who take part in the tradition, as they need to give it the form and shape that is relevant in their context. The consequence of this approach is that it enables us to see that it is concrete practices that mediate the relationship between individual, community, and tradition.[536]

Under the conditions of modernity, practices that tend to solidify either the origin of the tradition or the community through which it is mediated, has come under scrutiny, sometimes even under attack, because references to these instances have been made in order to secure authority, and thereby, obedience to one specific interpretation and use of the text. I argue that if texts are to mediate relationships to something ultimate, it is important to perform this type of criticism. Neither the text as such, nor the church or community that interprets it, or the specific uses of the text for this or that purpose, can be seen as ultimate. Therefore, the text must be employed in *reflective* practices. By this, I mean practices that help reflect on the present situation of the readers. It cannot simply be used as a *Vorlage* for what convictions one should hold, or what one should do, without any reflection of how and why to use it in this or that way. Then the text would provide no more than an authoritarian and arbitrary model for human conduct, that requires no more than the obedience of its readers. But in practice, this is not possible, because all text is read in the context of communities and individuals conditioned by their experiences and other sources of knowledge as well – both of which cannot be ignored.

When one engages the text, the most important question is, therefore, "in what ways does it tell me something about what should be my ultimate concerns?" This question opens up the reader's responsibility because it engages her in a continuous quest for what matters and not. Of course, the community to which she belongs may provide guidance and suggestions, but if reading is genuinely reflective and responsible, it cannot foreclose the quest by demanding obedience to an already established practice of reading without providing opportunities for alternatives. Engaging a text for the purpose of exploring it as

---

Wesen des Christentums: In Wahrheit und aus Gnade leben (Tübingen: Mohr Siebeck, 2017), 6f.

[535] I use the notion "chain of memory" with reference to Danièle Hervieu-Léger, *Religion as a Chain of Memory* (New Brunswick, N.J.: Rutgers University Press, 2000).

[536] Cf. Henriksen, *Christianity as Distinct Practices: A Complicated Relationship*, 91–92.

a representation of ultimacy is different from using it as a tool for compliance and obedience – then it is simply a means for the desire of control and conformity, which does not take into account the vulnerability that should make the reader a responsible user of it.

My point in underscoring the above is that it is the only way in which one can secure the connection between freedom and responsibility in reading. Reflective reading implies using the text in order to make transparent the reasons one has for one's own conduct. Texts should provide guidance and understanding. If religious texts are used for no other purpose than to secure conformity and obedience, they lose the possibility to engage readers' relation to the ultimate and their ability to take responsibility for their own reading and use. this is most obvious in cases where people act in ways that oppress others – without any cognitive understanding or moral warrant for doing so – simply by reference to their reading of the text. We see this in cases like theological legitimation of apartheid, the denial of women's access to ordination, or of the rights for gays and lesbians to enter into marriage with their partners on equal terms as their heterosexual peers.

When one rejects to absolutize either the tradition or the Bible, this is not only a way to open to the ultimate beyond the text and provide chances for reflective and responsible (read: transparent) practice. Existing readings and concomitant practices may also be challenged by an alternative reading that establishes alternative interpretations of tradition based on convictions held by individual believers who find it necessary to express their disagreements through an alternative practice. One tradition and one text do not necessarily lead to only one type of interpretation, community, and practice; rather, different communities, practices, and interpretations emerge from a tradition that is under constant negotiation concerning its content and how it should be practiced. The continued, active use of text in different practices to open up the present and the future in a constant negotiation process that expresses its orientation towards the future, is what makes it meaningful to employ religious resources for reflection.

Today, more than ever before, we have access to a flow of information that is insurmountable and impossible to oversee. There is simply too much information. This is also the case on the religious scene: I can get access to information about the diversity of religious traditions and denominations, practices, and beliefs by sitting in my living room and using my computer. Although it is not the same as meeting the practices and the materiality of the religious traditions first hand or face to face, it nevertheless creates the awareness that there is so much to know, relate to, and try to understand, that it will take a lifetime to do so.

The response to this situation can be withdrawal. It can also be oversimplifications: Either claiming that all religions are basically about the same, no matter how this same is defined, be it in a secular or psychological sense or with respect to religious ultimacy. Or, the response can be ignoring religion altogether, to avoid overload or confusion. It can also be withdrawing to your own tradition, often the one you grew up as part of, and keeping other traditions at a distance, with pragmatic or religious excuses for doing so.

In most of these cases, religious texts play a role: they provide something to which one can recur in order to find legitimation for one's choice of strategy, be it rejection, withdrawal, or worship ("the Bible is violent, nonsense, wisdom, the word of God, a text among other religious texts, inspiring," etc.). Against this backdrop, scriptures can be seductive: they may suggest that here you have, ready at hand, what you need. However, as should be obvious from what is already said, that is exactly what is not the case.

As indicated above, no reading takes place in an interpretative and experiential vacuum. Humans have their basic point of orientation in what they take to be their community. Their orientation is based on where they think they belong. In other words, *orientation is relationally defined.* When they want to orient themselves, they ask what would be right in the eyes of their (idealized, not necessarily actual) peers.[537] It is in recognition of relationships with others, *as well as* in the capacity to overcome or transcend the perceived, required, or just assumed normative expectations of loyalty, normativity, and conformity, that the Christian tradition and individual Christian identity emerges and expresses itself in different practices. Thus, identity emerges from partaking in the practices of the tradition, and it is based on this participation that one gains the knowledge and know-how necessary to perceive shortcomings and defects that are in need of correction within that tradition and community. Thus, participation in the practices of tradition is more often than not a necessary condition for its further development and adjustment. It is always a tacit or explicit negotiation between the individual and the group, be it in the context of a political party, in a football club, or in a religious community. Furthermore, I hold that this "negotiation" creates important dynamics in all these groups and that

---

[537] The addition in brackets here is to suggest that peers can be of various kinds for humans, but that it would be incomplete to understand the choice of orientational features without having peers in mind. Peers need not be idealized to still have influence, though (e.g., communities with strong relational bonds and concomitant control mechanisms).

such dynamics are important because it allows for the development of new types of interaction. Conformity alone does not provide sufficient opportunities for renewal. Discussion, controversy, and difference are therefore to be valued, and necessary for development and growth.

Against the backdrop of the analysis so far, it is obvious that one should expect to find a diversity in ways of using the Bible among Christians and a concomitant plurality of purposes for which it is used. There is no reason why one should consider this situation inherently problematic. However, to expect agreement, or to establish one use and/or interpretation is therefore not easy.

Differences in interpretation are not solved merely by claiming that one group has a more authoritative or adequate understanding of scripture than has another. There can be radically different interpretations of how texts could be used, based on similar attitudes regarding the authority ascribed to a given text. This does not mean, however, that there is no difference between how Christian groups consider the authority of the texts they have received from the past, which is often the case. How this authority is established and perceived is itself a question closely related to practice, and to contextual elements that contribute to different uses of the text. What a text can identify as points of ultimacy is crucial here. The authority of the text here actually lies in or is dependent upon the extent to which the text can be used in concrete practices that provide such identification and thereby either shape and develop a specific practice, or to legitimize, justify, or criticize a specific practice. The text is usually taken for granted as providing basic points of orientation, but how it is used is still dependent on the contextual circumstances for interpretation and use. Concerning moral questions, it is, for example, how the text stimulates or ignites already existing moral intuitions that make it a moral source for orientation and/or transformation.[538]

---

[538] Cf. for this point also the reflections offered by Jeffrey Stout: "Imagine that you ascribe infallible authority to the Bible and consult it regularly in forming your own opinions. Suppose further that all members of your society are similarly committed to conforming their opinions to what the Bible says, and you know this. It does not follow that it will make sense for you to appeal to the Bible in settling disputed questions in a public forum. Why? Perhaps you know that members of your society do not have compatible views of what the Bible says on political and economic matters. You notice that when members of the group use reasoned discussion to forge consensus on questions of biblical interpretation, they almost always fail. You therefore conclude that it will be unwise for any of you to appeal to the Bible as an infallible authority even though each of you believes that it is. Any such appeal, in this sort of setting, is going to be useless, and anyone who makes it is going to appear foolish." Jeffrey Stout, *Democracy and Tradition* (Princeton, N.J.: Princeton University Press, 2004), 94.

Now, what if one is *not* able to make use of the text? The decision that a text is "unusable" arises when practices in the community context become so at odds with what the text says, that one must ignore it. Again, this is a decision made by the community about how to use (or not) the text. Most Christians today do not accept polygamy, although some of the biblical patriarchs practiced it. Furthermore, most (but not all) are opposed to capital punishment because cultural conditions have favored the development of a version of Christian practices where it is rendered as inhuman and un-Christian. However, it is a sociological fact that the more a specific community separates itself off from its environment and the higher the costs for adherence to the group, the easier it is to maintain a preference for practices that are at odds with the rest of society. Given such circumstances, it is important to see that, when actual practices are legitimized by texts, these legitimations are not only related to the convictions and practices of a specific group, but to how the group relates to its cultural and societal environment.

On the practice of using texts (mainly normative): Six theses

1. A religious text must primarily be understood and used as a representation. Neither itself nor some form of its use can be reified or petrified without losing sight of the relationship the text may have with the ultimate or the divine. To ignore the text's character of representation is concomitant to making it an object of idolatry (what G.E. Lessing called bibliolatry).

2. Religious uses of text are primarily for illocutionary purposes. When read as simply matters of fact about the world, its transformative and orientational character gets lost, and often, they are mistaken for conflicting with other sources of knowledge.

3. Religious texts open humans to the awareness of their own historical being as much as a similar awareness of the text's need for interpretation and the diversity of its potential uses.

4. When texts are employed for the purpose of orientation and guidance, this happens under historical and social conditions that make such practices an unending task. As long as it is realized that such practices are unending, texts provide means for reflection that can contribute to the formation of the readers' moral and religious responsibility and subjectivity. Texts are in this sense instrumental for developing prudence, and not for suspending it.

5. Readings for reflective, orientational, and transformative purposes see texts as sources of wisdom, and are critical to, or resist, uses of them for power

purposes. The criteria for adequate uses of text can be found in how texts provide means for thriving and flourishing by relating humans to the ultimate in a just community that takes care of the most vulnerable, and guides its members' desire towards the common good.

6. To acknowledge that a religious use of the text is mainly constituted of its ability to instigate illocutionary actions (the text addresses me, promises me, exhorts me, asks or commands me, etc.) means that the religious significance of a religious text is not primarily what it communicates of facts – be they about nature or historical events – but in how the text opens human practices of faith, hope, and love.[539] Thereby, it achieves its authority by what it makes possible, and one can avoid all the strange movements that literalists may find necessary in order to secure textual authority.[540]

---

[539] Cf. the following, with which I mostly agree, although I would have liked to see the reference to "human success" exchanged for something more substantial. "As regards content, the distinctive power of scripture lies in providing guidance embraced by a community, guidance of the most profound practical interest and unlimited practical relevance in that community. This Guidance is taken as commanding, exhorting, advising, inviting, even teasing, but in any case decisive – in some way necessary and in some way sufficient – for ultimate human success." Smith, *Scriptures and the Guidance of Language : Evaluating a Religious Authority in Communicative Action*, 162.

[540] Cf. again Stout: "The idea that what the Bible says must be true exerts pressure on the interpreter to read the Bible in such a way that it does not conflict with his or her strongest commitments. The strongest proponents of biblical authority therefore often have the strongest reasons, from their own point of view, for being what we might call 'strong' readers of the biblical text. They proclaim the primacy of the Bible at one moment and then a moment later push the text hard in the direction of truths with which it must in the end prove compatible, given that God is no author of falsehoods." Stout, *Democracy and Tradition*, 96.

.

God as the ultimate in human reality

Religion is about what matters – or at least, it should be. It is about ultimacy. It is about how to live, and live well, in the tension between desire and vulnerability, as an individual and in community. However, this claim does not mean that religion can be reduced to morality. Religions, including Christianity, offer resources for reflecting on what matters – on from what we orient ourselves – and it points to what needs transformation. Hence, it is not only dealing with questions about morality, or with questions about what we can know and how. This is the reason why the question of ultimacy is so important. Hence, contrary to empirical approaches that will "explain" religion due to this or that function, religion cannot be "explained" unless one takes the issue of ultimacy into account. In the words of Robert Neville,

the new combinations of scientific inquiries into religion usually define themselves as sciences in part by the fact that they do not and cannot deal vulnerably with ultimacy. But this means that they are tone deaf to the distinction between authentic religion and religion that fails to engage ultimacy and is reduced to the dynamics of its historical cultures, social organization, and psychological states. They do not hear the prophets' cry against dead symbols and liturgical forms, against social structures that are only power plays, and against supposedly divine madness that is only pathological madness. They cannot take at face value the disciplines in so many religions focused on spiritual discernment and on the vetting of allegedly religious engagements with ultimacy as to whether they are the real thing.[541]

That authentic religion has as its purpose to mediate ultimacy, and thereby – from a Christian perspective – the relationship between God and human beings, implies a critical approach to anyone who wants to hijack religion for political purposes, even if these may appear as laudable from the outset. Religious representations must serve the task of keeping open critical approaches to human life and to specific understandings of what can count as ultimate. Thus, such representations are employed in the indefinite task of serving the good for all humans. Consequently, representations must, as indicated, be understood as that, and not as ultimate in themselves. Neither the Church, the Bible, any human or any other instance can serve as anything else than a preliminary representation of God. As long as history goes on, the quest for what matters is kept

---

[541] Neville, *Defining Religion : Essays in Philosophy of Religion*, 34.

open – as no final representation of God that relates us in a definite way to God is possible. To speak of God as the ultimate in human reality means a continuous quest to find new ways to practice God. True worship of God can be nothing else than to love others. In this final chapter, I will develop a philosophical backing for this claim, which I think can be related to the content of the previous chapters.

The importance of what we care about: H. Frankfurt as philosophical theology

The *Vorlage* for this sub-section is Harry Frankfurt's article "The importance of what we care about."[542] Although the main elements in the article are not about religion, it makes use of examples related to religion and theology and provides important insights into the topics discussed in this book. The following is, therefore, a commentary to most of its content, written from the point of view of philosophical theology.

Frankfurt starts out with the claim that we can distinguish between three different sorts of inquiry, namely what he calls the epistemological, which seeks to clarify what we should *believe*, the moral, which is about how to *behave*, and finally, the question of what we should care about. He argues that the last is the most fundamental aspect of human life and cannot be solved by referring it to any of the other two lines of inquiry.[543]

Already here, Frankfurt arguably points to elements of relevance to philosophy of religion. Because it would be a mistake to reduce it to dogmatics (what we believe) or to matters of morality (what it would be right to do), the perspective of what we should care about presents itself as relevant also within a context that theorizes about religion. What matters, what we *should care about* is directly related to the topic of ultimacy.

Moreover, when Frankfurt delineates the question of what we should care about as distinct for questions in ethics, it has immediate relevance for what we have been analyzing previously with regard to the necessary first-person-perspective involved in a religious mode of life. Inquiry into what matters occupies itself with questions related to evaluation and action, and therefore, implies "an intimate connection between what a person cares about and what he will, generally or under certain conditions, think it best for himself to do."[544] However,

---

[542] Harry G. Frankfurt, "The Importance of What We Care About," *Synthese* 53, no. 2 (1982).
[543] Ibid., 257.
[544] Ibid.

it is not primarily oriented towards our relationship with other people, as is ethics. Contrary to ethics, questions about what matters are about "deciding what to do with ourselves," and accordingly, "we therefore need to understand what is important or, rather, what is important *to us*."[545] This does not imply that one does not care about moral matters. Frankfurt's point is simply that what we care about cannot and should not be reduced to morality, because people "may care more, for instance, about their own personal projects, about certain individuals and groups, and perhaps about various ideals to which they accord commanding authority in their lives but which need not be particularly of an ethical nature."[546] This statement is clearly open to a perspective that takes religion into account: religious people care about the group to which they belong, and to ideals and values that influence them and from which they orient their lives, without these ideals and values necessarily being of a moral character. Sometimes non-moral concerns may even override moral concerns, simply because we think the non-moral concerns are more important.[547] The main point here is that such examples make it clear that we may have opinions about what matters (most) that are not possible to identify by means of moral reasoning.

Frankfurt strengthens the claim that the importance of what we care about is distinct from morality with another case, namely that it is necessary to distinguish between moral judgments and the fact that someone cares about them. The conviction that certain courses of action should be dictated by ethical considerations can be distinguished from the conviction that no other considerations are as important as these.[548]

However, what does it mean that something is important? In the context of this treatise, this question is relevant because it is closely connected to the question of ultimacy. It is what matters more than anything else, i.e., what is considered the most important, that constitutes convictions about ultimacy. Frankfurt, however, admits that it is difficult to define importance without ending up with a circular argument of the type which will be referred to shortly. He also suggests that a traditional pragmatic approach, which considers the importance

---

[545] Ibid. My italics.
[546] Ibid., 258.
[547] Cf. ibid. An obvious example of this is Kierkegaard's discussion of the possibility of a teleological suspension of the ethical. See Søren Kierkegaard and Alastair Hannay, *Fear and Trembling*, Penguin Books (New York: Penguin Books, 2006). Another example, related to the previous section on forgiveness, is that forgiveness may be offered even under circumstances that may seem contrary to moral intuitions.
[548] Frankfurt, "The Importance of What We Care About," 259.

of something only in virtue of the differences it makes, is insufficient. His argument on this matter is as follows:

> If it would make no difference at all to anything whether a certain thing existed, or whether it
> had certain characteristics, then neither the existence of that thing nor its characteristics would
> be of any importance whatever. But everything does actually make some difference. How is it
> possible, then, for anything to be genuinely unimportant? It can only be because the difference
> such a thing makes is itself of no importance. Thus it is evidently essential to include, in the
> analysis of the concept of importance, a proviso to the effect that nothing is important unless the
> difference it makes is an important one.[549]

In other words, the importance of something must be defined in a certain respect, and this respect must, therefore, be determined as important. If we relate this point to religion, we get the following picture: religions, as clusters of practices for orientation, transformation, and reflection, contribute the resources that identify something as more important than anything else. Importance is related to my first-person perspective on what matters in life. However, such importance cannot be perceived apart from the fundamental conditions of life. I have defined some of these in terms of love, the power to be, desire, and vulnerability – as things that matter, and as something of crucial importance to come to terms with. Thus, religious interpretations and practices do not only ascribe importance to these elements but also imply a claim about coming to terms with these elements as the most crucial or ultimate for orientation if one is to lead a good life.

In his theology, Paul Tillich defined religious faith as an *ultimate concern*.[550] This notion fits rather well with Frankfurt's notion of the importance of what we care about. When we care about something important, this comes close to relating to what are our ultimate concerns – because this importance may not only override other concerns we might have, but they may also orient and transform our way of life.

At the end of the previous chapter, I referred to Steven Smith's work on Scripture as a tool for guidance and orientation. Scriptures can provide suggestions about what to care about because they can serve as such tools. Frankfurt argues that caring, "insofar as it consists in guiding oneself along a distinctive

---

[549] Ibid.
[550] Cf. Paul Tillich, D. Mackenzie Brown., *Ultimate Concern : Tillich in Dialogue* (London: SCM Press, 1965), and the recent contributions that relate Tillich's notion to some of the topics I have discussed earlier, in Adam Pryor and Devan Stahl, *The Body and Ultimate Concern : Reflections on an Embodied Theology of Paul Tillich* (Macon, GA: Mercer University Press, 2018).

course or in a particular manner, presupposes both agency and self-consciousness."[551] Caring is essentially a reflexive activity, and we could add, it presupposes that one has appropriated resources or principles on which to guide oneself. To care for oneself in some respect is to guide one's life according to such principles. Thus, caring as a reflexive activity shows many parallels to what happens in the context of religious beliefs. "This is not exactly because the agent, in guiding his own behavior, necessarily does something to himself. Rather, it is more nearly because he purposefully does something with himself."[552] The parallel to religious belief becomes even more obvious in the following description:

A person who cares about something is, as it were, invested in it. He identifies himself with what he cares about in the sense that he makes himself vulnerable to losses and susceptible to benefits depending upon whether what he cares about is diminished or enhanced. Thus he concerns himself with what concerns it, giving particular attention to such things and directing his behavior accordingly. Insofar as the person's life is in whole or in part devoted to anything, rather than being merely a sequence of events whose themes and structures he makes no effort to fashion, it is devoted to this.[553]

To care about something is not the same as to desire it. We can like, want, or desire something without caring about it. Caring has a temporal direction towards the future, whereas these other attitudes do not necessarily have any relation to one's future existence. Caring constitutes a continuity in life that is not similar with regard to more contingent desires and beliefs.[554] Here, the reflexive dimension in caring becomes apparent: "The moments in the life of a person who cares about something, however, are not merely linked inherently by formal relations of sequentiality. The person necessarily binds them together, and in the nature of the case also construes them as being bound together, in richer ways. This both entails and is entailed by his own continuing concern with what he does with himself and with what goes on in his life."[555]

In this book, I have used the notion of orientation to point to the practices that place the individual, in his or her self-understanding, within a definite context that can be experienced as meaningful and purposeful. Practices of orientation provide what Frankfurt calls guidance. Guidance implies caring and has

---

[551] Frankfurt, "The Importance of What We Care About," 260.
[552] Ibid.
[553] Ibid.
[554] Cf. ibid., 260–61. "Desires and beliefs have no inherent persistence; nothing in the nature of wanting or of believing requires that a desire or a belief must endure" (261)
[555] Ibid., 261.

some consistency or steadiness of behavior as its consequence. Thus, it also presupposes some degree of persistence, which comes to expression in temporal continuity.[556]

Frankfurt makes a distinction between making a decision about caring and the actual act of caring. This distinction I would hold as parallel to deciding to believe in something and continuing to hold and practice that belief. The decision is never a guarantee for the continuation of neither caring nor belief. But a decision forms a person's intentions about what to care about from here on, without being sufficient in itself to make it happen. That is up to the practice that follows (or not) after the decision is made.[557]

What one cares about is what shapes the content of one's will. This needs to be distinguished from what one decides under given circumstances. This distinction makes it possible to identify the choices we make as expressions of what we *intend* to be our will, but these decisions may not necessarily express our true will.[558] This point is especially relevant in relation to religious convictions and beliefs, which people may sometimes find it hard to hold on to or practice consistently, for different reasons. We may find ourselves bereft of the possibility to carry out in action the intentions that our belief entails. The reasons for it may be of diverse kinds: it may be due to contextual and contingent circumstances and need not imply that we give up or forget our decisions and intentions to pursue our beliefs or the conviction that they matter more than anything else. Frankfurt describes the causes that can deprive a person of the capacity to carry out his intentions along several lines, all of which have bearings also for the difficulties in maintaining a religious belief through expressions in different actions or practices:

Without changing his mind or forgetting anything, he might find either that he is moved irresistibly to pursue the other course of action instead or that he is similarly constrained at least to forbear from the course he has chosen. Or he might find that he is actually able to perform the actions he has chosen to perform, but only by forcing himself to do so against powerful and persistent natural inclinations. That is, he might discover that he does not have and that he does not subsequently develop the feelings, attitudes and interests constitutive of the sort of person which his decision has committed him to being.[559]

---

556 Ibid. Accordingly, Frankfurt holds that a person who only cares for something for a moment is indistinguishable from a person who acts on impulse and without guidance.
557 Cf. ibid., 261.
558 Ibid.
559 Ibid.

Let us rephrase Frankfurt's analysis here with reference to religious beliefs: without giving up these beliefs, one might be tempted to ignore them, or something may impede the practices it would usually entail. That is, realistically speaking, something that many people involved in religious practices may experience. Moreover, in the subsequent example he mentions, one may be able to do what is requested, demanded, or expected, but this requires that one is able to impede one's own natural tendencies. Abstention from drink, food, or sex presents obvious instances where one is not able to conform to the ideals one has committed oneself to. From a realistic religious point of view, this points not only to the necessity of allowing for processes of transformation that may take considerable time, but it also implies that one must acknowledge that one always has to reckon with the possibility of a distance between one's decisions and intended commitments and what one actually practices. Hence, a decision for a religious commitment may only be the start of a long process of transformation, sometimes with no end within sight.

One could, furthermore, ask how wise it is for religious traditions to introduce ideals for a commitment that can only be carried out by forcing oneself to do so against powerful and persistent natural inclinations. If there are some concerns for ultimacy behind such ideals and commitments, these may be hard to realize and/or bring in accordance with experientially accessible insights into the conditions for human flourishing. Hence, to motivate for such practices, and finding ways out of the dilemmas they represent, cannot be solved simply by a decision that one should do it. Frankfurt maintains that they can only be solved if a person really cares more about something than something else. "It requires that he really care more about one of the alternatives confronting him than about the other, and it requires further that he understand which of those alternatives it is that he really cares about more."[560] Hence, a decision for religiously motivated practices must be followed up by insight and reflexivity.[561]

Frankfurt makes clear that we care about something due to a composite array of cognitive, affective, and volitional dispositions and states.[562] This insight applies to religious beliefs, as well. To overlook this complexity is not recommendable. Neither is the insight into the "wide variations in how strongly

---

[560] Ibid., 262.

[561] The last point here is also relevant in relation to what I discussed with reference to the problem of "obedience to commands" in the previous chapter.

[562] Cf. Frankfurt, "The Importance of What We Care About," 262.

and how persistently people care about things."[563] A similar thing goes for religious beliefs. Furthermore, when he points to the possibility to "discriminate different ways of caring, which are not reducible in any obvious manner to differences of degree,"[564] we can again say that similar things apply to belief. The varieties of love are good examples of this insight.

Sometimes it is entirely up to us what we care about or believe, and how much or how intensely we do it. But sometimes we may experience that we believe or care about something out of necessity, simply because we cannot imagine any other alternative. Frankfurt here refers to Luther's famous declaration: "Here I stand; I can do no other."[565] This example is especially relevant in the present context because it represents the consequence of a religious conviction – something that religion has mediated the reasons for caring more about than any other concerns or thing to care for. The necessity is not due to Luther's deficient capacity, but rather his experience of "having no choice but to accede to the force by which he is constrained even if he thinks it might be better not to do so."[566] However, "the impossibility to which Luther referred was a matter neither of logical nor of causal necessity."[567] Frankfurt calls this situation for *volitional necessity*. A person who finds himself in such a situation must act as he does. However, this does not imply any passive state in which one is a helpless bystander to one's own behavior. People in such situations may regard it as actually enhancing both their autonomy and their strength of will. They do not accede to the constraining force because they lack sufficient strength of will to defeat it. Frankfurt describes a person in this situation thus: "He accedes to it because he is unwilling to oppose it and because, furthermore, his unwillingness is itself something which he is unwilling to alter. Not only does he care about following the particular course of action which he is constrained to follow. He also cares about caring about it."[568]

Frankfurt's analysis here is interesting also because it sheds some light on the formation of desire that situations like those of volitional necessity entail – also in a religious context. Such necessity is not perceived as an external force that threatens to dissolve the person's autonomy of sense of self by installing him in a situation that cannot be otherwise. The reason is that this situation

---

[563] Ibid., 263.
[564] Ibid.
[565] Ibid.
[566] Ibid., 263–64.
[567] Ibid., 264.
[568] Ibid., 264–65.

coincides with – and is, indeed, partly constituted by – desires which are not merely his own but with which he actively identifies himself. Moreover, the necessity is to a certain extent self-imposed. It is generated when someone requires himself to avoid being guided in what he does by any forces other than those by which he most deeply wants to be guided. In order to prevent himself from caring about anything as much as he cares about them, he suppresses or dissociates himself from whatever motives or desires he regards as inconsistent with the stability and effectiveness of his commitment. It is in this way that volitional necessity may have a liberating effect: when someone is tending to be distracted from caring about what he cares about most, the force of volitional necessity may constrain him to do what he really wants to do.[569]

Consider this analysis against the backdrop of what I have developed earlier about how we are, as humans, shaped by forces and relationships that extend beyond ourselves but nevertheless causes us to become ourselves and establish our identity. Identity has to do with what you innermost and deepest hold to be important, and from what you desire to orient the fundamental features of your life – even if you sometimes fail in doing so. This instigates the person in a continuous or unending struggle to manifest the convictions that shape the decisions in which this identity is at play. And, as Frankfurt suggests, sometimes volitional necessity may come to help us here.[570]

Not only the reference to Luther as an instance of volitional necessity but also the subsequent component in Frankfurt's analysis suggests that he deals with a topic of strong interest to religious reasoning. In William James' definition of religious experience, he says that we are saved "by making a proper connection with the higher powers."[571] This statement, which will not concern us much here, is echoed in Frankfurt's identification of a theme which is both morally and religiously persistent, namely that "a person may be in some sense liberated through acceding to a power which is not subject to his immediate voluntary control."[572] He addresses this topic with special reference to the two human capacities that seem to be of utmost importance for the realization of human flourishing, including the experience of freedom: rationality and love.

---

[569] Ibid., 265.

[570] For the sake of a consistent answer to some of the questions that this position raises, cf. the following: "It may seem difficult to understand how volitional necessity can possibly be at the same time both self-imposed and imposed in-voluntarily, or how it is possible to avoid the conclusion that an agent who is constrained by volitional necessity must be simultaneously both active and passive with respect to the same force. Resolution of these difficulties lies in recognising that: (a) the fact that a person cares about something is a fact about his will, (b) a person's will need not be under his own voluntary control, and (c) his will may be no less truly his own when it is not by his own voluntary doing that he cares as he does." Ibid., 266.

[571] See James, *The Varieties of Religious Experience : A Study in Human Nature*. Here quoted from the original, 508.

[572] Frankfurt, "The Importance of What We Care About," 266.

Both love and rationality "require a person to submit to something which is beyond his voluntary control and which may be indifferent to his desires." Being moved by logic or by love does not cause an experience of dispirited impotence but "a sense of liberation and of enhancement."[573] These phenomena move a person beyond herself. Frankfurt writes:

[W]hen a person is responding to a perception of something as rational or as beloved, his relationship to it tends towards selflessness. His attention is not merely concentrated upon the object; it is somehow fixed or seized by the object. The object captivates him. He is guided by its characteristics rather than primarily by his own. Quite commonly, he feels that he is overcome – that his own direction of his thoughts and volitions has been superseded.[574]

Remember: Frankfurt is writing as a philosopher, and not as a Christian theologian. However, what he articulates are the selfsame insights that the Christian tradition has struggled to articulate through the centuries; "that we find ourselves to be most fully realised, and consider that we are at our best, when – through reason or through love – we have lost or escaped from ourselves."[575]

This does not mean that personal elements are absent. Love is the clearest and most profound example of how a first-person position is required in order to realize it. However, Frankfurt makes some important distinctions in this regard as well, when he claims that "rationality and love equally entail selflessness."[576] However, whereas rationality is essentially impersonal, love cannot be. Rational claims or judgments are impersonal because they are not dependent on or limited to the person who makes them and entail that anyone who holds a different opinion is wrong. On the other hand, a declaration of love is "a personal matter [...], because the person who makes it does not thereby commit himself to supposing that anyone who fails to love what he does has somehow gone wrong."[577] I would like to add here, that this claim suggests that the character of freedom connected to love is of another kind than the freedom articulated in making a rational argument or claim. Moreover, this suggests that a specific type of integrity emerges from love, which cannot be explained by reference to moral ideals only:

---

[573] Ibid., 267.
[574] Ibid.
[575] Ibid.
[576] Ibid.
[577] Ibid. Subsequently, Frankfurt also argues that moral judgments must be considered as impersonal. See ibid., 268. His argument in that context is not of specific relevance for what I want to say about religion here, though.

Especially with respect to those we love and with respect to our ideals, we are liable to be bound by necessities which have less to do with our adherence to the principles of morality than with integrity or consistency of a more personal kind. These necessities constrain us from betraying the things which we care about most and with which, accordingly, we are most closely identified. In a sense which a strictly ethical analysis cannot make clear, what they keep us from violating are not our duties or our obligations but ourselves.[578]

The above analysis indicates how the relationship between love, what one personally cares for and holds as ultimate, personal identity and integrity, and religion is quite tight. Hence, the previous analyses developed in this book are confirmed, or better: it turns out that the Christian understanding of love and human life is possible to formulate as features that are common to human life in general.

It follows from Frankfurt's reasoning that insofar as humans are caring about things or involved in finding things to care about, they are also by necessity involved in processes of formation and transformation. "The formation of a person's will is most fundamentally a matter of his coming to care about certain things, and of his coming to care about some of them more than about others."[579]

The formation of the will has been an important element in the Christian tradition since Augustine and is closely related to the previous considerations about the formation and shaping of desire. Not only in a religious perspective, but also in general, one needs to acknowledge that such processes cannot be fully under one's own control. But, as Frankfurt points out, because people care about what they care about, they nevertheless have some interest in affecting these processes, because their outcome has large consequences for their identity and self-evaluation.[580]

The final topic relevant for religious reasoning in Frankfurt's article, is that he points out that despite the fact that what a person cares about (or what he believes, J-OH) is a personal matter and therefore involves the first-person position, it does not entail that anything goes. It is still "possible to distinguish between things that are worth caring about to one degree or another and things that are not"[581] – or, in our perspective, discussing what kind of beliefs appear as justifiable and is not excluded because it relies on personal convictions. Critical inquiry is recommendable and useful. To ask "what makes something worth

---

[578] Ibid., 268.
[579] Ibid.
[580] Cf. Ibid., 268–69.
[581] Ibid., 269.

caring about – that is, what conditions must be satisfied if something is to be suitable or worthy as an ideal or as an object of love – and into how a person is to decide, from among the various things worth caring about, which to care about"[582] should not be avoided. He goes on, writing; "Although people may justifiably care about different things, or care differently about the same things, this surely does not mean that their loves and their ideals are entirely unsusceptible to significant criticism of any sort or that no general analytical principles of discrimination can be found."[583] And, I would add: similar conditions go for what we believe in. Why people believe what they do, and what these beliefs entail for how they lead their lives, can be the subject of discussion. Unless such critical inquiry takes place, people's beliefs may not only become opaque to others who want to understand them, but believers may also lose the ability to articulate the content of their beliefs, as well as why they have them, to themselves and others.

In the following, I will try to employ Frankfurt's analysis by making a productive re-phrasing of his insights with reference to a specific case: the importance of caring about, and therefore, believing in God. When Frankfurt says that "people often do not care about certain things which are quite important to them," this is an insight that makes perfect sense from the point of view of Christian belief. Many people do not recognize the importance of believing in God. Note here that nothing is said yet about why this should be important. The point so far is simply to state, with Frankfurt, that "if there is something that a person does care about, then it follows that it is important to him. This is not because caring somehow involves an infallible judgment concerning the importance of its object. Rather, it is because caring about something *makes* that thing important to the person who cares about it."[584]

When one believes in and cares about God (whatever that means), one cannot be indifferent to matters of faith. When someone, e.g., attacks one's faith or one's community, it "will make a difference to a person who cares about it, and the difference it makes must itself be important to him."[585] Hence, it is important to people not only what they care about, but what they believe in, because belief, or faith, relates to those things which are of ultimate importance. Care and belief make a difference. Therefore, it is important not only what we care about

---

[582] Ibid.
[583] Ibid.
[584] Ibid.
[585] Ibid.

and what we believe in, but also whether or not we care or believe in any-thing.[586] Underlying this line of reasoning is the valid claim that "if anything is worth caring about, then it must be worth caring about what to care about."[587]

Frankfurt distinguishes between two ways in which something may be im-portant to a person. They are not incompatible. First, something may be of im-portance to someone "due to considerations which are altogether independent of whether or not he cares about the thing in question. Second, the thing may become important to him just because he does care about it."[588] This distinction may, from the point of view of religious reasoning, be articulated as the "objec-tive, doctrinal point of view" about the importance of believing in God, versus the personal and existential importance that such belief has for the believer.

From this distinction follows two different lines of reasoning for justifying the importance of what one cares about – or, in my perspective, believes in. With regard to the first line, the "objective one," something may be worth car-ing about or believing in exactly because it has importance for someone inde-pendent of his or her acknowledging it. The second line of reasoning is, how-ever, the one that has the most traction in a religious context: the position that one is justified in caring or believing because caring or believing is itself some-thing that is important to him.[589] However, in this latter case, when importance is exclusively dependent on the fact that someone cares, that fact is an insuffi-cient measure of the extent to which his caring about the thing is justified. Sim-ilarly, the fact that the belief in God means something for someone is not in itself sufficient justification for that belief.

So, to offer reasons for why it is important to care about God, the critical question must be whether someone is justified in making God important by car-ing about God. Frankfurt argues that "the only way to justify doing this is in terms of the importance of the activity of caring as such."[590] At this point Frank-furt points to how there are central elements in human experience that suggest this point: "It is manifest that the varieties of being concerned or dedicated, and of loving, *are* important to us quite apart from any antecedent capacities for affecting us which what we care about may have. This is not particularly be-cause caring about something makes us susceptible to certain additional grati-fications and disappointments. It is primarily because it serves to connect us

---

[586] Cf. Ibid.
[587] Ibid., 270.
[588] Ibid.
[589] Cf. ibid.
[590] Ibid.

actively to our lives in ways which are creative of ourselves and which expose us to distinctive possibilities for necessity and for freedom."[591]

Caring connects us with life, with others. So does love, and so does belief. Therefore, it matters what we care about, who or what we love, and what we believe in. "Even when the justification for caring about something rests upon the importance of the caring itself, rather than being derivative from the antecedent importance of its object, the choice of the object is not irrelevant or arbitrary,"[592] says Frankfurt. He illustrates this with reference to God as love – and it is therefore also not arbitrary why I present this example on the last pages of this book, because it can also be read against the backdrop of how human beings can understand themselves as images of God, called because of God's love to realize that image:

According to one theological doctrine, divine love is in fact bestowed without regard to the character or antecedent value of its objects. It is God's nature to love, on this view, and He therefore loves everything regardless of any considerations extrinsic to Himself. His love is entirely arbitrary and unmotivated - absolutely sovereign, and in no way conditioned by the worthiness of its objects. Perhaps it is possible only for an omnipotent being – to whom nothing is antecedently important – to love altogether freely and without conditions or restrictions of any kind.[593]

To love another is the most profound way to care about him or her. However, against the backdrop of the theological line of reasoning Frankfurt presents in the quote just given, and his insistence that care makes a difference, it is also worth referring his answer to the question about what makes it more suitable "for a person to make one object rather than another important to himself?" His answer to this question is related to the *possibility* we have for caring, in ways that make it possible either to care about one and not about the other or the possibility to care about someone *in a way* that is more important than it is for him to care about some other. According to Frankfurt, from this follows that, "When a person makes something important to himself, [...], the situation resembles an instance of divine agape at least in a certain respect. The person does not care about the object because its worthiness commands that he do so. On the other hand, the worthiness of the activity of caring commands that he choose an object which he will be able to care about."[594]

---

[591] Ibid., 270–71.
[592] Ibid., 271.
[593] Ibid., 271–72.
[594] Ibid., 272.

To resemble the divine agape is in some respects a consequence of practic- ing what it means to bear the divine image. It means relating to others in terms of grace. But it also implies that one has to take up the responsibility of caring by caring for that which one will be able to care about. In this lies the recogni- tion of human finitude, and therefore, under the human condition, agape can only be practiced by bearers of this image with the acknowledgment of the fact that this finitude also implies our fundamental difference from the God who is represented in human practices. Hence, the relevance of God for human life is revealed. This relevance is, however, dependent on a composite notion of God as the creative power to love, care, and desire community.[595]

***

If God exists, one could assume that it is important to care about God. Hence, religious practices of reflection, orientation, and transformation must make vis- ible why it is important to care about God. If not, God cannot be the ultimate reality that provides meaning to human life. The only reason we should care more about God than about anything else is that loving ourselves just as much as our neighbors and God is the best way to lead a life. We are called to live in God and to love because God, as love, cares about us. There is nothing more important to care about than God and love. For if there is, then it is not worth caring about, or believing in, God.

---

[595] Cf. Robert C Neville, in *Defining Religion,* 233–234: "To love in the purest sense is not to have a sentiment about something but to make something good, or, in less pure contexts, to make some- thing better. God, on my view, does not create the world for a reason. God creates in an act of pure, unbounded love that provides its justification in the things created. God does not love us because we are lovely – quite the opposite – nor does God love us because we are unlovely. God creates us with our own loveliness, and this creation is God's pure, unbounded love."

Conclusion

The present study has tried to show how deeply intertwined are the three central topics religion, God, and humanity. Religion represents the practices in which humans relate to the ultimate, and in Christianity, this ultimate is primarily expressed in the symbol God as love. God is the ultimate reality that comes to expression in human life by means of representations of ultimacy as these are expressed in rituals, practices, symbols, and texts. Humans thematize the ultimate conditions of their lives when they employ the representations provides by religious practices and resources. These ultimate conditions are, in the Christian religion, primarily mediated by the representation of God in Jesus Christ, who is, at the same time, also understood as the true human.

The interplay among these three topics suggests that they are all part of a process that takes place in the course of history. God realizes Godself by relating to and mediating Godself in human history, through and by means of, human practices and religious representations that mediate faith, hope, and love as these features shape and motivate human action. Hence, the ways in which humans understand and practice God is an open process that one will have to expect remains unfinished as long as history continues. Because God is no part of the empirical world, but rather its origin and its ultimate condition, God is only accessible in representations. This feature means that any attempt to reify God amounts to idolatry and that any representation of God that is not acknowledged as such may lead humans astray when it comes to an understanding of what matters most in human life. One can even see the fact that the Bible, as one of the main representations of God in the Christian tradition, is in constant need of interpretation in new contexts and in relation to new experiences and historical conditions, as a testimony to this fact. Relating to God via such representations always represents something open-ended, something still to be done, some unfinished business.

Religion, or religions, must, accordingly, be understood as processes and practices instead of being reified as entities that represent fixed states, doctrines, rituals, or specific experiences that can be delineated, validated, and ritualized once and for all. This understanding, in turn, also suggests that humans need to take this open-ended character of life and religion-as-life into consideration when they orient themselves. Religion is an opportunity for orienting oneself in relation to the important aims for transformation, and not an opportunity to end development, growth, and maturation. I have suggested that the basic features of human life, as they come to expression in desire and vulnerability, are best shaped by the phenomenon of love. This suggestion is an attempt to express how love (and God as love) is intrinsically linked to such processes.

Against this backdrop, we can summarize the main points that I have developed above thus: By understanding religion as clusters of practices that relate humans to ultimacy and what they should care about (Frankfurt), Christian religion articulates its belief in God as creator (manifest in the power to be) and redeemer (manifest in the ministry of Jesus Christ as love). These two features condition and manifest themselves in human experience. They are closely related to the human features of desire and vulnerability, as these express elements that shape, form, and articulate challenges for human life. As life constantly facing challenges, humans are in need of orienting themselves and in need of different types of transformation. Christian religion articulates a specific mode of how to cope with challenges presented by desire and vulnerability: by living in love. Hence, love is what matters. Love expresses itself in the power to create new conditions for life, as well as in practices of forgiveness that can restore broken relationships or allow humans to understand themselves as more than their actions.

To practice love is not a task ever finished. By understanding human beings as representatives of God – as *imago Dei,* modeled in Jesus Christ as the true human being and as such the true representative of God, Christianity brings to expression the following: Human life represents God and relates to God when God as love is practiced and understood as the ultimate reality from which human life springs, by which it is transformed, and towards which it is oriented.

Literature

Afdal, Geir. *Religion Som Bevegelse: Læring, Kunnskap Og Mediering*. Oslo: Universitetsforlaget, 2013.

Althaus, Paul. *The Theology of Martin Luther*. Philadelphia: Fortress Press, 1996.

Anselm, *Cur Deus Homo*. Chicago: The Open Court Publishing Company, 1926.

Baker, Lynne Rudder. *Naturalism and the First-Person Perspective*. Oxford ; New York: Oxford University Press, 2013.

Bash, Anthony. *Forgiveness and Christian Ethics*. New Studies in Christian Ethics. Cambridge, UK ; New York: Cambridge University Press, 2007.

Blue, Daniel. *The Making of Friedrich Nietzsche : The Quest for Identity, 1844-1869*. Cambridge, United Kingdom: Cambridge University Press, 2016.

Bracken, Joseph A. *The World in the Trinity: Open-Ended Systems in Science and Religion*. Minneapolis, MN: Fortress Press, 2014.

Brierley, Michael. "Naming a Quiet Revolution: The Panentheistic Turn in Modern Theology." In *In whom we live and move and have our being*, edited by Philip Clayton and A. R. Peacocke, 1–15. Grand Rapids, Mich.: William B. Eerdmans Pub., 2004.

Brock, Rita Nakashima. *Journeys by Heart: A Christology of Erotic Power*. New York: Crossroad, 1988.

Brown, Brené. *I Thought It Was Just Me (but It Isn't) : Making the Journey from "What Will People Think?" To "I Am Enough"*. New York: Avery (Penguin Random House), 2008.

Brudholm, Thomas. *Resentment's Virtue : Jean Améry and the Refusal to Forgive*. Politics, History, and Social Change. Philadelphia: Temple University Press, 2008.

Brudholm, Thomas, and Thomas Cushman. *The Religious in Responses to Mass Atrocity : Interdisciplinary Perspectives.* Cambridge ; New York: Cambridge University Press, 2009.

Bubbio, Paolo Diego. "Hegel, the Trinity, and the 'I'." *International Journal for Philosophy of Religion* 76, no. 2 (2014): 129–50.

Butler, Judith. *Subjects of Desire. Hegelian Reflection in the Twentieth-Century France.* New York: Columbia University Press, 1999.

Caputo John D.; Michael J. Scanlon (Eds.), *God, the Gift, and Postmodernism.* Bloomington, IN: Indiana Univ. Press, 2006.

Clayton, Philip. *Mind and Emergence : From Quantum to Consciousness.* Oxford, UK; New York: Oxford University Press, 2004.

————."Panentheism Today: A Constructive Systematic Evaluation." In *Whom We Live and Move and Have Our Being : Panentheistic Reflections on God's Presence in a Scientific World*, edited by Philip Clayton and A. R. Peacocke, 249–264. Grand Rapids, Mich.: William B. Eerdmans Pub., 2004.

Clayton, Philip, and A. R. Peacocke. *In Whom We Live and Move and Have Our Being : Panentheistic Reflections on God's Presence in a Scientific World.* Grand Rapids, Mich.: William B. Eerdmans Pub., 2004.

Coakley, Sarah. "Kenosis and Subversion: On the Repression of 'Vulnerability' in Christian Feminist Writing." In *Swallowing a Fishbone?Feminist Theologians Debate Christianity*, edited by Margaret Daphne Hampson, 83–111. London: SPCK, 1996.

————. *Powers and Submissions Spirituality, Philosophy and Gender.* Oxford, UK Malden, Mass.: Blackwell Publishers, 2002.

Cross, F. L., and Elizabeth A. Livingstone. *The Oxford Dictionary of the Christian Church.* London; New York: Oxford University Press, 1974.

Dalferth, Ingolf U. *Becoming Present : An Inquiry into the Christian Sense of the Presence of God.* Leuven: Peeters, 2006.

————. *Die Wirklichkeit des Möglichen: hermeneutische Religionsphilosophie.* Tübingen: Mohr Siebeck, 2003.

————. "God, Time, and Orientation." In *The Presence and Absence of God*, edited by Ingolf U. Dalferth, 1–20. Tübingen: Mohr Siebeck, 2009

─────, ed. *The Presence and Absence of God*. Tübingen: Mohr Siebeck.

Danermark, Berth, and Mats Ekström. *Explaining Society : Critical Realism in the Social Sciences*. Routledge Studies in Critical Realism. Second edition. Abingdon, Oxon ; New York, NY: Routledge, 2019.

Davies, P. C. W., and Niels Henrik Gregersen. *Information and the Nature of Reality : From Physics to Metaphysics*. Cambridge, UK ; New York: Cambridge University Press, 2010.

Depoortere, Frederiek, and Magdalen Lambkin. *The Question of Theological Truth : Philosophical and Interreligious Perspectives*. Currents of Encounter. Amsterdam ; New York: Rodopi, 2012.

Derrida, Jacques. *On Cosmopolitanism and Forgiveness*. Thinking in Action. London ; New York: Routledge, 2001.

Deuser, Hermann, Hans Joas, Matthias Jung, and Magnus Schlette. *The Varieties of Transcendence : Pragmatism and the Theory of Religion*. American Philosophy. New York: Fordham University Press, 2016.

Engedal, Leif Gunnar. "Ecce Homo : En Studie av psykovitenskapelige identitetsteorier med særlig henblikk på identitetserfaringens konstituerende elementer og de metateoretiske forutsetningenes funksjon i teoriutformingen." Dissertation, Faculty of Arts, University of Oslo, 1999.

Feuerbach, Ludwig. *The Essence of Christianity*. New York: Continuum, 1990.

Fiddes, Paul S. "Memory, Forgetting and the Problem of Forgiveness. Reflecting on Volf, Derrida and Ricoeur." In *Forgiving and Forgetting : Theology and the Margins of Soteriology*, edited by Hartmut von Sass, Johannes Zachhuber,. Tübingen: Mohr Siebeck, 2015.

─────. *Participating in God : A Pastoral Doctrine of the Trinity*. London: Darton Longman & Todd, 2000.

─────. *Seeing the World and Knowing God : Hebrew Wisdom and Christian Doctrine in a Late-Modern Context*. First edition. ed. Oxford, United Kingdom: Oxford University Press, 2013.

Frankfurt, Harry G. "The Importance of What We Care About." *Synthese* 53, no. 2 (1982): 257–72.

Gadamer, Hans-Georg, Joel Weinsheimer, and Donald G. Marshall. *Truth and Method*. 2nd, rev. ed. London ; New York: Continuum, 2004.

Garrard, Eve, and David McNaughton. *Forgiveness*. Durham: Acumen, 2010.

Gestrich, Christof. *The return of splendor in the world: the Christian doctrine of sin and forgiveness*. Grand Rapids, Mich.: W.B. Eerdmans Pub. Co, 1997.

Gregersen, Niels. "From Anthropic Design to Self-Organized Complexity." In *From complexity to life: on the emergence of life and meaning*, edited by Niels Gregersen. New York: Oxford University Press, 2003, 206–234

———. "The Emotional Christ: Bonaventure and Deep Incarnation." *Dialog* Fall 2016.

———. "From Laws of Nature to Natural Capacities: A Theological Thought Experiment." In *Essays in Naturalism & Christian Semantics*, edited by Troels Engberg-Pedersen and Niels Henrik Gregersen. 167–199. (Copenhagen University, 2010).

———. "Three Varieties of Panentheism." In *Whom We Live and Move and Have Our Being: Panentheistic Reflections on God's Presence in a Scientific World*, edited by Philip Clayton and A. R. Peacocke. Grand Rapids, Mich.: William B. Eerdmans Pub., 2004.

———. "The Twofold Assumption: A Response to Cole-Turner, Moritz, Peters and Peterson." *Theology and Science* 11:4 (November 2013), 455–468.

Gregersen, Niels Henrik, ed. *Incarnation : On the Scope and Depth of Christology*. Minneapolis: Fortress Press, 2015.

Grube, Dirk-Martin, and Walter Van Herck. *Philosophical Perspectives on Religious Diversity Bivalent Truth, Tolerance and Personhood*. London: Routledge, 2018.

Hampson, Margaret Daphne. *Swallowing a Fishbone?Feminist Theologians Debate Christianity*. London: SPCK, 1996.

Hart, David Bentley. *The Experience of God : Being, Consciousness, Bliss*. New Haven ; London: Yale University Press, 2013.

Hegel, Georg Wilhelm Friedrich. *Werke in Zwanzig Bänden*. Theorie - Werkausgabe. neu ed. Ausg. ed. Frankfurt am Main: Suhrkamp, 1976.

Hegel, Georg Wilhelm Friedrich, and Peter Crafts Hodgson. *Lectures on the Philosophy of Religion : The Lectures of 1827.* One-volume ed. Berkeley: University of California Press, 1988.

Heidegger, Martin. *Sein Und Zeit.* 11. unveränderte Aufl ed. Tübingen: M. Niemeyer, 1967.

Heidegger, Martin, John Macquarrie, and Edward Robinson. *Being and Time.* Malden: Blackwell, 2013.

Henriksen, Jan-Olav. *Christianity as Distinct Practices: A Complicated Relationship.* London: Bloomsbury, 2019.

———. "Creation and construction. On the theological appropriation of post-modern theory." *Modern Theology* 18, no. 2 (2002): 153–169.

———. "The Crucifixion as Realisation of Identity: The Gift of Recognition and Representation." *Modern Theology* 22, no. 2 (2006): 197–220.

———. *Desire, Gift, and Recognition : Christology and Postmodern Philosophy.* Grand Rapids, Mich.: William B. Eerdmans Pub. Co., 2009.

———. "Distinct, Unique, or Separate? : Challenges to Theological Anthropology and Soteriology in Light of Human Evolution." *Studia Theologica* 67, no. 2 (2013): 166–83.

———. "The Experience of God and the World: Christianity's Reasons for Considering Panentheism a Viable Option." *Zygon* 52, no. 4 (2017): 1080–97.

———. "Everyday Religion as Orientation and Transformation: A Challenge to Theology." *Nordic Journal of Religion and Society*, no. 01 (2016): 36–51.

———. *Finitude and Theological Anthropology : An Interdisciplinary Exploration into Theological Dimensions of Finitude.* Studies in Philosophical Theology. Leuven ; Walpole, Mass.: Peeters, 2011.

———. "God Revealed through Human Agency – Divine Agency and Embodied Practices of Faith, Hope, and Love." *Neue Zeitschrift für systematische Theologie und Religionsphilosophie* 58, no. 4 (2016): 453–72.

———. "God, Semiosis and Experience." In *Talking Seriously About God : Philosophy of Religion in the Dispute between Theism and Atheism*, edited by Asle Eikrem Atle Søvik. Nordische Studien Zur Theologie, 37–54. Münster; Zürich: LIT Verlag, 2016.

———. *Imago Dei. Den teologiske konstruksjonen av menneskets identitet.* Oslo: Gyldendal Academic Press, 2003.

———. *Life, Love, and Hope : God and Human Experience.* Grand Rapids, Michigan: Eerdmans Publishing Company, 2014.

———. "Love as the Power with Which God Shapes the World: Theological Anthropology and Human Experience." *Louvain studies.* 41, no. 3 (2018): 269–85.

———. "Mennesket som natur : en systematisk-teologisk analyse av forholdet mellom antropologi og naturforståelse i Wolfhart Pannenbergs teologi." Oslo: Det teologiske Menighetsfakultet, 1989.

———. "Panentheism without the Supernatural? On a Perichoretic Trinitarian Conception of Reality." *Philosophy, Theology and the Sciences* 3, no. 1 (2016): 51–71.

———. *Relating God and the Self : Dynamic Interplay.* Burlington: Ashgate, 2013.

———. *Religion as Orientation and Transformation : A Maximalist Theory.* Religion in Philosophy and Theology,. Tübingen: Mohr Siebeck, 2017.

———. *Religious Plurality and Pragmatist Theology – Openness and Resistance.* Leiden: Brill, 2019.

———. "Thematizing Otherness." *Studia Theologica - Nordic Journal of Theology* 64, no. 2 (2010/12/01 2010): 153-76.

———. "Åpenbaring, Erfaring Og Teologi." *Teologisk Tidsskrift* 2, no. 4 (2013).

Henriksen, Jan-Olav; Karl Olav Sandnes. "The Vulnerable Human and the Absent God the Stories About Gethsemane as a Possible Source for Theological Anthropology." *Kerygma und Dogma : Zeitschrift für theologische Forschung und kirchliche Lehre* 64, no. 3 (2018): 163–77.

Herms, Eilert. *Systematische Theologie: Das Wesen Des Christentums: In Wahrheit Und Aus Gnade Leben.* Tübingen: Mohr Siebeck, 2017.

Hervieu-Léger, Danièle. *Religion as a Chain of Memory*. New Brunswick, N.J.: Rutgers University Press, 2000.

Hodgson, Peter Crafts. *Hegel and Christian Theology : A Reading of the Lectures on the Philosophy of Religion*. Oxford ; New York: Oxford University Press, 2005.

Hogarth, Steve. "Marillion's Steve Hogarth." Interview by Dennis Cook. *Dirty Impound*, 31 October 2012.

Irenaeus, and James R. Payton. *Irenaeus on the Christian faith: a condensation of Against heresies*. Eugene, Or.: Pickwick Publications, 2011.

James, William. *The Varieties of Religious Experience : A Study in Human Nature*. Penguin Classics. New York ; London: Penguin Books, 1985.

Jeanrond, Werner G. *A Theology of Love*. London: T. & T. Clark, 2010.

Jenkins, Scott. "Hegel's Concept of Desire." *Journal of the History of Philosophy* 47 (2014), 103–130.

Johnson, Elizabeth A. *She Who Is: The Mystery of God in Feminist Theological Discourse*. New York: Crossroad, 2002.

Johnson, Dominic D. P., Hillary L. Lenfesty, and Jeffrey P. Schloss. "The Elephant in the Room: Do Evolutionary Accounts of Religion Entail the Falsity of Religious Belief?" *Philosophy, Theology and the Sciences* 1, no. 2 (2014): 200–231.

Jones, W. Paul. "Suffering into Wholeness: Vulnerability and the Imprisoned Child Within." *Quarterly Review* 15, no. 3 (Fall 1995): 275–85.

Jónsson, G. A. *The Image of God. Genesis 1, 26-28 in a century of Old Testament Research*. Stockholm: Almquist & Wiksell, 1988.

Kaag, John, and Kipton E. Jensen. "The American Reception of Hegel (1830–1930)." In *The Oxford Handbook of Hegel*, edited by Dean Moyar, 670–96. Oxford: Oxford University Press, 2017.

Karle, Isolde. "Die Suche Nach Anerkennung – Und Die Religion." *Evangelische Theologie* 76 (2016).

Kearney, Richard. "Desire of God." In: *God, the Gift and Postmodernism*, edited by Caputo and Scanlon; Bloomington, IN: . Indiana Univ. Press, 2006.

Keener, Craig S. *Miracles: The Credibility of the New Testament Accounts*, 2 vols. Grand Rapids, Mich.: Baker Academic, 2011.

Kierkegaard, Søren, and Alastair Hannay. *Fear and Trembling*. New York: Penguin Books, 2006.

Koopman, Nico. "Vulnerable Church in a Vulnerable World? Towards an Ecclesiology of Vulnerability." *Journal of Reformed Theology* 2, no. 3 (2008): 240–54.

Lash, Nicholas. *The Beginning and the End of 'Religion'*. Cambridge; New York: Cambridge University Press, 1996.

Lévinas, Emmanuel. "The paradox of morality." In *The Provocation of Levinas: Rethinking the other*, edited by Robert Bernasconi and David Wood

———. *Totality and Infinity. An Essay on Exteriority*. Pittsburg: Duquesne UP, 1969.

Laird, Martin. *Gregory of Nyssa and the Grasp of Faith : Union, Knowledge and Divine Presence*. Oxford: Oxford University Press, 2014.

Lewis, Thomas A. "Overcoming a Stumbling Block: A Nontraditional Hegel for Religious Studies." *The Journal of Religion* 95, no. 2 (2015): 198–212.

———. *Religion, Modernity, and Politics in Hegel*. Oxford ; New York: Oxford University Press, 2011.

———. *Why Philosophy Matters for the Study of Religion–and Vice Versa*. New York, NY: Oxford University Press, 2015.

Løgstrup, Knud E. *Metaphysics*. Marquette Studies in Philosophy. 2 vols. Milwaukee: Marquette University Press, 1995.

———. *Skabelse og Tilintetgørelse: Religionsfilosofiske Betragtninger*. Metafysik. Copenhagen: Gyldendal, 1978.

MacIntyre, Alasdair C. *After Virtue : A Study in Moral Theory*. 2nd ed. Notre Dame, Ind.: University of Notre Dame Press, 1984.

———. *Dependent Rational Animals : Why Human Beings Need the Virtues*. Chicago: Open Court, 2006.

———. *Ethics in the Conflicts of Modernity : An Essay on Desire, Practical Reasoning, and Narrative*. New York: Cambridge University Press, 2016.

Marion, Jean-Luc. *The Erotic Phenomenon.* Chicago: University of Chicago Press, 2007.

McFadyen, Alistair I. *Bound to Sin : Abuse, Holocaust, and the Christian Doctrine of Sin.* Cambridge: Cambridge University Press, 2000.

McGowan, John. *Democracy's Children : Intellectuals and the Rise of Cultural Politics.* Ithaca, N.Y.: Cornell University Press, 2002.

Merleau-Ponty, M. *Phenomenology of Perception.* London: Routledge, 1994.

Merklinger, Philip M. *Philosophy, Theology, and Hegel's Berlin Philosophy of Religion, 1821-1827.* Albany: State University of New York Press, 1993.

Murphy, Jeffrie G., and Jean Hampton. *Forgiveness and Mercy.* Cambridge Studies in Philosophy and Law. Cambridge ; New York: Cambridge University Press, 1988.

Müller, Friedrich Max. *Einleitung in Die Vergleichende Religionswissenschaft.* Strassburg: Trubner, 1874.

Nagel, Thomas. *Mind and Cosmos : Why the Materialist Neo-Darwinian Conception of Nature Is Almost Certainly False.* New York: Oxford University Press, 2012.

Neville, Robert C. *Defining Religion : Essays in Philosophy of Religion.* Albany, NY: State University of New York, 2018.

———. *The Truth of Broken Symbols.* Suny Series in Religious Studies. Albany: State University of New York Press, 1996.

———. *Ultimate Realities.* The Comparative Religious Ideas Project. Albany: State University of New York Press, 2001.

Nordling, Cherith Fee. *Knowing God by name: a conversation between Elizabeth A. Johnson and Karl Barth.* New York: Peter Lang, 2010

Pannenberg, Wolfhart. *Anthropology in Theological Perspective.* Edinburgh: T. & T. Clark, 1985.

———. *Systematische Theologie.* 3 vols. Göttingen: Vandenhoeck & Ruprecht, 1988.

Paulson, S. "Luther's Doctrine of God." In *The Oxford Handbook of Martin Luther's Theology,* edited by Kolb, Dingel and Batka, 187–200. Oxford: Oxford University Press, 2014.

Peacocke, Arthur. "Sciences of Complexity: New Theological Resource?" In *Information and the Nature of Reality: From Physics to Metaphysics,* edited by P. C. W. Davies and Niels Henrik Gregersen, 249–281. Cambridge, UK ; New York: Cambridge University Press, 2010.

Peirce, Charles Sanders. "How to Make Our Ideas Clear." In *Peirce on Signs: Writings on Semiotic by Charles Sanders Peirce,* edited by James Hoopes. Chapel Hill: University of North Carolina Press, 1991.

Pelikan, Jaroslav, ed. *Luther's Works.* St. Louis: Concordia Publishing House, 1955.

Phillips, D. Z. *Belief, Change, and Forms of Life.* Atlantic Highlands: Humanities Press International, 1986.

Pihlström, Sami. *The Bloomsbury Companion to Pragmatism.* Bloomsbury Companions. London: Bloomsbury Academic, 2015.

———. "A New Look at Wittgenstein and Pragmatism." *European Journal of Pragmatism and American Philosophy* IV, no. 2 (2012).

Proudfoot, Wayne. *Religious Experience.* Berkeley: University of California Press, 1985.

Pryor, Adam, and Devan Stahl. *The Body and Ultimate Concern : Reflections on an Embodied Theology of Paul Tillich.* Macon, GA: Mercer University Press, 2018.

Puntel, Lornez B., and Alan White. *Structure and Being: A Theoretical Framework for a Systematic Philosophy.* University Park, Pa.: Pennsylvania State University Press, 2008.

Pyysiäinen, Ilkka. *Supernatural Agents: Why We Believe in Souls, Gods, and Buddhas.* Oxford ; New York: Oxford University Press, 2009.

Reckwitz, Andreas. "Toward a Theory of Social Practices: A Development in Culturalist Theorizing." *European Journal of Social Theory* 5, no. 2 (2002): 243-63.

Ricœur, Paul. *The Symbolism of Evil.* Religious Perspectives,. 1st ed. New York,: Harper & Row, 1967.

Riesebrodt, Martin. *The Promise of Salvation : A Theory of Religion.* Chicago: University of Chicago Press, 2010.

Riis, Ole, and Linda Woodhead. *A Sociology of Religious Emotion.* Oxford ; New York: Oxford University Press, 2010.

Rizzuto, Ana-Maria. *The Birth of the Living God : A Psychoanalytic Study.* Chicago: University of Chicago Press, 1979.

Robinson, Andrew. *God and the World of Signs : Trinity, Evolution, and the Metaphysical Semiotics of C.S. Peirce.* Philosophical Studies in Science and Religion. Leiden ; Boston: Brill, 2010.

———. *Traces of the Trinity. Signs, Sacraments and Sharing God's Life.* Cambridge: James Clarke & Co, 2014.

Sanderson, Christiane. "The Role of Forgiveness after Interpersonal Abuse - Danger or Road to Recovery and Healing?". In *Forgiveness in Practice*, edited by Stephen Hance, 137-46. London ; Philadelphia: Jessica Kingsley Publishers, 2019.

Schilbrack, Kevin. *Philosophy and the Study of Religions : A Manifesto.* Wiley Blackwell Manifestos. Chichester, West Sussex: Wiley Blackwell, 2014.

Schleiermacher, Friedrich. *Christian Faith: A New Translation and Critical Edition*. Louisville, Kentucky: Westminster John Knox Press, 2016. German ed: Friedrich Schleiermacher: *Der Christliche Glaube*, 2. Aufl., Berlin: de Gruyter, 1960.

Schwöbel, Christoph. "Divine Agency and Providence." *Modern Theology* 3, no. 3 (1987): 225–44.

Selak, Annie. "Orthodoxy, Orthopraxis, and Orthopathy: Evaluating the Feminist Kenosis Debate Orthodoxy, Orthopraxis, and Orthopathy." *Modern Theology* (2017): 529–548.

Shults, F. LeRon. *Theology after the Birth of God: Atheist Conceptions in Cognition and Culture*. New York: Palgrave Macmillian, 2014.

Smith, Christian. *Religion : What It Is, How It Works, and Why It Is Still Important.* Princeton: Princeton University Press, 2017.

Smith, Jonathan Z. "Religion, Religions, Religious." In *Critical Terms for Religious Studies*, edited by Mark Taylor, 269–284. Chicago: University of Chicago Press, 1998.

Smith, Steven G. *Scriptures and the Guidance of Language : Evaluating a Religious Authority in Communicative Action.* Cambridge; New York: Cambridge University Press, 2018.

Southgate, Chris. "Depth, Sign and Destiny: 'Thoughts on Incarnation.'" In *Incarnation: On the Scope and Depth of Christology*, edited by Niels Henrik Gregersen. Minneapolis: Fortress Press, 2015.

Springhart, Heike. "Exploring Life's Vulnerability: Vulnerability in Vitality." In *Exploring Vulnerability*, edited by Heike Springhart and Günter Thomas, 13-33. Gottingen: Vandenhoeck & Ruprecht, 2017.

———. "Vulnerable Creation: Vulnerable Human Life between Risk and Tragedy." *Dialog* 56, no. 4 (2017): 382–90.

Steinbronn, A. J. *The masks of God: the significance of larvae Dei in Luther's theology.* Diss. Concordia Theological Seminary, 1991.

Stenmark, Mikael. *Scientism: Science, Ethics, and Religion.* Aldershot; Burlington: Ashgate, 2001.

Stout, Jeffrey. *Democracy and Tradition.* Princeton, N.J.: Princeton University Press, 2004.

Stålsett, Sturla J. "Prayers of the Precariat? The Political Role of Religion in Precarious Times." *Estudos Teológicos* 58, no. 2 (2018): 313–25.

———. "Towards a Political Theology of Vulnerability: Anthropological and Theological Propositions." *Political Theology* 16, no. 5 (2015): 464–78.

Tanner, Kathryn. *Christ the Key.* Cambridge: Cambridge University Press, 2010.

Taves, Ann. *Religious Experience Reconsidered : A Building Block Approach to the Study of Religion and Other Special Things.* Princeton, N.J.: Princeton University Press, 2009.

Taylor, Charles. *A Secular Age.* Cambridge, Mass. ; London: Belknap Press of Harvard University Press, 2007.

———. "The Validity of Transcendental Arguments." In *Philosophical Arguments*, 21–33. Cambridge, MA: Harvard University Press, 1995.

———. *Varieties of Religion Today: William James Revisited.* Cambridge, Mass. ; London: Harvard University Press, 2002.

Thøgersen, Ulla. *Krop Og Fænomenologi : En Introduktion Til Maurice Merleau-Pontys Filosofi.* Århus: Systime, 2003.

Tillich, Paul. *Love, Power, and Justice : Ontological Analyses and Ethical Applications.* New York: Oxford University Press, 1960.

———. *Systematic Theology.* 3 vols. London: SCM, 1978.

Tillich, Paul, D. Mackenzie Brown, and University of California Santa Barbara. *Ultimate Concern : Tillich in Dialogue.* London: SCM Press, 1965.

Torrance, Thomas F. *The Christian doctrine of God, one being three persons.* Edinburgh ; New York: T&T Clark, 2001.

Tracy, David. "Augustine Our Contemporary." In *Augustine Our Contemporary : Examining the Self in Past and Present*, edited by Willemien Otten and Susan Elizabeth Schreiner. Notre Dame, Indiana: University of Notre Dame Press, 2018, 27–74.

Turner, Bryan S. *Vulnerability and Human Rights.* University Park, Pa.: Pennsylvania State University Press, 2006.

Vanhoozer, Kevin J. *Remythologizing Theology : Divine Action, Passion, and Authorship.* Cambridge Studies in Christian Doctrine.

Vetlesen, Arne Johan. *The Denial of Nature : Environmental Philosophy in the Era of Global Capitalism.* Ontological Explorations. London: Routledge, 2015.

Volf, Miroslav. *Exclusion and embrace: a theological exploration of identity, otherness, and reconciliation.* Nashville: Abingdon Press, 1996.

Wahlberg, Mats. *Revelation as Testimony: A Philosophical-Theological Study.* Grand Rapids, Michigan: William B. Eerdmans Publishing Company, 2014.

Wenz, Gunther. *Gott.* Studium Systematische Theologie Bd. 4. Göttingen: Vandenhoeck und Ruprecht, 2007.

Westhelle, Vitor. "Luther's Theologia Crucis." In *The Oxford Handbook of Martin Luther's Theology*, edited by Robert Kolb; Irene Dingel; Lubomir Batka, 156–67. Oxford: Oxford University Press, 2014.

Williams, Rowan. *Lost Icons : Reflections on Cultural Bereavement.* London: Continuum, 2000.

Wolterstorff, Nicholas. *Divine Discourse : Philosophical Reflections on the Claim That God Speaks.* Cambridge UK ; New York, NY: Cambridge University Press, 1995.

Index

Agape 88,126, 184, 246–247

Agency (God's) 66, 67, 72, 84–85, 87–89, 133, 200, 201–203

Agency (human) 10, 24–26, 37, 40, 41, 46–48, 68–71, 78, 84–85, 87–89, 133, 150–153, 162, 183, 197– 202, 204–206, 237

Améry, Jean 213, 220

Appearance (Schein) 46, 58,

Arendt, Hannah 209

Atrocities 135, 139, 213, 215, 218–222

Augustine, Aurelius 185, 192, 243

Bash, Anthony   207, 211, 215

Beauty 40, 56–57, 65, 93, 100, 178

Bible (see also Scripture) 156, 201, 209, 225, 227–229, 233 249

Body, embodied 37, 89, 108,110, 113–115, 125–127, 129, 134, 140–143, 145–146, 148, 159–161, 163, 170, 172, 175, 183, 189, 195, 197–199, 201, 205

Brock, Rita Nakashima 219–220

Brudholm, Thomas 215, 218, 220–222

Care, caring 109–110, 126, 137, 154, 163, 171, 174, 189, 192, 195, 201, 205, 206, 219, 234–247

Clayton, Philip 198–199

Coakley, Sarah 166, 180

Complexity 114, 123, 199

Concept (Begriff) in Hegel 20–22

Cross 65, 114, 168, 182, 189

Dalferth, Ingolf U. 62–64, 179

Dawkins, Richard 55

Deacon, Terrence 94

Death 65, 76, 163, 165, 169, 182

Deep incarnation 112–116

Dependence 10, 54, 69–73, 84, 85, 96, 105, 163, 165, 176, 179–181

Dependence (feeling of) 70, 72–73

Derrida, Jacques 148, 211–217

Desire 10, 13, 38, 55, 84, 104, 111, 129, 136–137, 139–162, 178, 180, 182–195, 197, 223, 227, 240–243

Destruction, destructive 167–170, 207, 222

Deus vulnerabilis 176

Dewey, John 51

Dignity 169, 190, 191

Divine action (see God's agency)

Doctrine, doctrinal 15, 25, 57, 59, 72, 79, 82, 83, 128, 136–138, 190–192, 194, 223, 245, 246, 249

Emergence (theory) 197–200, 203

Emotion, emotional 11, 38, 74, 76–79, 81–84, 90, 96, 140, 143, 146, 164, 175, 180, 198, 203, 204, 219

Engagement (of ultimacy) 15, 35, 41–46, 49, 54, 224, 233

Eros. Erotic 141–143, 192–194

Eucharist (Last supper) 64, 91, 101

Evolution 11, 111–112, 114–116, 124, 127, 129, 130, 186, 192, 195, 199, 200, 202–23, 206

Existential (in Heidegger) 45, 47

External position (towards religion) 43, 44

Feuerbach, Ludwig 54

Fiddes, Paul S. 184, 198, 211, 213, 216

Finite-infinite contrast 63

Finitude 10, 100, 142, 143, 145–147, 157, 164, 165, 169, 173, 181, 192, 247

Firstness 55

First-person perspective 108, 142, 196, 234, 236, 242, 243

Flesh 112–115, 145

Flourishing, human 9, 11, 25, 28, 31, 78, 79, 110, 117, 127, 130, 136, 137, 139–141, 152, 163, 164, 171, 172, 196, 207, 222, 231, 239, 241

Forgiveness 135, 206–222, 250

Foucault, Michel 151

Frankfurt, Harry 13, 234–246, 250

Freedom 9, 62, 69–73, 86, 89, 129, 227, 241, 242, 246

Freud, Sigmund 74, 76, 77

Fundamentalism, fundamentalists 11, 177

Fulfillment 71, 86, 105, 110, 115, 125, 128, 131, 136, 141, 142, 144, 155, 156, 160, 195, 203, 205

Gethsemane story 181–182

Gift 106, 121, 130, 132, 134, 148–150, 152–154, 161, 184, 186, 195, 208, 211, 212, 215–217

Goodness 40, 43, 53, 56, 57, 109, 110, 126, 131, 132, 134, 139, 140, 144, 147–149, 151–154, 169, 186, 187, 191–195, 202

Grace 106, 110, 121, 125, 128, 153, 154, 158, 184, 193, 194, 202, 208, 217, 222, 247

Gratification 143, 147, 153, 156, 157–160, 162, 182, 188

Gregersen, Niels Henrik 106, 112–115, 123, 127, 128–130

Guilt 167–168, 212

Habits 24, 27

Harrison, George 55

Hart, David Bentley 50, 97–99, 101, 103–104

Hegel, Georg Wilhelm Friedrich 11, 13, 19–24, 35, 38, 42, 45, 48, 51, 53, 57–61, 63, 65–66, 68, 69, 71, 73, 75, 77, 82, 84, 85, 96, 104, 106, 118, 136, 143–144, 148, 193.

Heidegger, Martin 45–50, 75, 80

Hogarth, Steve 55–57, 64, 65, 74

Human identity 138, 144, 159, 161, 191, 195

Hume, David 17

Icon, iconic 56, 93, 94, 99, 100–102, 104

Idol, idolatry 10, 44, 70, 133, 155, 159–160, 230, 249

Imagination, imaginaries 31, 74, 76, 78, 80, 84, 141, 146

Imago Dei 10, 13, 85, 86, 87, 158, 159, 181, 190, 250

Immediacy 20, 22, 46, 69

Incarnation (see also Deep incarnation) 111, 112, 116–118, 125–127, 131, 160, 170, 189

Index, indexical 56, 93, 94, 99, 100, 101, 102

Infinity 64, 99, 148, 149, 157, 200

Injustice 65, 155, 174, 210

Institution 23, 33, 34–36, 41,174–175, 210

Intentionality 32, 46, 60, 144, 146, 147

Irenaeus 130, 194

James, William 28–30, 33, 35, 241

Jankelevitch, Vladimir 211

Jeanrond, Werner 110, 185, 187

Jesus Christ 62, 65, 84, 85, 87–89, 91, 93, 99, 100, 104, 111–115, 135, 158, 170, 181–182, 188–189, 192, 201, 209, 211, 224, 249

Johnson, Elizabeth A. 128–129

Justice 40, 144, 151–154, 158, 174, 177, 187, 189, 194, 198, 206, 209, 212–214, 221

Karle, Isolde 178–179

Kearney, Richard 156–157, 159, 160

Koopman, Nico 174

Lessing, Gotthold Ephraim 230

Lewis, Thomas A. 19, 21, 23, 24, 59,

Lopez, Jennifer 9

Luther, Martin 132–134, 168, 240, 241

Løgstrup, Knud E. 102, 107–109, 132

Marillion 55

Marion, Jean-Luc 148, 184,

Mediation 11, 62, 79, 92, 95, 96, 98, 99, 102, 105, 107, 120, 138, 145

Merleau-Ponty, Maurice 140, 143, 145

Mozart, Wolfgang Amadeus 121

Müller, Max 20

Natural theology 64–65

Neville, Robert Cummings 12, 25, 40, 41–44, 54, 63–64, 155, 233

Nietzsche 137

Normativity, normative 9, 16, 23, 27, 28, 37, 39, 49, 78, 150, 151, 152, 176, 228, 230

Otherness 102, 142, 144, 156, 160–162, 182, 190, 193, 195

Panentheism 104–107, 109, 113, 116, 118–120, 126

Pannenberg, Wolfhart 138, 183

Passivity 140, 144, 150

Paul, the apostle 150, 151, 170

Peacocke, Arthur 200–201

Peirce, Charles Sanders 12, 15, 55, 92–94, 97, 108, 119

Perichoresis 128–131

Phillips, Dewi Z. 37–38

Piety 16, 69, 71, 219,

Plato 45, 48, 49

Pragmatism, pragmatic 12, 15, 17, 21, 22, 24, 26–29, 35–38, 40, 42, 44, 45, 47, 49, 51, 64, 106, 120, 136, 138, 207, 228, 235

Praying, prayer 15, 177, 179–180, 182, 209, 223

Promissory (religion) 35, 37

Quality 96–100, 102, 108, 119

Receptivity 70, 72

Reckwitz, Andreas 203, 205, 207

Recognition 82, 86, 138, 150, 155, 162, 164, 168, 170, 177, 178, 185, 194, 205, 206, 213, 219, 220, 222, 228

Reconciliation 62, 213, 217, 218, 220–221

Relationality 10, 55, 68, 96, 151, 164, 178–179

Religions as clusters of practices 16, 25, 32, 34, 40, 236, 250

Responsibility 171, 174, 176, 210, 219, 226, 227, 230, 247

Revelation 60, 62, 65–68, 76, 84, 85, 87–89, 94, 98, 126, 200, 203, 205, 224

Ricoeur, Paul 56, 59, 145–147

Riesebrodt, Martin 28, 29, 35

Rizzuto, Ana-Maria 74–78, 80–84

Robinson, Andrew 92, 95–97

Salvation 29, 35, 112, 127, 173, 193

Sanderson, Christiane 219

Schilbrack, Kevin 12, 18, 35–41

Schleiermacher, Daniel Ernst Friedrich 20, 68, 69–73, 75, 77,83–86, 96, 104, 179

Schwöbel, Christoph 84–85, 87, 88

Scripture (see also Bible) 10, 15, 58, 98, 126, 222, 223, 228, 236

Self-consciousness 21, 69–72, 144, 237

Self-transcendence 142, 193

Semiosis, semiosis 11, 12, 27, 41, 43, 47, 50, 56, 58, 60, 71, 85, 89–92, 94, 97–99, 101–103, 105–106, 116, 120, 137, 138, 170, 179

Semper Major, God as 10, 11, 44, 110

Sex, sexual 76, 77, 141, 160, 172, 173, 239

Shame 167, 173, 189

Signs 18, 42, 44, 49, 51, 56, 59, 80, 85, 91–97, 99, 100, 102–104, 106, 107, 116–117, 120, 152, 153, 170

Sin 88, 138, 152, 156, 164, 167–168, 173, 183, 191–194, 202

Smith, Christian 28–35

Smith, Jonathan Z. 16–17

Smith, Steven G. 223

Springhart, Heike 163–170, 172, 173, 175, 188, 189

Stålsett, Sturla 176–177, 187–189

Subjectivity 34, 50, 69, 71, 141, 144–146, 150, 153, 220, 230

Substantive definition of religion 35–37, 39, 40

Suffering 65, 104, 113, 114, 128, 163, 164, 168, 174, 176, 180–182, 222

Superempirical 12, 40–41, 96,

Superhuman powers 21, 24, 28–34,

Supernatural 21, 30, 32, 101, 103, 117–118, 120–125, 127, 201

Symbol 10, 15, 25, 40, 50, 51, 56–58, 60, 63–64, 71, 74–78, 80, 81, 83–85, 93–94, 100–102, 120, 126, 129, 136, 144, 161, 165, 166, 169, 174, 176–177, 179, 184, 186, 187, 190, 233, 249

Tanner, Kathryn 129–130

Theologia crucis 65, 168

Theology (Christian) 62, 64, 65, 72, 99, 100, 104, 107, 109, 111, 116–118, 123–127, 156, 170, 176, 184, 188, 202, 219

Tillich, Paul 195, 196, 236

Tradition (Christian) 135, 151, 176, 190, 206, 215, 227–228, 242, 243, 249

Tragedy, tragic 162–163, 168, 171

Transcendental, transcendentals 10, 21, 24–27, 43, 56, 58–59, 64, 68, 70, 73, 91–92, 95–98, 100–104, 107, 109, 125, 131, 184, 185, 190

Trinitarian panentheism 113, 117, 125

Trinity, trinitarian 87, 105, 113, 114, 116–118, 124, 128, 129

Truth and Reconciliation Commission (TRC) 213, 220–222

Turner, Bryan S. 174–175

Tutu, Desmond 220, 221

Ultimates 25, 32, 41, 50, 56, 59

Value commitments 23–24

Volitional necessity 240–241

Vulnerability 10, 13, 65, 112, 135–137, 158, 162–193, 195, 197, 201, 215, 219, 220, 227

Vulnerability, ontological 165–169

Vulnerability, situated 165–169

Williams, Rowan 158–162, 185

Wisdom 115, 129, 160, 175, 198, 219, 223, 228, 230

Wolterstorff, Nicholas 224

Wrongness 28–30, 35

Nordic Studies in Theology / Nordische Studien zur Theologie
Edited by / Prof. Dr. Kirsten Busch Nielsen (University of Copenhagen),
Prof. Dr. Dr. Jan-Olav Henriksen (MF Norwegian School of Theology),
Dr. Hans Bringeland (NLA University College, Bergen)

Frederik Saxegaard
Realizing Church
Parish Pastors as Contributors to Leadership in Congregations
vol. 6, ca. 2020, ca. 280 pp., ca. 39,90 €, br., ISBN-CH 978-3-643-91177-3

Asle Eikrem; Atle O. Søvik (Eds.)
Talking Seriously About God
Philosophy of Religion in the Dispute between Theism and Atheism
Talk about God is often the source of controversy. Theists and atheists are equally passionate when making their stand for or against belief in God.
In this book a wide range of philosophers of religion have come together to discuss how serious talk about God ought to be conducted for theists and atheists alike in what should be their common pursuit for truth. The essays both address methodological questions and provide a range of concrete samples of serious God-talk, spanning from political religion and classical proofs of God's existence to the problem of evil.
Bd. 4, 2016, 184 S., 29,90 €, br., ISBN 978-3-643-90741-7

Hans Bringeland
Die Theologie Ole Hallebys
Norwegischer Pietismus in erfahrungstheologischer und kantianischer Prägung
Bd. 3, ca. 2020, ca. 256 S., 39,90 €, gb., ISBN-CH 978-3-643-90385-3

Gunnar Innerdal
Hans Urs von Balthasar on Spirit and Truth
A Systematic Reconstruction in Connection to the Theoretical Framework of Lorenz B. Puntel
The doctrine of *the Spirit of truth* (cf. John 16:13) stands at the center of *Hans Urs von Balthasar on Spirit and Truth*. To articulate a coherent systematic theology of this aspect of pneumatology, Gunnar Innerdal analyzes Balthasar's *Theo-Logic* and related texts, followed by critical assessments in connection to the theoretical framework of Lorenz B. Puntel's structural-systematic philosophy and in dialogue with other contemporary theological proposals. In Part I philosophical questions concerning truth are discussed. Part II shows the relevance of Christology and Trinity for theological truth talk, discussing the doctrine of analogy and negative theology. Part III elaborates on the relationship of Son and Spirit, and the Spirit's work as the Spirit of truth inside and outside the Church. The Spirit, as breath of life and Spirit of Christ, has ontological and epistemological significance for all truth.
Bd. 2, 2016, 328 S., 49,90 €, br., ISBN 978-3-643-90628-1

Jonna Bornemark; Mattias Martinson; Jayne Svenungsson (Eds.)
Monument and Memory
A century after the Great War broke out, studies on politics of memory and commemoration have grown into a vast and vital academic field. This book approaches the theme "monument and memory" from architectural, literary, philosophical and theological perspectives. Drawing on diverse sources – from the Augustine to Freud, from early photographs to contemporary urban monuments – the contributing authors probe the intersections between memory and trauma, past and present, monuments and memorial practices, religious and secular, remembrance and forgetfulness.
Bd. 1, 2015, 272 S., 49,90 €, gb., ISBN 978-3-643-90467-6

LIT Verlag Berlin – Münster – Wien – Zürich – London
Auslieferung Deutschland / Österreich / Schweiz: siehe Impressumsseite

Nordic Studies in Religion and Culture / Nordische Studien zur Religion und Kultur

edited by /Dr. Hans Bringeland (NLA University College, Bergen),
Prof. Dr. Ingvild S. Gilhus (University of Bergen)

Kai Merten
Färöische Religionsgeschichte
Von den Anfängen bis zur Gegenwart
Die Inselgruppe der Färöer bildet den kleinsten selbständigen Teil Skandinaviens. Dennoch weist sie
eine mehr als tausendjährige Geschichte und Kultur auf, die von Anfang an ein eigenes Gepräge ent-
wickelt hat. Besonders auffällig ist die außerordentlich starke Bindung der Menschen an die Religion.
Rund 23% der Färinger besuchen jeden Sonntag einen Gottesdienst!
Das vorliegende Buch bietet deshalb einen umfassenden Überblick über die gesamte Religionsge-
schichte der Färöer.
Bd. 4, 2017, 320 S., 29,90 €, br., ISBN 978-3-643-13580-3

Peter Nynäs; Ruth Illman; Tuomas Martikainen (Eds.)
On the outskirts of "the church"
Diversity, fluidities and new spaces of religion in Finland
Through exploring the diversity of contemporary religious phenomena, this volume sheds new light
on religion in the twenty-first century: Is religion going through a decisive change? What are the resources that make religion so persistent and what happened to secularisation? How do the traditional
religious institutions fare? How do people identify themselves with regard to religion?
Firmly rooted in analyses of the rich and fluid spiritual life on the outskirts of religious institutions –
from angel healing and prayer clinics to LGBT activists and yoga entrepreneurs – this volume engages with topical discussions on religious change and post-secularity. The book suggests that there
are profound changes occurring in the ways in which religion is involved in people's lives today and
looks at how religious institutions have responded to these changes.
Bd. 3, 2015, 288 S., 34,90 €, br., ISBN 978-3-643-90571-0

Nils G. Holm
The Human Symbolic Construction of Reality
A Psycho-Phenomenological Study
The book sums up several years of research into religion from a perspective informed by history,
phenomenology and psychology. It is typical of humans to create forms of understanding at a symbolic level of the biological and physiological reality which confronts them. This gives meaning and
a coherent structure to the often chaotic nature of that reality. Religion has been a means of creating
such symbolic understandings. The similarities between various religions are actually very great, although their differences tend to dominate our view of them. Everything in the world of religion can
be traced back to everyday and simple circumstances which, through the construction of symbols at
both the cognitive and the behavioural levels, acquire a more elevated and "sacred" character. This
book provides an introduction to the key aspects of a psycho-phenomenological study of the forms of
expression within religions.
Bd. 2, 2014, 152 S., 34,90 €, br., ISBN 978-3-643-90526-0

Hans Bringeland; Arve Brunvoll (Hg.)
Die Religion und das Wertefundament der Gesellschaft
Studien zum 200. Jahrestag des norwegischen Grundgesetzes 2014
Diese Aufsatzsammlung, die anlässlich des 200. Jahrestages des norwegischen Grundgesetzes ent-
standen ist, besteht aus Beiträgen von norwegischen Forschern in Fächern wie Theologie und Philo-
sophie, Religionswissenschaft und Soziologie, Jura und Literaturwissenschaft. Die Aufsätze sind den
Themenbereichen „Werte, Grundgesetz und Menschenrechte", „Religion und Wertefundament" und
„Christliche Ideologen, Nationaltagsfeier" zugeordnet. Obwohl der Primärkontext nordisch ist, dürfte
diese Anthologie auch für deutschsprachige Leser von Interesse sein.
Bd. 1, 2015, 278 S., 34,90 €, br., ISBN 978-3-643-90466-9

LIT Verlag Berlin – Münster – Wien – Zürich – London
Auslieferung Deutschland / Österreich / Schweiz: siehe Impressumsseite

Theorizing the Postsecular
International Studies in Religion, Politics and Society
edited by Christoph Jedan (Groningen), Arie Molendijk (Groningen) and
Justin Beaumont(Groningen)

Ville Päivänsalo; Taina Kalliokoski; David Huisjen, Jr. (Eds.)
Tolerance
Human Fragility and the Quest for Justice
Bd. 3, 2017, 278 S., 39,90 €, br., ISBN 978-3-643-90871-1

Renée Wagenvoorde
Is Citizenship Secular?
Conceptualising the relation between religion and citizenship in contemporary Dutch society
Bd. 2, 2015, 268 S., 34,90 €, br., ISBN 978-3-643-90683-0

Christoph Jedan (Ed.)
Constellations of Value
European Perspectives on the Intersections of Religion, Politics and Society
Bd. 1, 2013, 200 S., 19,90 €, br., ISBN 978-3-643-90083-8

LIT Verlag Berlin – Münster – Wien – Zürich – London
Auslieferung Deutschland / Österreich / Schweiz: siehe Impressumsseite

Theorizing the Postsecular
International Studies in Religion, Politics and Society
edited by Christoph Jedan (Groningen), Arie Molendijk (Groningen) and
Justin Beaumont(Groningen)

Hans-Gerd Janßen; Julia D. E. Prinz; Michael J. Rainer (Hg..)
Theologie in gefährdeter Zeit
Stichworte von nahen und fernen Weggefährten für Johann Baptist Metz zum
90. Geburtstag
Bd. 50, 2. Aufl. 2019, 600 S., 39,90 €, br., ISBN 978-3-643-14106-4

LIT Verlag Berlin – Münster – Wien – Zürich – London
Auslieferung Deutschland / Österreich / Schweiz: siehe Impressumsseite